# China Currents
## 2017 Special Edition

# China Currents
# 2017 Special Edition

*James R. Schiffman and Penelope B. Prime, Editors*

*China Research Center, Atlanta, Georgia*
*www.chinacenter.net*

*Sponsored by the School of History and Sociology*
*and the Ivan Allen College of Liberal Arts*
*at the Georgia Institute of Technology*

*Cover design: Vanessa F. Garver*

For electronic browsing and ordering of this, and other China Research Center titles, visit www.chinacenter.net

For more information, please contact:
China Research Center
Atlanta, Georgia
info@chinacenter.net

*China Currents: 2017 Special Edition*
James R. Schiffman and Penelope B. Prime, Editors

© 2017 China Research Center – All Rights Reserved
No part of the contents of this book may be reproduced in any form or by any means without the written permission of the publisher.

ISBN: 978-0-9826415-6-9

Published in the United States by China Research Center

Design and Production: Carbon Press, Inc.
Manufactured in the United States of America

First Edition

# Contents

## Politics and International Relations

# Preface

Economic reform and development in China and China's rising role in global affairs are reshaping the global system in the 21st century and fueling an unprecedented social transition within China itself. China Currents is a forum for thoughtful, concise articles analyzing society in contemporary China, published by the China Research Center at ChinaCurrents.com. Periodic printed special editions include selections from past issues, organized by topic. The 2017 Special Edition includes articles covering religion, philanthropy, international trade, education, business, corruption, international relations and more.

The Center gratefully acknowledges financial support from our institutional sponsor, the School of History and Sociology, and the Ivan Allen College of Liberal Arts, at the Georgia Institute of Technology. Beginning in 2017, the Center is based at Georgia Tech and is directed by Dr. Hanchao Lu, Professor of History.

We also thank East West Manufacturing and Project Success, Inc. for their support as Gold sponsors. Our dedicated editorial team includes Dan Williams, Stephen Herschler, Clifton Pannell, Shu-chin Wu and Lisa Guthrie. The views expressed in these articles are those of the authors.

Founded in 2001, the China Research Center is dedicated to promoting understanding of greater China based on research and experience and to working collaboratively on events and projects with the public and private sectors. The Center draws much if its expertise from educational and service institutions around the southeast U.S., including Agnes Scott College, The Carter Center, Dalton State

University, Emory University, Georgia College & State University, Georgia Institute of Technology, Georgia State University, Kennesaw State University, Mercer University, Oglethorpe University and the University of Georgia. The Center is a founding member of the International Consortium for China Studies based at the National School of Development, Peking University.

The associates of the Center believe that favorable U.S.-China relations are crucial for promoting economic development in the U.S. and greater China and peace in the region. One of the foundations of favorable relations is mutual understanding based on knowledge and open communication. The associates specialize in the study of a wide variety of aspects of Chinese society, including language, culture, history, politics, economics, business, society, international relations, demographics, geography, and the environment. The Center's goal is to make knowledge and expertise available to a wide variety of constituents within and beyond our academic communities, as well as to enhance our academic work via cross-disciplinary and cross-institutional collaboration.

*James R. Schiffman, Ph.D.*
*Penelope B. Prime, Ph.D.*
*June 2017*

# Protestant Christianity in the People's Republic of China

*Linlin Victoria Lu*
*Vol. 15, No.1*
*2016*

The history of Christianity in China is a remarkable tale of the encounters between two very different civilizations and of how a foreign religion survived, revitalized, and became a vibrant torrent in China today. The main focus of this essay is to evaluate the feature of Protestant Christianity in China after the Communist takeover in 1949, comprehend its process of cross-cultural movement, and testify how the simultaneous replication and transformation of the faith in a new cultural setting has finally been indigenized.

## Before 1950: A Century of Missionary Work

Historically, Christianity has made several forays into China, first with Persian Nestorian monks in the seventh century, followed by Catholic Franciscans in the 12th century, and Jesuits in the 16th century, but failed each time to establish a lasting presence as anti-foreign politics and culture played a big role in how Christianity was accepted and rooted in Chinese soil. [1]

The arrival of missionary Robert Morrison (1782-1834) to China in 1807 marked the introduction of Protestantism and the fourth major entrance of Christianity to China. Coinciding with the most violent period of expansion into Asia by all the Western imperialist nations, the Protestant missionary movement remained in China for almost 150 years before the Communist takeover. Gunboats indirectly enabled the missionaries to penetrate all levels of Chinese society, but the message of their barking cannons deafened many Chinese to the serene sound of the Gospel. [2] Nevertheless, by 1920 rapid Christian expansion had resulted in not only Protestant churches with 500,000 partisans, but also a burgeoning sense of nationalism that manifested with the birth of indigenous churches.[3] In 1922, the Church of Christ in China (CCC) organized its first National Christian Council (NCC) in Shanghai with the inaugural announcement of the Chinese Christian Movement under the "Three Self" Principles: self-support, self-governance, and self-propagation.[4] Chinese Protestant leader Cheng Jingyi (C.Y. Cheng, 1881-1939) was elected as the General Secretary and strived to promote an independent, unified, and non-denominational base for Christianity in China.[5]

The turbulent forces of history in first half of the 20th century, which shaped all aspects of China's politics, economy, and culture, once again changed the fate of Protestant missionaries and Chinese Christians. In October 1949 the Communists took power, and under the banner of patriotism the new regime started rooting out the influence of Christianity in China. As Wolfgang Franke commented, "The Christian missionaries had to pay a particularly heavy price for the mistakes of their predecessors, and reaped the hatred that had been sown in the past."[6] All 130 foreign missionary institutions and organizations, including schools and universities, were shut down; the missionary funds were frozen, and all foreign missionaries were expelled. By 1951 not a single Protestant missionary remained in mainland China, marking the ending of 150 years of Protestant missionary work. Left behind were 700,000 Chinese Protestants facing an uncertain future.[7]

## 1950-1966: From Liberation to the Cultural Revolution

In keeping with Marxist orthodoxy, the Chinese Communist Party (CCP) declared itself atheist. Maoism or Mao Zedong Thought (as it is known in China) was the dominant, state-enforced ideology. As such, the Communists condemned religion as "the opiate of the people." Christianity in particular was seen as something brought to China under the protection of Western gunships, and foreign missionaries, as its propagators, were representatives of imperialist powers. The activities of missionaries in modern Chinese history were not so much a religious or social problem as they were an international political problem, that is, "cultural imperialism."

However, when this "foreign religion" became an integral part of the culture and life of the people, it was impossible for the government to eradicate it. Therefore, a political compromise was made. As former Premier Zhou Enlai (1898-1976) stated, the CCP government allowed domestic churches to function after 1949 as long as they would not collaborate with Western imperialism and were loyal to the government.[8] In 1954, the proclamation of the Chinese Constitution *Article 88* declared that Christians as "citizens of the People's Republic of China enjoy freedom of religious belief," but they were placed under the jurisdiction of state and party bodies.[9]

No doubt, Protestant Christianity faced serious challenges when the churches desperately needed to remove the historical stigma of their religion by distancing it from its foreign heritage. As early as December 1949, Protestant church leaders had signed a long open letter entitled "Message from Chinese Christians to Mission Boards Aboard" that declared an end to the missionary era in China and the contestation of its legacy:

> We Christians in China feel the urgent necessity of re-examining our work and our relationship with the older churches abroad in the light of this historical change…The Christian movement will have its due place in the future Chinese society and will have a genuine contribution to make. Its future road will not be a bed of roses… It will suffer a purge, and many of the withered branches will be amputated.[10]

Six months later, "The Christian Manifesto" was issued by the CCC in response to pressure from Premier Zhou as a "Declared Direction of Endeavor for Chinese Christianity in the Construction of New China":

> Recognize clearly the evils that have been wrought in China by imperialism; recognize that in the past imperialism has made use of Christianity itself; and be vigilant against imperialism, especially American imperialism, in its plot to use religion in fostering the growth of reactionary forces.[11]

Forty Protestant church leaders initially signed the document, followed by 180,000 members; eventually a total of 400,000 signatures would support this declaration of independence from the churches in the West.[12] The CCC also pleaded unconditional compliance by accepting the direct supervision of the State Administrations of Religious Affairs (SARA), which operated underneath the United Front Work Department (UFWD) to manage the government's relations with domestic religious organizations. In addition, the CCC called for a new Three-Self Church that was as ecumenical as it was indigenous, a church that was patriotic while remaining committed to the tenets of global Protestantism. After the Korean War, at the first National Christianity Conference in July 1954, the CCC rebranded the Three-Self Reform Movement (TSRM) as the Three-Self Patriotic Movement (TSPM). It called all Christians in China to unite under the leadership of the CCP government. At the conference Wu Yaozong (Wu Yaotsung or Y.T. Wu, 1890-1979) was elected chairman.[13]

Despite a few discordant voices inside of the TSPM, Protestant churches continuously operated. In 1958 the churches started "joint worship services" to enter a so-called post-denomination period.[14] For 17 years, Protestant Christians survived numerous political campaigns. Then the Cultural Revolution broke out.

## 1966-1976: The Cultural Revolution

The "Great Proletarian Cultural Revolution" ironically turned out not to be cultural, proletarian, or even a revolution. It was instead a manmade disaster affecting the whole country, and Protestantism was just one of its victims. Like all other religious institutions in China, the Protestant National CCC and TSPM stopped operating. Local churches, YMCAs, and YWCAs were closed. Christian life was banned, Bibles were destroyed, church buildings were confiscated, and Christian homes were looted. Christians were subjected to public humiliation, beatings, and labor camps. The catastrophe lasted for 10 years, but in the end Protestant Christians survived by practicing their faith underground.

## 1978 – Present: The Reform Era

The death of Mao Zedong in 1976 marked the end of the Cultural Revolution and the era of fanatical Maoism. Under Deng Xiaoping's (1904-1997) leadership, sweeping changes took place in China that had a profound impact on Protestants.

Deng Xiaoping initiated the "Four Modernizations" movement to reform the economy, agriculture, national defense, and science and technology. He adopted a new stance on the issue of church-state relationships by calling for "seeking unity, preserving differences" through a fully utilized United Front to make constructive use of religion. Deng wanted his party to rally all positive features and social strength to advance the reform movement.[15]

In so doing the Party relaxed its ideological control in *Document 19*:

> What is primary at the moment is the common goal of building a modernized powerful Socialist State, so the difference between believers and nonbelievers at this time is secondary…According to Marxism, the religion will naturally disappear when the people are sufficiently educated and understand the secrets of science. It is useless then to persecute religion as was done during the Cultural Revolution.[16]

In *Article 36* of the 1982-implemented Constitution, the government promulgated religious freedom:

> Citizens of the People's Republic of China enjoy freedom of religious belief. No state organ, public organization or individual may compel

citizens to believe in, or not to believe in, any religion; nor may they discriminate against citizens who believe in, or do not believe in, any religion. The state protects normal religious activities. No one may make use of religion to engage in activities that disrupt public order, impair the health of citizens or interfere with the educational system of the state. Religious bodies and religious affairs are not subject to any foreign domination.[17]

The government also formulated several important documents to further clarify the intent of the constitutional clause of religious freedom, such as the Regulation on the Management of Places for Religious Activities (1994), the Regulation on the Management of Foreigners' Religious Activities in the PRC (1994), the laws for normal missionary affairs and religious services, and the principle of separating religion from state education. The government conceded the fact that over the country's long period of historical development, religious culture in China had become a component of traditional Chinese ideological culture.[18]

**Growth of Protestantism**

The CCP's new religious policy allowed Christianity to surge once again. In September 1979, the first Protestant church reopened in Shanghai, followed by 11 others in addition to four in the outskirts of the city. Every Sunday morning the total congregation worshiping at these churches was more than 20,000 people.[19] In 1980, the third National Protestant Christian Conference (NPCC) was held in Nanjing and estimated that the total number of Protestants in China exceeded two million. The NPCC called all Protestants to unite under biblical scripture while applying the "Three-Self" principles to guide church activities. The NPCC also reopened the Nanjing Theological Seminary (NTS) and, as a parallel to the National TSPM, formed the China Christian Council (new CCC) to manage church international affairs such as Bible printing and distribution, hymnal publications, and building church leadership. The Anglican bishop Ding Guangxun (K.H. Ting, 1915-2012) was appointed chairman.[20]

Reopening more churches was hardly a straightforward endeavor. Recovering church property that had been occupied by other organizations during the Cultural Revolution often proved difficult. With the aid of new policies, however, church properties were returned to respective churches with repair costs and daily operating budgets covered by the state. The reopened NTS enrolled 52 students including 20 women selected from more than 1,000 applications. Despite its small size, the NTS regularly published more than 20,000 course syllabi for use in rural areas and some cities through short-term training institutes organized for volunteers and laypersons.[21]

By 1982 more than 1,100 Protestant churches had reopened nationwide. In 1991 the CCC joined the World Christian Council (WCC).[22] The number of Chinese Christians continued to grow. In 2002, the Three-Self churches had 15 million baptized Protestant Christians. There were 50,000 TSPM churches and registered "preaching points" in the country.[23] According to the national TSPM and the CCC, by 2010 there were 53,000 TSPM churches, of which 70 percent were newly built, with almost 20 million Protestant partisans, 70 percent of them in rural areas. To date the TSPM has opened 19 theological seminaries nationwide with a large number of young clergy.[24]

In 2014, the national conference for the 60th anniversary of the Three-Self Church claimed that China has about 23.05 million to 40 million Protestants, or about 1.7 percent to 2.9 percent of the total population. Each year, about 500,000 people are baptized as Protestants.[25] The figures released by the TSPM or the CCC are routinely quoted around the world. However, they are still an extremely conservative estimate as they exclude all youth and children under the age of 18 who may attend church worship but are not regarded as church members.[26]

**Political Harmonization**

The 1982 Constitution provided new breathing space for the revival of Protestantism. The CCP is aware of the current popularity of Christianity in China as well as the historical contribution of Christianity to the economy in the West. It hopes that Christian faith along with Chinese traditional values can foster social stability and economic development in order to balance the pervasive materialism in Chinese society.[27] Therefore it encourages Chinese scholars to reassess the ecumenical value of Christianity and its potential impact on Chinese economic reforms.

Many Chinese scholars have answered the call. Researchers from the Chinese Academy of Social Sciences (CASS) found that Christianity can be an important strength in Chinese society. They report that Christianity has shaped the structure of Western society from the bottom up and has been beneficial to the development of Western civilization. They believe that Christianity could bring similar benefits to China to promote economic growth, social stability, and common morality. Among them, the market economist and ethicist Peter Zhao was the first to argue that China's economy would benefit from the spread of Christianity.[28] His article, "The Real Story behind Chinese Economic Growth", was approved by Premier Zhu Rongji (1928- ) as required reading for the State Council's economist conference in 2002. Later Zhao converted to Christianity and started the Business Christian Fellowship (BCF), focusing on the urban Christianity movement in order to find roles for Christianity in China's social transformation. Zhao claimed "God is My Chairman of the Board" and openly praised the contribution of Christianity to the expansion of world civilization and the impact by Christian missionaries in 19th century Chinese history. The BCF published Ten Commandments for Business People:

> No fraudulent accounting book; no tax evasion; no adultery; treat employees fairly; no destruction of the environment; not to engage in immoral business (in terms of both products and service); no violation of covenants (including oral and written covenants); honoring your father and mother; loving your spouse, children and family; and loving your community, the earth and justice.[29]

Some government officials have echoed the CASS scholars' perceptions of Christianity. These CCP cadres, although bonded with the atheist Communist ideology, also believe that the borrowing of Christian practices from the West will bring positive effects on Chinese society. In his Religious Media and Social Harmony, Zhuo Xinping, director of the Institute of World Religion of the Chinese Academy of Social Sciences (CASS), stresses the ecumenical values of Christianity in the current Chinese society as these values help with social harmony.[30] Wang Zuoan, director of the SARA, also points out that Christianity promotes love, peace, and mutual understanding among peoples, which makes it a facilitator to enhance the relationship between China and the United States.[31]

**Methods of Religious Control**

The receptiveness of Christianity in Chinese society seems to not be in conflict with the CCP political agenda of building the "Harmonious Society," although the churches are still under the direct supervision of the SARA and subjected to national, provincial, and local regulations. In fact, the CCP has not relinquished control of religion, as it still believes that religion is the social ideology opposite to Marxism, and Christianity is one of the major elements among foreign enemy forces to subvert Communism and undermine the regime. Therefore "peaceful evolution" and foreign infiltration of Christianity must be condemned and the government must control and supervise the degree and extent of religious activities.[32]

Indeed, the Chinese state tolerates Christianity only if it is developed along the principles of the TSPM without any outside interferences, such as foreign missionary work, in the administration. This is particularly true regarding the nation's numerous underground churches.[33]

The underground churches organized as independent churches in the 1950s. Most of them are rural or urban house churches not registered with the official TSPM. The government views them as legal entities. Some unregistered churches, such as True Jesus Church, Little Flock, and Seventh Day Adventists, are not registered but still operate in the TSPM format. The CCP certainly knows the exact locations of these churches and their respective organizers, but their non-affiliation with the TSPM does not seem to endanger operations. These churches actually enjoy a limited autonomy. However, unregistered churches, such as the Conditional Church, Basement Church, the Shouters, the Established King sect, the Disciples Sect, Three Grades of Servants, the Lightning of the East, Weepers, China Gospel Fellowship, and Fangcheng Church, do not enjoy the same tolerance from the government and are constantly watched by the local police. The leaders of these churches are frequently interrogated, their teaching materials are confiscated, and members are persecuted. The government claims that the punishment is "meted out in accordance with the law to those who know of the matter but did not report and to those who masterminded the scheme."[34]

## Conclusion

Protestant Christianity has a burdened past in China, yet it not only has survived but also has become the fastest-growing religion in contemporary China. Today, Protestant Christianity is a significant part of Chinese culture. Combined from all denominations, this vibrant Chinese Christian Church has become the most diverse religious institution in the world.

Nevertheless, popular Protestant Christianity also brings tensions between nationalism and cosmopolitanism.[35] In 2013, the National Committees of the CCC and TSPM announced a five-year campaign of indigenization of Protestant Christianity through the construction of Chinese Christian theology.[36] At the 2014 Shanghai Forum of "Sinicization of Christianity," SARA Director Wang Zuoan reminded the TSPM leaders that the implementation of the government's religious policy made possible the fast development of Protestant churches in China. The government would continue to boost the development of a unified indigenized Protestantism with Chinese characteristics. Thus, the five-year campaign of construction of Chinese Christian theology must adapt to China's national condition and integrate with Chinese culture.[37]

Apparently, the rapid growth of Protestantism in China and the popularity of Christian culture are particular troublesome for the CCP given the fact that its own virtual abandonment of Marxism has created an ideological vacuum. In its place, the CCP has increasingly turned to Chinese nationalism as the ideational complement to economic growth and prosperity. Thus, a five-year campaign of "Sinicization of Christianity" would be consistent with its drive to push Chinese nationalism. On the other hand, the campaign could simultaneously help the government to crack down on the large network of underground churches in China, especially 14 "evil cults" listed for eradication. Moreover, the drive to nationalize Christianity could be aimed at cracking down on foreign religious influences in China.

Currently, Protestant Christianity is following the TSPM's principles to harmonize with the Chinese political and cultural climate. It is ironic that in an era of continuing restrictions on the freedom of religion, Protestantism in China recognizes its ultimate challenge is not about survival or religious freedom, but a meaningful and realistic evangelization to "encourage more believers to make contributions to the country's harmonious social progress, cultural prosperity and economic development."[38]

## Notes

1   Kenneth Scott Latourette, *A History of Christian Missions in China* (New York: MacMillan Company, 1929).

2   David Aikman, *Jesus in Beijing: How Christianity is Transforming China and Changing the Global Balance of Power* (Washington, DC: Regnery Publishing, 2003), 44.

3   Daniel H. Bays, *A New History of Christianity in China* (UK: Wiley-Blackwell Publication, 2012), 94.

4   National Christian Conference in Shanghai 1922: *The Chinese Church as Revealed in the National Christian Conference, Shanghai, 1922* (Shanghai: Oriental Press, 1922), 495-503.

5   Ibid., 19-22.

6   Wolfgang Franke, *China and the West: The Cultural Encounter, 13th to 20th Centuries* (New York: Harper Torchbook, 1967), 138

7   The Central People's Government of PRC. "History of Christianity in China," accessed July 18, 2015, http://www.gov.cn/test/2005-07/26/content_17214.htm.

8   Louis K. Ho, *The Dragon and the Cross: Why European Christianity Failed to Take Root in China* (UK: Xulon Press, 2009), 108-09.

9   Bays, *A New History of Christianity in China*, 159.

10  Wallace C. Merwin and Francis P. Jones, *Documents of the Three-Self Movement: Source Materials for the Study of the Protestant Church in China* (New York: National Council of the Churches of Christ in the USA, 1963), 18.

11  Merwin and Jones, *Documents of the Three-Self Movement*, 19-20.

12  Bays, *A New History of Christianity in China*, 162.

13  China Christian Council Three-Self Patriotic Movement, "History of the NCC and the CCC," accessed July 18, 2015, http://www.ccctspm.org/.

14  Ibid.

15  Ho, *The Dragon and the Cross*, 110.

16  Shen Guiping, "Long-term Policy of Religious Freedom - Commemorate 30th anniversary of Document 19 Issued by the CCP in 1982," *Chinese Nationalities*, March 13, 2012.

17  State Administration for Religious Affairs of PRC, "Religious Freedom in China," accessed November 11, 2015, http://www.sara.gov.cn/zwgk/17839.htm.

18  Ibid.

19  Jiang Wenhan, "The Present Situation of Christianity in China," in *Missiology: An International Review*, Vol. XI, ed. Rich Starcher (CA: Biola University Press, 1983), 259-65.

20  China Christian Council Three-Self Patriotic Movement. "The Third National Christian Conference Resolution," accessed July 18, 2015, http://www.ccctspm.org/.

21  Jiang, "The Present Situation of Christianity in China," 264.

22  State Administration for Religious Affairs of PRC, "Religious Freedom in China."

23   Tony Lambert, "Counting Christians in China: A Cautionary Report," *International Bulletin of Missionary Research, Vol. 27, (CA: Biola University Press, 2003), 1:7.*

24   China Christian Council Three-Self Patriotic Movement, "History of the NCC and the CCC."

25   Wang Hongyi, "China Plans Establishment of Christian Theology," *China Daily, August 7, 2014.*

26   Patrick Johnstone, *Operation World (London, Paternoster, 2001), 165.*

27   Wang Zuoan, "Protestantism We Want to See," *China Religions, No. 12, 2006; Joseph Tse-Hei Lee and Christie Chui-Shan Chow, "Christian Revival from Within," in Christianity in Contemporary China: Socio-cultural Perspective, ed. F.K.G. Lim (New York: Routledge, 2013), 45-58.*

28   Zhao Xiao, "Christianity and China's Transformation," *accessed January 15, 2015,* http://www.brookings.edu/~/media/events/2014/06/03-christianity-in-china/zhao-xiao-ppt.pdf.

29   *Ibid.*

30   Zhuo Xinping, "Religious Media and Social Harmony," *China Religions Academic Network, accessed November 11, 2015,* http://www.sara.gov.cn/zwgk/17839.htm.

31   Wang, "Preaching, Expansion, and Future of Christianity in China," *China Religions (Beijing: State Administration for Religious Affairs of PRC, 2010), No. 11.*

32   "Religious Policies by the CCP," *The National Committee of the Chinese People's Political Consultative Conference, accessed November 11, 2015,* http://www.cppcc.gov.cn

33   Wang, "Protestantism We Want to See."

34   Ho, *The Dragon and the Cross, 116.*

35   Jacqueline E. Wenger, "Official vs. Underground Protestant Churches in China: Challenges for Reconciliation and Social Influence." *Review of Religious Research, Vol. 46, No. 2 (2004):169-82; Yang Fenggang, "Between Secularist Ideology and Desecularizing Reality: The Birth and Growth of Religious Research in Communist China," in The Association for the Sociology of Religion, vol. 65, no.2 (2004):101–19.*

36   Wang, "China Plans Establishment of Christian Theology."

37   *Ibid.*

38   *Ibid.*

## Primary Sources

Central People's Government of PRC. "History of Christianity in China." *Accessed July 18, 2015.* http://www.gov.cn/test/2005-07/26/content_17214.htm.

China Christian Council Three-Self Patriotic Movement. "History of the NCC and the CCC." *Accessed July 18, 2015.* http://www.ccctspm.org/.

"The Third National Christian Conference Resolution."

Merwin, Wallace C. and Francis P. Jones. *Documents of the Three-Self Movement: Source Materials for the Study of the Protestant Church in China.* New York: National Council of the Churches of Christ in the USA, 1963.

National Christian Conference in Shanghai 1922: *The Chinese Church as Revealed in the National Christian Conference.* Shanghai: Oriental Press, 1922.

National Committee of the Chinese People's Political Consultative Conference. "CCP's Religious Policies." *Accessed November 11, 2015.* http://www.cppcc.gov.cn.

State Administration for Religious Affairs of PRC. "Religious Freedom in China." *Accessed November 11, 2015.* http://www.sara.gov.cn/zwgk/17839.htm.

## Secondary Sources

Aikman, David. *Jesus in Beijing: How Christianity is Transforming China and Changing the Global Balance of Power.* Washington, DC: Regnery Publishing, 2003.

Bays, Daniel H. *A New History of Christianity in China.* UK: Wiley-Blackwell Publication, 2012.

Franke, Wolfgang. *China and the West: The Cultural Encounter, 13th to 20th Centuries.* New York: Harper Torchbook, 1967.

Ho, Louis K. *The Dragon and the Cross: Why European Christianity Failed to Take Root in China.* UK: Xulon Press, 2009.

Johnstone, Patrick. *Operation World.* London, Paternoster, 2001.

Lambert, Tony. "Counting Christians in China: A Cautionary Report." *International Bulletin of Missionary Research,* Vol. 27:1. CA: Biola University Press, 2003.

Latourette, Kenneth Scott. *A History of Christian Missions in China.* New York: MacMillan Company, 1929.

Lee, Joseph Tse-Hei and Christie Chui-Shan Chow. "Christian Revival from Within." *Christianity in Contemporary China: Socio-cultural Perspective,* ed. F.K.G. Lim. New York: Routledge, 2013.

Shen, Guiping. "Long-term Policy of Religious Freedom - Commemorate 30th anniversary of Document 19 Issued by the CCP in 1982." *Chinese Nationalities,* March 13, 2012.

Wang, Hongyi. "China Plans Establishment of Christian Theology." *China Daily,* August 7, 2014.

Wang, Zuoan. "Protestantism We Want to See. *China Religions,* No. 12, 2006.
--- "Preaching, Expansion, and Future of Christianity in China." *China Religions,* No.11. Beijing: State Administration for Religious Affairs of PRC, 2010.

Wenger, Jacqueline E. "Official vs. Underground Protestant Churches in China: Challenges for Reconciliation and Social Influence." *Review of Religious Research,* Vol. 46, No. 2, 2004.

Wenhan, Jiang. "The Present Situation of Christianity in China." *Missiology: An International Review,* Vol. XI, ed. Rich Starcher. CA: Biola University Press, 1983.

Yang, Fenggang. "Between Secularist Ideology and Desecularizing Reality: The Birth and Growth of Religious Research in Communist China." *The Association for the Sociology of Religion,* Vol. 65, No.2, 2004.

Zhao, Xiao. "Christianity and China's Transformation." Accessed January 15, 2015. http://www.brookings.edu/~/media/events/2014/06/03-christianity-in-china/zhao-xiao-ppt.pdf.

Zhuo, Xinping. "Religious Media and Social Harmony." *China Religions Academic Network.* Accessed November 11, 2015. http://www.sara.gov.cn/zwgk/17839.htm.

---

*Linlin Victoria Lu is the Campus College Chair for the University of Phoenix Atlanta Campus.*

# Why Giving is Harder than Earning: Philanthropy in China

*Yong Lu*
*Vol. 16, No.1*
*2017*

The year 2016 is an important milestone for China's social development. China's first charity law was passed in March and became effective in September. Moreover, China's Foreign NGO Management Law was passed in April and takes effect in January 2017. Both laws indicate the intention of the Chinese government to strengthen regulations of the emerging fields of philanthropy and civic engagement.

China has enormous potential for philanthropy. Forbes reported in 2016 China has 251 billionaires, second only to the United States' 540, and China has the most new billionaires, adding 70 to the list.[1] Beijing has become the "Billionaire Capital of the World" with 100 billionaires, five more than New York City.[2] Credit Suisse reported that China's middle class is the largest in the world: 109 million Chinese adults have wealth between $50,000 and $500,000, well ahead of the 92 million in the U.S.[3]

Despite the explosive wealth accumulation, charitable giving in China is lagging far behind the U.S. In 2014, giving as a percentage of China's GDP was only 0.1 percent, compared to two percent in the U.S.[4] Chinese giving was about one-hundredth of what Americans donated per person.[5] China ranked 144 among 145 countries in the 2015 World Giving Index; only Burundi ranked lower.[6]

Why such a huge gap between private wealth and private giving? Chinese billionaire Jack Ma, founder of Alibaba Group, said during the 2015 opening ceremony of a new degree program in nonprofit management at Peking University, "Giving donations to charities is much harder than earning money." Ma commented that in China, it is particularly tough to figure out to whom one should give. China lacks the infrastructure, training, and proper legal framework to en-sure that donations go to good use. Setting that up does not happen overnight.[7]

Ma's concern is widely shared by Chinese people who wish to contribute to social services – not only the super-rich but also the rapidly growing middle class. Private, modern philanthropic practices that are entrenched in Western culture are new to both Chinese donors and charities. Just 20 years ago, a distinct socio-economic middle class was virtually nonexistent in China[8], not to mention the ultra-rich philanthropist class. Only in recent years has China started the journey of modernizing philanthropy and social organizations. Like many other systems in China, Chinese philanthropy will take on its special characteristics in the pro-cess of modernization. The following discussion provides a deeper understanding of the current state, as well as the challenges and opportunities for such develop-ment in China.

## The Rebirth of Philanthropic Spirit

Philanthropy appears to be a new phenomenon in China, but it isn't. Conven-tional wisdom holds that the donation of money to good causes or to the general well-being of society is a modern Western concept to which China is not accus-tomed. But the fact is China has a long history of charitable behaviors. For both Confucianism and Buddhism, benevolence is a core value. Traditionally, "helping and caring for others" is held in high esteem by the Chinese. The value of philan-thropy has been rooted in Chinese culture for thousands of years.

China also has a tradition of government planning and guiding of charitable activities. Before the ninth century, charitable activities were largely religion-based and managed by temples or ancestral shrines, some of which functioned much like the civil society we know today. Since the mid-ninth century, the government has been playing a key role in funding charities, often appointing local notables as managers. In the early 20th century during the pre-Communist period, a number of prominent Chinese demonstrated remarkable generosity and charitable initia-tive. For example, former Premier of the Republic of China Xiong Xiling (1870-1937) pioneered China's modern philanthropy by helping establish educational and human service institutions to confront natural disasters and the Japanese in-vasion. A group of Western foundations and missionaries introduced American-style philanthropy to China, including the Rockefeller Foundation's contribution in medicine and John Leighton Stuart's work with Yenching University.

However, during the first quarter-century of the People's Republic – from the Socialist Revolution through the Cultural Revolution – wealth was completely na-tionalized. An ideal Communist state was believed to be able to provide compre-hensive public services and resolve all social problems, so almost any recognition of the need for private charity was considered a sign of government failure and was not encouraged. As Zhang Xin, one of China's richest women and billionaire CEO of the SOHO China real estate development company commented, "As children of that society we could not have imagined the possibility of becoming a philanthropist."[9]

It was not until 1978 that China turned to economic reform and reopened its doors to global markets. The most significant social consequence of China's economic growth is the increasing diversification of public resources, interests, and needs. A modern nation, regardless of its political system, must find a way to combine public and private efforts in providing social services for its citizens. The Chinese government has begun to realize the essentiality as well as the benefits of civic participation and private philanthropy. Now, the same entrepreneurial spirit that has been demonstrated in the business sector is beginning to have an impact in the civic arena.

In 2014, China received an estimated $16 billion from both domestic and overseas donors, surpassing the peak last seen in 2008, when Wenchuan earthquake killed nearly 70,000 people and triggered significant public giving.[10] Several successful entrepreneurs such as Jack Ma and Zhang Xin made strong commitments in philanthropy. In 2014, Jack Ma set up a $3 billion charitable trust, and Zhang Xin and her husband set up a $100 million endowment for underprivileged Chinese students to attend leading universities around the world.

We should not take China's philanthropic record of the last 60 years as proof that Chinese people are generally not philanthropic. With continued economic growth and social diversification, China's philanthropic spirit will likely flourish in the future.

### Philanthropy with Chinese Characteristics

Why has modern philanthropy been slow to take off in China? China faces unique challenges in cultivating philanthropy, not only because of historical and cultural factors, but also, more importantly, because of the underdeveloped social support system. Philanthropy in China today demonstrates three noteworthy characteristics.

One is that Chinese donors are more focused on addressing immediate social needs, as opposed to long-term issues. The latest Giving China report showed that the vast majority of donations – more than 75 percent – have been directed to urgent needs including medicine and disaster relief, education, and poverty alleviation.[11] According to the research by Harvard Kennedy School Ash Center, the top 100 philanthropists in China gave most often to education (58 percent of total donations) and least often to environmental causes (0.9 percent), despite that China faces serious environmental challenges.[12] Other long-term social areas such as public policy, international affairs, and arts, culture and humanities received little support. In education, most giving was in support of universities, and specifically focused on scholarships and building constructions. Areas such as research, teaching, and special initiatives received very limited funding.

Secondly, Chinese people tend to trust family members and neighbors much more than strangers, partly because of the country's long history as an agrarian society. This is true in China both for conducting business and for philanthropy. It works fine for traditional charitable behaviors – donors give to people in need and immediately see the result. But modern philanthropy does not work that way. The concept of modern philanthropy is not just about giving fish to feed a hungry person; it seeks to empower those in need to fish for themselves and even work to improve the entire ecosystem for fishing. In other words, the goal of modern philanthropy is to make sustainable, systematic change. We are helping people we do not know and it will often take years to measure our results. Many Chinese may find it difficult to adopt such concept. They are generally less concerned about tackling the long-term, root causes of the social problem. This pattern poses a direct challenge to the development of philanthropy in China.

Another characteristic is the widespread "trust crisis" of Chinese donors toward Chinese charities. Chinese social organizations are traditionally affiliated with the government, run by government personnel and supported by government funding. Such structure has proven to be inefficient and ineffective in providing many social services. In recent years, a series of scandals among major state-run charities, including the Red Cross Society of China, further undermined their credibility. Partly because of the reform of registration procedures for social organizations that came into force in 2013, a great variety of new organizations have sprung up in China. Currently there are more than 511,000 legitimately registered NGOs.[13] Many of them are still quasi-state institutions. Donors often find it difficult to identify appropriate or trustworthy organizations to which to contribute. At the same time, organizations that want to raise funds for meaningful causes do not have a clearly defined set of technical and ethical standards to conform to. Only 30 percent of registered charities in China meet basic international standards for transparency and disclosure.[14]

As a result, Chinese donors often choose to adopt a hands-on approach in giving, by establishing their own operating foundations to conduct charitable work by themselves, or even personally hand out donations to recipients. A great number of wealthy Chinese give to overseas nonprofits in the belief that investing in those reputable organizations will bring meaningful social returns. The new charity law attempted to address the issue by specifying some requirements in transparency and accountability for charities, as well as a few fundraising guidelines. However there is still a long way to go for Chinese social organizations to build professionalism and re-establish public trust.

**Road Ahead: Infrastructure Building and Professionalization**

Over the past 30 years, China has established a market economy system. The next critical agenda for China is to deepen the reform and open the social sector. China is in urgent need of philanthropic infrastructure.

First, the market economy needs to perform strongly, and personal wealth needs to be well-protected. People should not worry that giving to charities may draw public criticism or create trouble for themselves. For example, Chinese donors often choose to stay anonymous because they are afraid of public attention and jealousy about their wealth. Also, when Chinese donors give to the world's leading universities, their actions often generate wide criticism among the Chinese as if the donors were not "patriotic" or their motivations are simply to gain admission for their children. The society as a whole needs to develop a reasonable expectation about philanthropy, and respect that giving is a personal choice and reflects individual interests.

Second, China needs to develop a mature financial system to ensure the sustainable development of philanthropic funds and endowments. It should require that each nonprofit create a board that acts as trustee of public assets and ensures that the organization is well-managed and remains fiscally sound. Many Chinese social organizations do not have formal governance structures in place to fulfill fiscal and strategic responsibilities. A modern accountability system should be constructed to ensure that endowment assets will be in the hands of ethical and professional investment managers. Nonprofits should be required to hire professional public accountants to conduct independent auditing based on internationally accepted standards. Strong financial management correlates strongly with institutional quality and sustainability.

Lastly, China needs to establish a legal system to regulate the social sector concerning philanthropy. The new charity law confirms charities' legal status, makes it easier for charities to register and raise funds, and improves tax incentives. In the U.S., the tax-exempt status for public charities entails large obligations and heavy regulation of the sector. Nonprofits are regulated by the tax authority at the federal level, by law offices at the state level, and by independent industry associations and watchdogs, etc. In China, none of this is fully in place yet, and it remains unclear whether the Ministry of Civil Affairs can effectively perform all the regulatory and administrative functions designated in the new law.

In order to make philanthropy work, it is also critical for China to professionalize the governance and management process of social organizations. The Chinese nonprofit world is not yet an independent "sector." Fundraising is not yet an established "profession," nor is nonprofit management. China will need to nurture a new generation of professionals who are dedicated to social sector management. Research shows that the main reason individuals give is because they are asked to and are presented with opportunities that motivate them to give.[15] Nonprofit professionals are the servants of philanthropy. They provide essential guidance and service for people to donate. They teach people the joy of giving. They also need to steward the donation and assume responsibility for the public trust. China's for-profit corporations have been adopting many international management standards and skills. Today, China's social organizations are faced with an unprecedented opportunity to try the same. Without competent professional leadership that cares about the cause and properly runs the organizations, we will continue to hear the comments that it is easier to make money in China than to give it away.

### Notes

1    Forbes Corporate Communications, *Forbes' 30th Annual World's Billionaires Issue*, March 1, 2016.

2    USA Today, "Beijing Overtakes NYC as 'Billionaire Capital'," February 24, 2016.

3    Credit Suisse, Global Wealth Report 2015, October 2015.

4    Harvard Kennedy School Ash Center for Democratic Governance and Innovation, China's Most Generous 2015, January 2016.

5    The Economist, "Panda Power," December 19, 2015.

6    CAF World Giving Index, November 2015.

7    South China Morning Post, "'It's harder to donate money to Chinese charities than earn it,' says Alibaba billionaire Jack Ma" September 16, 2015.

8    Cheng Li edited, China's Emerging Middle Class, Brookings Institution Press, Washington, DC, 2010.

9    Zhang Xin, "The Rise of the Chinese Philanthropist," The New York Times, December 4, 2014.

10   China Charity Information Center, Giving China 2014, Chinese Society Press, Beijing, 2015.

11   Ibid.

12   Harvard Kennedy School Ash Center for Democratic Governance and Innovation, China's Most Generous 2015, January 2016.

13   He Dan, "Reforms Give NGOs a Level Playing Field," China Daily, March 31, 2014.

14   China Charity Information Center, China Charity Transparency Report, September 2013.

15   National Park Service, "Motivations for Giving," www.nps.gov/partnerships/fundraising_individuals_motivations.htm.

*Yong Lu is founder and CEO of Evergreen Asia Advisors, LLC.*

# Rural China's Fallen Children

*Mark Akpaninyie*
*Vol. 15, No.1*
*2016*

China has amazed the world once again, not with economic growth, but with the closing of its education gap. There has been tremendous transformation in Chinese education over the past three decades. With the elimination of school fees for the nine years of compulsory education, the Ministry of Education reports a near universal primary education rate at 99 percent.

But the figures mask a disturbing reality. The Chinese education system is vastly unequal. Despite the tremendous expansion in education, wide, well-documented differences remain in educational access and quality between rural and urban communities. Rural areas have been left behind.

While academic access for rural children has risen, many students are casualties of the system. Many rural schools lack the outreach necessary to remediate students falling behind or differentiate teaching styles and curriculum for students with learning disabilities or different learning styles. Low-performing students and students with disabilities are simply overlooked and equipped with the tools of failure, guaranteeing them bleak chances for future academic success.

## Admitting the Problem

Three years ago, I began a fellowship that brought me to a rural village school in southwest Yunnan, one of China's poorest areas. As a primary school English teacher, I was exposed to an educational setting far removed from the highly rated classrooms of Shanghai, where assessment is based on an internationally recognized rubric. It was here that I realized I was not in Shanghai anymore. I had an awakening about the real plight of children learning in rural China.

Having just completed a lesson, I called upon a student to assess general understanding. When it became clear that this student did not know the answer, I pointed to the Chinese translation on the board, instructing the student to read the correct response.

After a moment of hesitation and silence, the student stated that he was unable to read. Other students immediately confirmed this claim. I would soon learn that not only was this student illiterate but dozens of other students were as well. I would discover that students also lacked skills in other subjects such as math, with no fewer than 60 out of approximately 900 fourth and fifth grade students scoring zeroes on standardized exams each year.

Nevertheless, these students routinely were promoted to the next grade with the implicit expectation that by middle school, they will drop out. This is, by far, not a singular experience. Many of my colleagues in nearby village schools witnessed a similar phenomenon.

By accidentally shaming my student, I revealed a larger issue of illiteracy and learning problems that plague many rural schools and a lack the resources and willingness to address the issues. Many underlying factors produced these effects.

## Where Rural Systems Fail

China's strict language education was prohibitive for many students in the village. Classes were taught strictly in Mandarin by teachers often from outside the village, and therefore unfamiliar with the local dialect. I worked in a village where Mandarin was not used much or at all beyond the school grounds. Villagers mostly communicated in their own dialect. In an environment where Mandarin may not be a first or even second language, many students struggle.

To make matters worse, students with learning disabilities, emotional trauma, and other issues fare even worse. Many of my head teachers would identify these students and suggest I not worry too much about them, stating nothing could be done. With a lack of resources not only to diagnose but also to treat and address such instances, sadly there is very little done to accommodate these students.

There is also a conceptual component. During my three years of teaching, I was consistently advised to focus on high-performing students, who would conveniently be seated in the front of all my classes, and not waste time on tiao pi[1], or "mischievous" students, some of whom had clear learning disabilities or a different style of learning.

Mainstream beliefs hold that certain students possess a stronger proclivity for learning and academic success. Students from poorer and/or non-Han backgrounds are often regarded as underachievers. Resources are focused on high-achieving students to the detriment of low-achieving students.

Accordingly, there are clear structural problems that cause many students to fail. Students are knowingly promoted to the next grade without having grasped necessary core skills or mastering critical knowledge, and many lack basic literacy skills.

### Pathways Forward

China must enact deliberate policies to maximize learning outcomes for all students and incentivize rural school systems and educators to work with all students equitably. Municipal education bureaus should invest in soft teaching resources. Currently, investment is largely devoted to technology, real estate, and materials.

Many rural school systems invest little or nothing in counseling or special education services, despite the fact that research indicates children living in poverty are more prone to suffer emotional trauma and setbacks. Soft teaching resources include creating remediated curricula, training and embedding counseling professionals, and prioritizing the identification and diagnosis of disabilities.

Stanford University's Rural Education Action Program (REAP) has conducted preliminary research demonstrating how teacher performance pay can improve student achievement under proper implementation. The creation of a rewards system should focus more closely on student improvement rather than student performance, offering higher rewards for low-achieving students than high-achieving ones. Under this system, teacher performance pay is not strictly tied to the final scores of students but rather to their aggregate improvement over a given period. This system assesses teacher effort more precisely and encourages teachers to focus on every student.

Education for rural children is more necessary than ever if economic development in the rural southwest is to start to bear a resemblance to its eastern provincial counterparts. As more rural residents flock to urban centers all over the country, an uneducated population augurs badly for the Chinese labor force. If China wants continued economic development and sustainable growth, it desperately needs a well-educated labor force that is not just concentrated in its urban centers.

### Notes

1    **Tiao pi** *is often translated as "mischievous," which describes teachers' view of these students. But the word in this case also carries the connotation that a student is a low performer.*

---

*Mark Akpaninyie spent three years as a Fellow with Teach For China and as a lecturer at Baoshan University in Yunnan Province.*

# Review of The China-U.S. partnership to Prevent Spina Bifida

*Zhuo (Adam) Chen*
*Vol. 15, No.1*
*2016*

Let me say it right here: *The China-U.S. Partnership to Prevent Spina Bifida – The Evolution of a Landmark Epidemiological Study*, by Deborah Kowal (Vanderbilt University Press, 2015), is a monumental work. And here is why.

The book is a vivid account of a large epidemiological study spanning roughly 16 years, from the conversation that started the project in 1983 to the first published results in 1999. There were new cultural and physical environments to get used to, bureaucratic hurdles to overcome, and miscommunications to clear up. The dedicated public health professionals from the U.S. and China overcame these issues in order to achieve the common goal of preventing neural tube defects (NTDs), which can happen early in a pregnancy. All this is chronicled in the book, along with revealing anecdotes and side stories. Kowal, for example, notes how Centers for Disease Control and Prevention (CDC) visitors reacted to hearing the American cowboy song "Home on the Range" played on Chinese instruments — namely, "strange and eerily out of place."

The book starts with a conversation between an American doctor from the CDC, the premier public health agency in the United States, and a Chinese doctor who was trained at the Peking Union Medical School, one of the most prestigious medical schools in China. They note the unusual rate of spina bifida and anencephaly in China and an opportunity to study the epidemiology of neural tube defects, which later materialize as the China-U.S. Collaborative Project for NTD Prevention. As the story unfolds, the Chinese collaborators are puzzled by the CDC budgeting and funding process, and the scale of participation and coordination in China surprise the CDC researchers. The Chinese researchers learn new concepts such as informed consent and Institutional Review Board protocol, while their American counterparts acculturate to their host country, consuming potent rice liquor and strange foods. Given the project is a unique collaboration between teams from two very different countries, unexpected developments in domestic and international politics always lurk and indeed pose serious risks to the project at times.

Aside from paying homage to those who have made critical contributions to the project, this book is a thorough account of the epidemiology study, providing more information and lessons learned to epidemiologists and economists than the author may realize. The detailed information, gathered by the author from the original documents and personal narratives, can help those who are interested in conducting and evaluating similar studies to be prepared for pitfalls, to avoid complications, and to learn better ways to manage both people and projects.

As an economist, I appreciate Kowal's description of the cost-benefit equation. Just a year after the crackdown in Tiananmen Square, 1990 was not the best time for collaborative projects between public institutions from the U.S. and China. The U.S. Congress, however, approved the funding for this project in China, partly due to the cost-benefit considerations. From a practical standpoint, this was a bargain for the U.S. The project would have cost much more if it had been carried out in the United States. But the investment was an even bigger bargain when we consider how many children it enabled to grow up healthy and whole. In health economists' jargon, this is an economic evaluation with a societal perspective that led to positive policy change.

As fine as the book is, there is a drawback for researchers. Many people contributed greatly to the project, and Kowal provides a complete list. But there is no bilingual index of names, something that could pose a challenge to readers interested in knowing more about the Chinese researchers. The Chinese language contains a large number of homophones, and it could be difficult to locate the exact Chinese names if the readers are not familiar with the players.

Despite that minor flaw, anyone interested in learning more about the collaboration between China and the United States in public health will find this book highly informative. Those interested international studies likewise will gain invaluable insights. A reader's time will be well spent.

---

*Zhuo (Adam) Chen is a health economist with an expertise in China's agriculture, labor and health policies. He is an associate of the China Research Center.*

## Beijing United Hospital

*Michael C. Wenderoth*
*Vol. 16, No.2*
*2017*

*This year marks the 20th anniversary of Beijing United Family Hospital, the first western-standard joint-venture hospital to open its doors in China. Started as a women's and children's hospital, Beijing United has evolved into <u>United Family Healthcare (UFH)</u>, the premium, private healthcare network across in China, offering a full range of healthcare services through its hospitals, clinics, and centers of excellence.*

*Michael C. Wenderoth, who served from 1994 to 1997 as the hospital's project manager, spoke to Roberta Lipson, CEO and Chairman of the Board of UFH, about the hospital's challenges and successes, and how those reflect on a changing China.*

*When we started the journey to establish Beijing United Family Hospital in 1994 (I worked for Chindex International, Beijing United's parent company, in the 1990s), Lipson already had more than a decade of business experience in China. Arriving in Beijing in 1979, she established Chindex in 1981 and took it public on NASDAQ in 1992 as the largest independent American distributor of high-end western medical equipment in China.*

[The interview below has been edited for brevity.]

**WENDEROTH: *Roberta, first I want to take this opportunity to publicly thank you. In 1994, you hired a 22-year-old American history graduate to help you establish Beijing United Family Hospital (hereafter referred to as "Beijing United"). You gave me a chance, more responsibility than I was due, and put me through the school of hard knocks. Margaret Mead was right: "Never doubt that a small group of dedicated people can change the***

*world, indeed it is the only thing that ever has." Thank you.*

*Establishing and successfully running any business in China is hard, yet you consistently have done this over almost four decades since you founded Chindex, the parent company of Beijing United, in 1981. When we opened Beijing United in 1997, you shifted Chindex's business from medical equipment into healthcare provision. Beijing United has now become United Family Healthcare Network (hereafter referred to as "UFH"), blazing many firsts, including becoming the first non-U.S. hospital to receive the prestigious Joint Commission International's accreditation, as well as numerous accolades and attention from international media.*

*Your vision in 1993 was to provide women and children – primarily expatriates – better patient-centered healthcare options in China. Most people said you were crazy and laughed at you. Did you really envision then that United Hospital would become what it is today, in 2017? What, if anything, differs in how United Hospital looks today versus the vision you had for it in 1993?*

LIPSON: To be honest, I can't say I foresaw the true potential of UFH when we decided to build our first little hospital.  I knew at the time there was a very meaningful opportunity to model a new approach to healthcare for China.  I thought that if we could show that a different approach to healthcare was possible on the ground in China, there were 10,000 or 20,000 expats in Beijing who had a great need for an upgrade in the services that were then available.  I knew that this limited expat market could sustain our small 50-bed hospital.  I thought that perhaps one day the economy of China would evolve and there would be some demand among the local population. But I, like most others, had no full sense of the great pace of growth of the Chinese economy, the great pace of change in the preferences of the Chinese consumer, or the impact in the changing supporting policies from the Chinese government that would allow us to grow into the multicity healthcare system we are today.

**Wenderoth: So it was a little bit of a leap of faith?**

Lipson: Through the 1980s we had been leading delegations of Chinese officials to the U.S.

They appreciated much of what they saw at some of America's best hospitals, but they were uniformly sure that little of the best practices they saw could be implemented in China. Part of me wanted to just prove them wrong and set up a pilot model closer to home. On the other hand, we did build a model we believed could be sustainable and reproducible in China's major cities.

**Wenderoth: Can you give an example of the "best practices" the Chinese saw in the U.S. that they felt could not be implemented in China?**

Lipson: They failed to see how the American patient-centric approach, or one might say a viable market-based model, could work in China's State-run healthcare system. But even simple things, like how to make a hospital not smell like a hospital. How to have patients not line up for hours at the best hospitals [as was common in China… when there were] neighborhood clinics available they could go to. How to reduce the inappropriate overuse of antibiotics.

**Wenderoth: Setting up that pilot model proved challenging. Healthcare is highly regulated, and so-called "nonmarket" forces (dealing with government policy) are key. Managing government policy consistently ranks as one of the most difficult areas for western executives to get their arms around in China. Again, you have been a pioneer in this front (not only setting up Beijing United, but being the first to set up bonded warehouses, creatively using export-import loans, to name a few). You also continue your active involvement in the American Chamber of Commerce, policy groups, and are sought after by policy makers from many countries. Can you share a few strategies that are critical to making things work from a nonmarket perspective in China?**

LIPSON: China's economy for the past 40 yeas has been consistently growing at an unprecedented pace, and the society's needs are evolving as quickly. It has been impossible for policy to keep up with these changes. Policymakers are further hampered by a multitude of interest groups that can be resistant to changes, even if those changes might be better for society as a whole. Furthermore, central government policy reforms are implemented at a varying pace and in varying ways in different local geographies. Sometimes the clear policy declarations of one government organ will be contradicted by another government department of equal impact. All of this can make for a very challenging policy environment.

My cardinal rule in overcoming this potentially confusing environment is to keep in close communication with all stakeholders and policymakers in the government. This is challenging, but we have found that the feedback we can offer to policymakers truly has been appreciated and often reflected in subsequent policy reforms. I firmly believe that ultimately the government is working to improve the policy environment and make China a healthier country. Actually the big plan is always outlined in each five-year plan, and most recently by the State Councils Healthy China 2030. I have always felt that if United Family's strategies fit within this framework, the attendant policy specifics will eventually be in place to support our direction.

*Wenderoth: Talk about dealing with shifts. The concept of growing a business and "pivoting" (shifting one's business focus or model in reaction to the market) is a popular buzzword and is viewed as a critical skill to managing in complex, rapidly changing environments such as Silicon Valley or China. As you established and ran the hospitals over the past 25 years, do you even think in terms of "pivoting," and is that an important skill to working in China? If you do, was there any particularly important "pivot" that Beijing United or UFH made that you can share? A key lesson learned?*

Lipson: When we first opened, we relied on the business of the international community. As the Chinese economy developed and the local market became the largest growth opportunity for us, we had to figure out how to design our systems to deliver the best experience for our local patient base while not losing the international aspects of our offering that set us apart, never losing our core value of evidence-based practice. We continue to adapt as the mix and knowledge evolve.

The other important pivot developed as we grew from a single hospital to a hospital-plus-community clinic model, and then to a multicity system with the full continuum of care from clinic to acute-care hospital, to rehab, to home health, providing care along the full life cycle, from before birth to hospice care. We upgraded our management model while deploying technology to help us deliver the same standard of quality offerings over both geographic and temporal continuums.

*Wenderoth: On your "management model," UFH is unique in that it employs about every culture imaginable (China and foreign), and serves patients of many cultures in a very high-service environment (having your child is a more important event than say a wedding or five-star hotel experience). Getting it "right" on the people side and intercultural side is critical. Can you share what is key to getting the intercultural part right? For a foreigner coming to China, how would you recommend them to best prepare them-selves for working/leading effectively in China? For that matter, for your Chinese employees, what is most important in working with westerners?*

Lipson: Actually, this is one of the ingredients at the core of our "secret sauce." Our teams are not only multicultural in the Chinese plus foreigner sense, but also gender-balanced and balanced among educational backgrounds (medicine, nursing, management, etc.). Having a management team fostering an environment of mutual respect and appreciation has allowed us to glean learnings from multiple perspectives. Open dialogue among often varying viewpoints allows us to examine issues a multidimensional way, often coming up with innovative solutions. We celebrate this diversity and it is explicitly reflected in an element of our core values of ICARE (Innovation, Caring, Accountability, RESPECT and Excellence). Being a multilingual institution, almost all of our 2,000 plus employees can communicate with each other in either English or Chinese. We encourage language and culture study and make opportunities for further development available to all our team members.

*Wenderoth: Are there any big myths that foreigners (and especially the West) have about China?*

Lipson: That it is Communist? Actually, China is one of the liveliest market economies going that operates alongside an influential state-owned sector. That it is monolithic? Actually, China is a country full of diversity: linguistic, ethnic, cultural, culinary, even policy environment. But it is also tied together by a strong national identity.

*Wenderoth: In 20 years, there must have been many crucial moments for you and the hospital – something insightful, a failure, or a moment that tested your resolve as a leader. Surely the SARS crisis, weathering economic down-turns or changes in management would be obvious issues I could ask about. But they may not have been what tested you the most. Can you share one of those key moments for you and the organization, and specifically how you overcame it, what you learned from it?*

Lipson: I would say your first guess was the most clear. The SARS crisis was a real test for us, for all of China, and for that matter for the whole world's healthcare community. We realized that no matter how close we were as an organization to getting our own systems as close to perfect as possible, we were still reli-ant for so much on information from the government, and support from the wider healthcare community. We realized that we could only do our best for our patients if not only our systems were working but also if the information coming from the wider system was reliable. During SARS both we and the government realized that improvement was needed in these areas in order to prevent another crisis.

The period of SARS was frightening in revealing stages. In the beginning, although we had already diagnosed a high-profile case of SARS at our hospital outpatient department, there was no official recognition yet of the problem in China. By the time an official recognition of the problem happened and a referral system was set up for confirmed cases, all referral center hospitals were quickly overwhelmed. Many of us worked around the clock to upgrade systems to keep up with the evolving situation and find ways to keep our patients safe. Luckily by the time the epidemic passed, all parties – including the government, our hospital, and the wider healthcare community – realized a lot of [lessons] could be gleaned from the disaster and quickly took those [lessons] on board. As a result there is a lot more transparency and timeliness around public health data, hospitals are better designed for infection control, and we feel that the whole system can work in a more reliable way.

***Wenderoth: Tell us more about operating in China. Chinese firms move fast, operate lean, or benefit from understanding their native environment well. Some copy quickly, many innovate in their own right, and others benefit from quasi-government support. Even now Chinese are rapidly moving into upscale healthcare provision. Outside of China, management thinkers have gone so far to say that we are seeing the "end of (traditional notions of) competitive advantage," and that the only competitive advantage today is being adaptable and moving fast. Can you share how you think, or UFH thinks, about dealing with Chinese competitors? Do Chinese firms think, act, or manage differently from the conventional "western" view? If so, what can western business learn from the Chinese? What is the competitive advantage western firms need these days?***

Lipson: UFH has been innovating, adapting, integrating, and growing for 20 years. Our success has been rewarded with many admirers and imitators. We consider this confirmation of our success and celebrate our models of care that have found currency in both the public system as well as other private startups.

***Wenderoth: What do you do when you are blatantly copied?***

Lipson: We do not appreciate when imitators also pretend to "be us," by copying our logo, brand name, as well as surface design elements of our facilities. We have successfully sued many of these imitators.

Healthcare, however, is extremely complex (as Donald Trump recently discovered), and so new startups tend to start with the simplest, most lucrative segments. It is relatively simpler to start an obstetrics hospital than a full-blown general model of care. UFH's system of Continuity of Care for our patients has evolved over time. Having the complete integrated continuum of care – including community clinics, acute care general hospitals, home health, rehab and hospice – will take newcomers years to develop.

*Wenderoth: So, in the end, the key is building a long-term business that serves your customers' needs and fits the changing environment, period?*

Lipson: The UFH's full-service offerings allow us to become the lifelong healthcare partner for our customers. In response to the growing acceptance of commercial health insurance we are able, together with our insurance partners, to take on the risk of the health of whole population groups. This can only be done in a system with the full spectrum of offerings from primary care and prevention to acute care intervention capabilities.

No matter whether Chinese or foreign, the keys to a company's long-term success in my mind are not only nimble adaptability but persistence of principal in moving toward a goal, a strategy that is consistent with the betterment of society, and the ability to inspire passion in the whole workforce about achieving this goal. I believe that the promise of only financial rewards, no matter how rich, will always be trumped by sound financial rewards plus the satisfaction of producing a good or service that benefits society.

*Wenderoth: If you had a "do-over" what would it be? Any regrets? Hindsight is 20-20, of course!*

Lipson: It's hard for me to say that I have any regrets. Every misstep has been a learning experience.

*Wenderoth: You've interacted with policymakers, industry titans, company alumni, the new generation of millennial Chinese who were born after the 1980s, and a whole community outside the business world, and have for more than 40 years. What has most surprised you about China's transfor-*

*mation? What should we be watching most closely?*

Lipson: The huge personal wealth that has accumulated, and the entrepreneurial spirit that is everywhere. Perhaps we should have predicted this. Specifically, as it applies to our business, the increasing acceptance that – in addition to basic healthcare, which the government should provide – an increasing number of consumers are willing to see choice in healthcare as a private good.

*Wenderoth: Over the past 40 years you've been at the center of what many would argue has been the greatest transformation of a country in world history. If you had young kids (I know yours are older now), what do you feel they should be studying or learning to be best prepared for the future?*

Lipson: I feel like my kids have had a great education in China in the international school which really did prepare them well for today's world. I am a strong believer in the global community. Being able to communicate in several languages, including a deep understanding of the language of data will continue to be important. At the end of the day the world is made of people, and having the ability to understand and relate to people will remain the essential element for success no matter how the world changes.

*Wenderoth: Finally, you are successful on many metrics. CEO, happily married, great kids, active in the community. You are a woman, Jewish – and that adds a whole layer of complexity and bars to leap over that people don't see or appreciate. How do you strike the balance? How do you do it? There is a whole generation wondering, "Can I have it all?" or "Do I even want it all?"*

Lipson: That's a very personal question. I have always lived by the belief that striving to "have it all" means that I will get to have "most" of what life has to offer. Some elements may be more or less successful. However, no one can have it all solely relying on themselves. I have been blessed to have a husband, children, partners, colleagues, neighbors, and friends who have contributed to my success and allowed me to contribute to theirs.

*Wenderoth: Thank you for your time, Roberta.*

---

*Michael C. Wenderoth is Associate Professor at IE Business School in Madrid, Spain, and Senior Advisor with InterChina Consulting. He teaches, trains, and writes on China, sales and leadership.*

# U.S.-China Education Relations: past, present, and future

*Mary Brown Bullock*
*Vol. 16, No.2*
*2017*

*The following is an address Dr. Bullock prepared for the third annual Young Scholars Forum at Nanjing University. The forum, held on September 21-22, 2016, was sponsored by The Global Times and the Carter Center.*

Let me begin with a story. In 1978 Zhou Peiyuan, senior scientist-educator and president of Peking University, led a delegation to Washington to negotiate a new era in U.S.-China education relations. Trained in both China and the United States, he was determined to recreate for a new generation the educational experiences that had given him a Boxer Indemnity scholarship, that had enabled him to receive three degrees from the University of Chicago and California Institute of Technology, that had enabled him to study at Princeton University with Albert Einstein. His model was that of the Republican era when thousands of Chinese students studied with scholarships at elite American universities. As an observer I was somewhat surprised that American negotiators were hesitant, preferring a very limited, centralized Soviet-type program. Under the Soviet exchange program, American and Soviet universities did not have direct contact with one another, and the exchange numbers were negotiated and balanced each year. Zhou would have none of it, canceling the meetings and threatening to return to China.

After a few days the American side accepted all details of his proposal. The "Understanding on the Exchange of Students and Scholars," signed in October 1978, was appended as Agreement #1 to the January 1979 political normalization agreement between Jimmy Carter and Deng Xiaoping. Today, 38 years later, with 305,000 Chinese in the United States and an American number only limited by interest and funding, this remains the governing framework.

I begin with this story for two reasons. First, to underline the many different ways in which the legacy of an earlier era has influenced government officials, educators, and the Chinese and American public. Second, to remind us that the power of ideas flows continuously, over decades and centuries, and across oceans and continents. The British and German influences on American education continue to be felt even as Confucianism and the traditional shuyuan find expression in China's modern universities.

Today China is America's largest educational and scientific partner, and vice-versa. China has made many investments to become an international education destination. In addition to national scholarship funds, each province is working to attract more international faculty and students. It has funded upwards of 100 Confucius Institutes in the United States. The Fulbright Program is the signature American program. The United States continues as the number-one destination for Chinese students who number more than twice those from India, the second-largest group. They are relatively evenly divided between graduate and undergraduate students. Hundreds of American universities have research and exchange programs with China. More American students study in China than any other developing country. Eighty colleges and universities from 36 states are operating undergraduate degree programs in China while 30 offer graduate degrees. All Chinese provinces and autonomous regions have educational agreements with American universities, and all but Xinjiang, Tibet, and Qinghai have joint degree programs. Most of the Ivy League schools are sponsoring stand-alone research centers in China while three American universities – NYU, Duke, and Kean – have established comprehensive, joint venture, independent Chinese universities. The Schwarzman College, a fully American-funded graduate school, has just opened at Tsinghua University this fall.[1]

The sheer scale is hard to grasp. But beyond the scale I would like to note three key factors.

First, the importance of science. Since 1980 more than 90,000 Chinese have received Ph.D. degrees in the United States, approximately 70 percent in the STEM fields, and approximately 80 percent have stayed in the United States, contributing significantly to U.S. human capital needs. This has not necessarily limited their contributions to Chinese higher education and research. Telecommunications and the ease of trans-Pacific travel have changed the context of global knowledge creation: the boundaries between national and international science are far more blurred. Given these numbers and the extensive bilateral institutional research projects, it is not surprising that for both countries, scientific collaboration has been the most important result of the educational relationship. Richard P. Suttmeier, the foremost American student of the scientific relationship, has concluded that, "Measured by co-authored scientific research papers, U.S. collaboration now exceeds collaboration with traditional partners such as the United Kingdom, Germany, and Japan. China and the United States have become each other's main partner in scientific collaboration." (Italics added.)[2]

Second, some limitations in the fields of social science and the humanities. Almost all of the joint-degree programs are in scientific fields, and only a small percentage (c. seven percent) of Chinese students in the U.S. are in these fields. During the last three decades, American scholars have learned a great deal about China, historically and today. Information about Chinese history, economy and government has been passed on to American higher education and the broader public. The Chinese study of the United States has, however, been rather limited. Given the importance of our bilateral relationship one hopes that Chinese attention to the study of the United States, including more accurate high school and college textbooks, could be accomplished. The United States would welcome more Chinese students and scholars studying the United States.

Third, although student exchanges receive the most attention, it is arguable that institutional partnerships are more significant. For both countries, their institutional partnerships with each other greatly outnumber those with other countries. Some are superficial but one increasingly finds dual-degree programs and significant collaborative research.

Of particular significance are the ways in which two American university models – the liberal arts college and the research university – are influencing China's education sector. In 2012 leading American, Chinese, and European university leaders signed "The Hefei Statement on Ten Characteristics of Research Universities." While recognizing national difference, the university leaders concurred on key attributes including academic freedom, tolerance of competing views, and open and transparent governance.

Looking to the future, let me suggest an emerging new paradigm in Sino-American education relations. I look forward to your critique of these ideas.

First, the education relationship is no longer asymmetrical; it is becoming symmetrical. Gone are the days when China needed American educational assistance. Gone are the days when American faculty were always the senior partners in research collaboration. China is creating world-class universities and Chinese funds are building and sustaining the new joint venture universities in China. No longer do American universities provide free rides for underprivileged Chinese students. They now seek self-paying Chinese students. In 2015 these contributed $9.8 billion to the American economy.

Second, for the first time China is directly participating in research and education in America. In 2015 Tsinghua University, the University of Washington, and Microsoft announced the creation of a new research and education institution in

Seattle, the first such bilateral venture in the United States. Ten years earlier, the Chinese government-funded education agency, Hanban, began funding Confucius Institutes in American universities. Today there are perhaps 100.

The third change is ideological. In 2014 the Minister of Education called for a rejection of western learning and subsequent government documents have reinforced the importance of Marxist ideology and patriotic education. This rhetoric, which appears to exclude American values, has already had a chilling effect on some educational programs.

Taken together these three factors – the advent of Chinese world-class scholars and universities, the entry of China into the domestic American educational world, and China's current ideological campaign – point to a more complex and potentially contentious future. To offset this pessimism let me also point to ways in which the U.S.-China educational relationship can continue to flourish.

First, both countries are experiencing the presence of new institutional models introduced from each other. There is every indication that these will include educational innovations that will benefit higher education universally. In 2018 Duke Kunshan University will introduce a new undergraduate curriculum that may well become a transformative model for both countries. The Tsinghua collaboration with the University of Washington and Microsoft introduces a new model of industry/university cooperation that could well have a broader influence. In collaboration with Tianjin City, The Julliard School will introduce a music academy in 2018 that truly is of world renown. The sometimes-criticized Confucius Institutes are innovative university partnerships that promote linguistic and cultural collaboration.

Second, at a time of growing competition between the two countries, the extensive bilateral educational relationship takes on a new strategic role – for both countries. The growing parity between the educational and scientific establishments makes the China connection much more valuable for the United States. Americans must learn to welcome a more symmetrical relationship in which we have much to gain as well as to give. With its many collaborative programs in China, American scholars are well positioned to collaborate with Chinese scholars in forefront fields. Already the fields of medicine, environment, geology, and climate change are benefitting from this bilateral collaboration.

Finally, the educational relationship is in the DNA of U.S.-China relations, a strand of DNA that has served both countries well, during the Qing, Republican, and People's Republic eras. This relationship has survived earlier periods in which China has questioned western education. China's quest to form a distinctly Chinese modern education system is central to its modern history. We need to learn more about this emerging model. And, I believe we share more educational values than some realize. While I was vice chancellor at Duke Kunshan University, I always talked about a cluster of values: academic freedom, academic responsibility, and academic integrity. My Chinese counterparts loved Duke's motto: knowledge in service to society. Chinese educators understand that all of these values are central to the success of the vibrant American educational model. Academic freedom and university autonomy are frequently discussed in educational circles. China cannot expect American educators to abandon their core values, nor should Americans expect Chinese universities to "become just like us." A new Chinese model is emerging, one that draws on historic Confucian as well as more recent Marxist and western influences.

### Notes

1  *Open Doors Report on International Education Exchange, 2015; "Doctorates Awarded to citizens of the People's Republic of China, by doctoral field of study, 1980-2013," National Science Foundation; Susan Lawrence, Testimony before the House Committee on Foreign Affairs Subcommittee on Africa, Global Health, Global Human Rights, and International Organizations, June 25, 2015; Chang Xiaolin, Vice Chancellor for Government Affairs, Duke Kunshan University.*

2  *Richard P. Suttmeier, "Trends in U.S. – China Science and Technology Cooperation: Collaborative Knowledge Production for the Twenty-First Century?" Research Report Prepared on Behalf of the U.S.–China Economic and Security Review Commission, September 9, 2014, 4.*

---

*Mary Brown Bullock is president emerita of Agnes Scott College in Decatur, Georgia and Founding Vice Chancellor of Duke Kunshan University. She serves on the advisory board of the China Research Center.*

# Chinese Courtyard Housing under Socialist Market Economy

*Donia Zhang*
*Vol. 15, No.1*
*2016*

## The Fall of Chinese Courtyard Houses

China's rapid economic growth coupled with an unprecedented level of real estate development have resulted in an almost wholesale destruction of traditional *siheyuan* (四合院) courtyard houses since the 1990s. For example, until 1949, Beijing was a completely traditional courtyard city. In the early 1950s, Beijing's inner city had 11 square kilometers of single-story *siheyuan* floor space, of which only five-to-six percent was dilapidated. In 1990, the inner city had a total single-story *siheyuan* of 21.42 square kilometers floor space, of which almost 50 percent was decaying. The increased floor space from 11 to 21.42 square kilometers was because of the proliferation of improvised extensions, an indication that not much courtyard space was left. A large-scale demolition started between 1990 and 1999, when a total of 4.2 square kilometers of Beijing's *siheyuan* were demolished; by 2005, another 14 square kilometers disappeared, leaving only three (Tan, 1998; Yuan, 2005).

Table 1. Destruction and conservation of *siheyuan* in inner Beijing

| Year | Siheyuan (courtyard houses) |
|------|------------------------------|
| 1949 | A completely traditional courtyard city in the 62 sqkm inner-city land area |
| 1990 | 805 courtyard houses in relatively good condition in the conservation areas |
| 2003 | 658 courtyard houses in relatively good condition in the conservation areas |
| 2004 | 539 courtyard houses in relatively good condition in the conservation areas |

*Sources: the author's summary based on Abramson, 2001; **Beijing City Planning Chart**, 2007; Collins, 2005; Kong, 2004; Ornelas, 2006*

*Table 1 shows a drastic decline of siheyuan between 1949 and 2004. There is no current data on the number of siheyuan remaining in Beijing, as it is increasingly more difficult to count them because of their impoverished conditions. One can expect the number has further decreased since 2004.*

In 2002, the *Conservation Plan of Historic and Cultural City of Beijing* created 25 protected conservation zones and provided detailed guidelines for *siheyuan* preservation. In 2004, the State Council approved a revised *Beijing Master Plan 2004-2020*, which designated another eight conservation zones, making a total of 33 protected areas in the inner city (and 10 in the outer city). The zones occupy a land area of 18 square kilometers, about 29 percent of the old city area. The revised plan calls for an end to large-scale demolition and reconstruction and implementing small-scale, gradual, organic renewal (Beijing City Planning Chart, 2007, pp. 261-266).

Today, the few well-preserved *hutong* (lanes) with refurbished *siheyuan* serve only high-level officials and those who can afford such homes (Trapp, 2003; Zheng, 2005) because these houses are sold at soaring prices. In 2015, the price range for a *siheyuan* is ¥70,000 – ¥250,000 CNY ($11,000 – $39,288 USD) per square meter, depending on the location, condition, and total area of the house. In the eastern district of Beijing, for example, a 230-square meter (160 square meter floor space) *siheyuan* has an asking price of ¥19 million CNY (almost $3 million USD) before renovation or ¥25 million CNY (almost $4 million USD) after renovation (Beijing Shun Yi Xing Real Estate Brokers Ltd., 2015-9-10).

## History and Significance of Chinese Courtyard Houses

The Chinese have lived in courtyard-type houses for several thousand years. The earliest courtyard house unearthed by archaeologists so far was built during the Middle Neolithic period, represented by the Yangshao culture (5,000-3,000 BCE) (Liu, 2002). The ancient Chinese favored this housing form because enclosing walls helped maximize household privacy and protection from wind, noise, dust, and other threats; and the courtyard offered light, air, and views, as well as acting as a family activity space when weather permitted.

A distinctive variety of traditional courtyard houses exists because of China's wide-ranging climates, 56 ethnic groups, and notable linguistic and regional diversity even among the Han majority. Traditional Chinese courtyard houses were grouped as northern, southern, and western types according to their geographic locations in relation to the Yangzi River (Knapp, 2000). The shape and size of the courtyards are determined by the amount of sunlight desired in the space. For example, in southern China, the courtyards are smaller, called *tianjing* (天井), or "lightwells," to reduce the summer sunlight; in northern China, the courtyards are relatively large to allow abundant sunlight in the winter. A traditional Chinese courtyard house would normally host an extended family of three or four generations (Knapp, 2005; Ma, 1999).

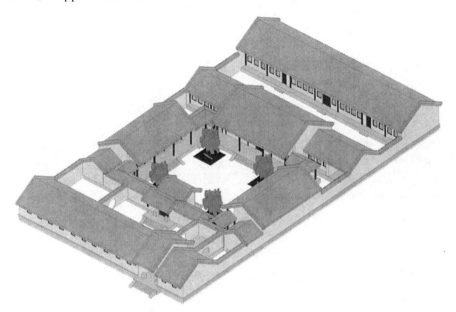

*Figure 1 A standard classical Beijing courtyard house (siheyuan) accommodating a single extended family. Computer model by Donia Zhang 2014*

## Chinese Housing in the Communist Era

Although China's population has more than doubled between 1953 and 2010 (Census 1953; Census 2010), the family structure has decreased from extended to nuclear families, a trend echoed elsewhere in the world (Amato, 2008; UN, 2003; Van Elzen, 2010). Statistics show that until recently, the average household size in China had remained relatively constant at about 5.2 persons (Jervis, 2005); it reduced to 3.96 persons in the 1990 Census, 3.44 persons in the 2000 Census, and 3.1 persons in the 2010 Census. The drop is due to the 35-year state-imposed one-child policy (introduced in 1978, enacted in 1980, and officially phased out in 2015), and free choices under circumstances of rapid modernization. The vertical, parent-son relationship typically found in traditional Chinese families is being replaced by the horizontal, conjugal tie as the axis of family relations in contemporary China (Yan, 2005). Thus, Chinese family structure evolved from a complex corporate organization to a relatively simple conjugal unit, in which family life revolves around a couple's pursuit of financial independence, privacy, and personal space (Cohen, 2005; Yan, 2005; Zhang, 2010). The change in Chinese family structure demands a change in the housing form, which has implications for new housing design (Cohen, 2005; Jervis, 2005).

Between 1949 and 1978, urban housing in China had been under a very strong centralized administration system. The urban housing policy, under the influence of socialist economic principles, was based on a centralized state housing provision and delivery system with socialist public ownership as a major characteristic (Dong, 1987). During the "Cultural Revolution" (1966-1976), the process of rationalization and the policy of low housing prices were driven to the extreme. All the construction elements of residential buildings were reduced in their dimensions to the utmost. A number of "Urban Village" kind of residential settlements were built in various parts of China at the time. The new concept was the ultra-economic habitation standard, praised as the "new socialist lifestyle" in political propaganda. The new housing type was basically 4-5-story parallel blocks, called "Socialist Super Blocks," constructed under the influence of the former Soviet Union in the late 1950s. The buildings were normally 12 meters deep, with all rooms standardized as 3-by-5-meter modules, with a 2-meter wide, centrally located corridor as the main circulation space for all the families. Several families shared the service facilities, such as a kitchen with a water tap and a single toilet, along the public corridor within the building (Dong, 1987; Gaubatz, 1995, 1999; Schinz, 1989). It was very communal-like.

Between 1974 and 1986, the Beijing Municipal Government built about seven square kilometers of new housing in the inner city which accounted for 70 percent of the city's total housing redevelopment since 1949 (Wu, 1999), most of which consisted of residential tower blocks of more than 10 stories made up of individual apartments. By the end of 1996, new housing projects numbered more than 200, covering 22 square kilometers of inner Beijing (Tan, 1997, 1998). For comparison, in Suzhou between 1994 and 1996, nearly three square miles of new housing were added each year (Zhu, Huang, and Zhang, 2000).

**Chinese Economic Reform and the Rise of Housing Market**

China's housing development has a direct link to its economic reform, which refers to the program called "Socialism with Chinese Characteristics" or "Socialist Market Economy" in the People's Republic of China, started in 1978 and led by Deng Xiaoping. China's economic reform has caused many of its sectors to privatize, one of which is the land and housing market.

In 1988, urban land leasing and housing privatization were introduced, with demands that the production of housing had to be commercialized. Subsequently, real estate development was increasingly drawn into national building and urban renewal processes. Nevertheless, work units were involved in housing provision until 1998. The result was a hybrid approach to housing provision, in which the work units purchased commodity housing and sold them to their employees at discounted prices (Wang and Murie, 1999; Wu, 2005).

In 1992, Beijing issued a policy statement entitled *Methods for Implementing the Central Government's Provisional Regulations for Leasing and Transfer of State-Owned Urban Land-Use Rights* (Wang and Murie, 1999). This policy significantly stimulated the development of a real estate industry in China and unleashed the value of urban land, especially land within the inner city. High land prices have led to larger-scale renewal projects and have made them increasingly market-driven. In 1994, the Beijing municipal government delegated the granting rights of dilapidated housing renewal projects to district governments, which became the leading actors in housing renewal, real estate development, and other urban construction projects (Wu, 1999).

Since 1998, work units have stopped welfare housing provision and allowed state workers nationwide to purchase their own apartments. This transaction primarily involved the subsidized sale of work-unit owned public housing to sitting tenants because reformers argued that housing shortages were caused by the housing welfare system, and the only effective way to solve the urban housing problem was to allow rents to increase and encourage urban dwellers to own their own housing units. This housing privatization was consistent with the broader market reforms that had already taken place in China since the 1980s. Commodity housing has become a major source of housing stock in China since the late 1990s. The Chinese government has planned to use commodity housing development as a catalyst to drive urban economic development (Wang and Murie, 1999; Wu, 2005; Zhou and Logan, 2002).

## The Issue of Housing Affordability

The success of China's economic policies and the manner of their implementation have resulted in immense changes in Chinese society. Although large-scale government planning programs with market characteristics have increased incomes and reduced poverty, income inequality has also increased (World Bank, 2013).

Commodity housing in Chinese real estate markets has created a significant financial constraint on affordability; housing prices are simply outside the range affordable to most urban workers without substantial state subsidies. In an entirely private housing market, only a small number of urban residents could afford housing at the construction costs. The annual house payment could exceed 70 percent of the average household income (Khan, 2012; World Bank, 1992). Thus, the actual pricing scheme for commodity housing is complex. It can be sold to work units or directly to urban workers at either the government-discounted standard price or the full standard price. Housing built or purchased by work units is usually sold to workers at further discounted prices; however, the purchaser owns only a proportion of the housing unit equivalent to the proportion of the full price they have paid, the remaining proportion of the property belongs to the work unit (Bray, 2005; Zhou and Logan, 2002).

## The Renewal and Redevelopment of Chinese Courtyard Houses

Since 2005, the Beijing municipal government has implemented a 25-year plan (2005-2030) to invest ¥0.5 billion CNY ($783 million USD) annually to renew dilapidated siheyuan, and to improve the living conditions of those households in the inner city. However, one third of the old-city population has to be relocated (Yuan, 2005).

For the 2008 Summer Olympic Games, 340,000 households in inner Beijing were required to leave their traditional homes (King, 2004, p. 120), to relocate to the suburbs, which have substandard educational, health care, and other service facilities. While in the inner city, new housing units in the redeveloped areas are sold at such high prices that only wealthy homebuyers can afford to pay. Relocation-related disputes have become a serious social issue since 1995 (Wu, 1999).

The author's 2007-2008 empirical research into one inner-Beijing traditional courtyard housing renewal project and five new courtyard housing redevelopment projects in Beijing and Suzhou likewise showed that gentrification has occurred in these Chinese cities. There was a breakdown of neighborhood structure due to the fact that only a small number of the original residents could afford to move back after redevelopment, and only the old residents socialized with one another; the new neighbors were unable to re-establish social networks as in the past (Zhang, 2013).

A more socially sustainable renewal and redevelopment method is urgently needed. For example, a participatory approach involving residents to create their own designs onsite and offer their own facility upgrade strategies in the renewal and redevelopment process may generate more satisfactory results as they are the final stakeholders for whom the housing product is ultimately intended. Moreover, reducing residents' socio-economic polarity can be an effective way to solve the social issues in housing renewal and redevelopment (Zhang, 2015b). This matter is critical for Beijing before the 2022 Winter Olympic Games, and for China to move forward in the 21st century.

As traditional Chinese courtyard houses with their established social relationships are fading away, maybe a new courtyard housing form could help restore them. The author here offers two evidenced-based designs based on her research findings (Zhang, 2013, 2015a).

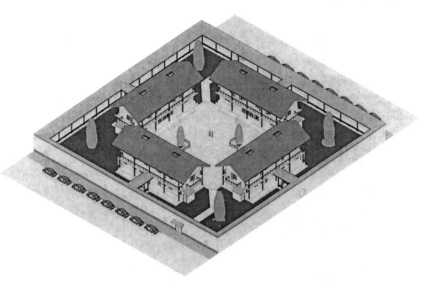

*Figure 2 shows Scheme A, a design for a new courtyard garden house compound based on a system of 60 m × 60 m standard block size, a communal courtyard of 26 m × 26 m shared by eight nuclear families, with each household enjoying a private garden at the back. Each housing unit measures 6 m × 10 m (total 180 square meters) with a semi-basement and two-and-a-half stories. Design and computer model by Donia Zhang based on her doctoral research findings (Zhang, 2013)*

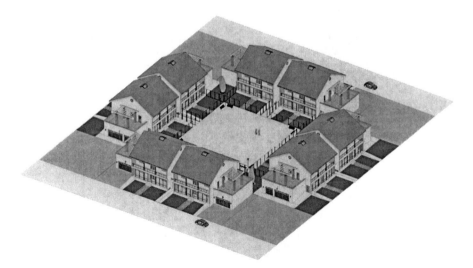

*Figure 3 shows Scheme B, a design for a new courtyard garden house compound based on a system of 78 m × 78 m standard block size, the communal courtyard is 26 m × 26 m shared by eight nuclear families, with each household enjoying a private garden of 12 m × 6 m at the front and the back. Each housing unit measures 10 m × 12 m (total 240 square meters) with a semi-basement and two-and-a-half stories. Design and computer model by Donia Zhang based on her postdoctoral research findings (Zhang, 2015a)*

## Acknowledgement

The author would like to thank Dan Williams for his careful editorial reviews and constructive comments on the essay.

## References

Abramson, D.B. (2001). *Beijing's preservation policy and the fate of the siheyuan. Traditional Dwellings and Settlements Review: Journal of the International Association for the Study of Traditional Environments, 13(1), pp. 7-22.*

Amato, P.R. (2008). *Recent changes in family structure: implications for children, adults, and society. National Healthy Marriage Resource Center. Retrieved May 30, 2011 from: http://www. healthymarriageinfo.org/docs/changefamstructure.pdf*

Beijing City Planning Chart (2007). *Beijing Municipal Planning Commission, Beijing Municipal Urban Planning and Design Institute, Beijing City Planning Institute.*

Beijing Shun Yi Xing Real Estate Brokers Ltd. (2015-9-10). *Beijing courtyard house price quote (*《北京四合院报价大概多少》 ，北京顺益兴联行房地产经纪有限公司*). Retrieved November 9, 2015 from: http://www.siheyuan.cc/Article/bbjdgd_1.html*

Bray, D. (2005). *Social space and governance in urban China: the danwei system from origins to reform. Palo Alto: Stanford University Press.*

Cohen, M.L. (2005). *House united, house divided: myths and realities, then and now. In R.G. . Knapp and K.-Y. Lo (Eds.), House home family: living and being Chinese (pp. 235-257). Honolulu: University of Hawai'i Press.*

Collins, M. (2005). *Protecting the ancient alleys of Beijing. Contemporary Review, 286(1668), pp. 34-38.*

Dong, G. (1987). *Beijing: housing and community development. Ekistics, 54(322), pp. 34-39.*

Gaubatz, P. (1995). *Changing Beijing. Geographical Review, 85(1), pp. 79-97.*

Gaubatz, P. (1999). *China's urban transformation: patterns and processes of morphological change in Beijing, Shanghai and Guangzhou. Urban Studies, 36(9), pp. 1495-1521.*

Jervis, N. (2005). *The meaning of jia: an introduction. In R.G. Knapp and K.-Y. Lo (Eds.), House home family: living and being Chinese (pp. 223-233). Honolulu: University of Hawai'i Press.*

Khan, T.S. (2012). *Asian housing markets: bubble trouble? (Report Number 67883: An Eye on East Asia and Pacific. World Bank: East Asia and Pacific Economic Management and Poverty Reduction). Retrieved November 5, 2015 from: http://documents.worldbank.org/curated/ en/2012/01/16211688/asian-housing-markets-bubble-trouble*

King, A.D. (2004). *Spaces of global cultures: architecture, urbanism, identity. London: Spon.*

Knapp, R.G. (2000). *China's old dwellings. Honolulu: University of Hawai'i Press.*

Knapp, R.G. (2005). *Chinese houses: the architectural heritage of a nation. North Clarendon, VT: Tuttle Publishing.*

Kong, F. (2004). *Dilapidated housing renewal and the conservation of traditional courtyard houses (*《危房改造方式与传统四合院保护》*). 北京市文物局 Beijing Municipal Administration of Cultural Heritage. Retrieved February 13, 2008 from http://www.bjww. gov.cn/2004/12-7/3717-2.shtml*

Liu, X. (2002). *The origins of Chinese architecture. In X. Fu et al., Chinese architecture (pp. 11-31). New Haven: Yale University Press.*

Ma, B. (1999). *The architecture of the quadrangle in Beijing (*《北京四合院建筑》*, Chinese edition). China: Tianjin University Press.*

Ornelas, M. (2006). *Beijing's rapid urbanization and the hutong. La Voz de Esperanza, 19(8), pp. 7-9.*

Schinz, A. (1989). *Cities in China. Stuttgart: Borntraeger Science Publishers.*

Smith, A. (1776). *The wealth of nations. London: W. Strahan and T. Cadell.*

Tan, Y. (1997). *Research into reconstruction of the old residential area of Beijing: from the residents' perspective. PhD thesis, Tsinghua/Qinghua University, China.*

Tan, Y. (1998). *Relocation and the people: a research on neighbourhood renewal in the old city of Beijing*. Department of Urban Planning and Design, Tsinghua/Qinghua University School of Architecture, China.

Trapp, M. (2003). *A Comparison of the relationship between urban development and the natural environment in Beijing, Tokyo, and Curitiba*. Retrieved March 5, 2007 from http://www. rd.msu.edu/ugrad/greenpieces/2003/Trapp.pdf

UN (2003). *Demographic and social trends affecting families in the south and central Asian region*. Retrieved May 30, 2011 from: http://www.un.org/esa/socdev/family/Publications/mt-desilva.pdf

Van Elzen, S. (2010). *Dragon and rose garden: art and power in China*. Hong Kong: Timezone 8/ Modern Chinese Art Foundation.

Wang, Y.P. and Murie, A. (1999). *Commercial housing development in urban China*. Urban Studies, 36(9), pp. 1475-1494.

World Bank (1992). *China: implementation options for urban housing reform (A World Bank Country Study)*. Washington, DC: The World Bank.

World Bank (2013). *The challenge of high inequality in China (Report Number 82522: Inequality in Focus, 2(2). World Bank: Poverty Reduction and Equity Department)*. Retrieved November 5, 2015 from: http://documents.worldbank.org/curated/en/2013/08/18485456/challenge-high-inequality-china

Wu, F. (2005). *Rediscovering the 'gate' under market transition: from work-unit compounds to commodity housing enclaves*. Housing Studies, 20(2), pp. 235-254.

Wu, L. (1999). *Rehabilitating the old city of Beijing: a project in the Ju'er Hutong neighbourhood*. Vancouver, BC: University of British Columbia Press.

Yan, Y. (2005). *Making room for intimacy: domestic space and conjugal privacy in rural north China*. In R.G. Knapp and K.-Y. Lo (Eds.), House home family: living and being Chinese (pp. 373-395). Honolulu: University of Hawai'i Press.

Yuan, Y. (2005). *Preserving the soul of Beijing*. Retrieved March 5, 2007 from http://www.china-today.com.cn/English/e2005/e200502/p28.htm

Zhang, D. (2013). *Courtyard housing and cultural sustainability: theory, practice, and product*. Farnham: Ashgate.

Zhang, D. (2015a). *Courtyard housing for health and happiness: architectural multiculturalism in North America*. Farnham: Ashgate.

Zhang, D. (2015b). *Courtyard houses of Beijing: lessons from the renewal*. Traditional Dwellings and Settlements Review, 27(1), pp. 69-82.

Zhang, L. (2010). *In search of paradise: middle-class living in a Chinese metropolis*. Ithaca, NY: Cornell University Press.

Zheng, J. (2005). *Rescue hutong (Chinese edition)*. Ming Bao (Brightness Newspaper) Saturday Supplement, 504, pp. 21-30.

Zhou, M. and Logan, J.R. (2002). *Market transition and the commodification of housing in urban China*. In J.R. Logan (Ed.), The new Chinese city: globalization and market reform (pp. 137-152). Oxford: Blackwell Publishers.

Zhu, X.D, Huang L., and Zhang, X. (2000). *Housing and economic development in Suzhou, China: a new approach to deal with the inseparable issues*. Seminal paper from Joint Center for Housing Studies, Harvard University.

---

*Donia Zhang is the Director at the Neoland School of Chinese Culture in Ontario, Canada.*

# Assignment China: An Interview with Mike Chinoy

*Penelope B. Prime*
*Vol. 15, No.2*
*2016*

*Penelope Prime, Founding Director of the China Research Center, talked with former CNN correspondent, Mike Chinoy, via Skype on April 15, 2016, about his recent project on the process of understanding China through the media. This interview has been edited for length and clarity.*

**Penelope Prime: To begin, please explain what the project is and where the idea came from.**

**Mike Chinoy**: The idea for Assignment: China came out of discussions at the University of Southern California's U.S.-China Institute that Clayton Dube, who runs the Institute, and I, were having about how Americans and others understand or misunderstand China. One of the things that became very evident was that most Americans get most of the information that shapes their views of China from the media.

As we looked at this and thought about it, having been a foreign correspondent for many years, it became very evident that most people don't have the slightest idea how foreign correspondents actually work. The process of how correspondents gather information shapes the final product people see on TV or hear on the radio or read in the newspaper or a website.

So we began this very ambitious project to tell the story of the people who have told the China story for the American media over the last 70 years. Who were these people, how did they end up in China, what did they do when they were the AP correspondent in Nanjing or Shanghai in 1949 at the time of the revolution, or the Time Magazine correspondent in Hong Kong in 1959, or trying to make sense of the Cultural Revolution in the '60s without being able to go there? What was it like to go to China with Nixon? What was it like to open the first U.S. news bureaus in Beijing after normalization?

We began by tracking down as many as possible of the current and former China correspondents and people who interacted with them. In the end we did well over 100 interviews. The series ended up being a narrative of Chinese history from 1945 to 2015, but from the perspective of the people who were on the ground trying to make sense of it as it happened. People talk about journalists writing the first rough draft of history, and so this is essentially an attempt to tell that first rough draft of history through the eyes and voices of people who were standing there experiencing it as it played out.

Some of these people have written books and memoirs but others had never written anything or spoken very much about their experiences. And so in those cases this was really precious material that hadn't come to light. People were able to give us home movies and private photo collections and all kinds of documents, and then we dug very deeply into the archives of the American television networks, and archives of presidential libraries, and places like Pathé, and old photo agencies, and so on. So we were able to assemble what, even to us, turned out to be an astonishing collection of material.

**PP: In the end, you did 10 or 12 episodes?**

MC:  We started out doing interviews for a documentary but after we did the first bunch of interviews, we said, Wow, this is more than just one single film. And it kept growing. One of the joys of doing a documentary in this way is not being a prisoner of a network, and able to distribute it through the U.S.-China Institute website and YouTube channel. In this day and age you don't need CNN to have a distribution mechanism. You can put it on YouTube and spread the word through social media and that's what we've tried to do. And if it warrants a dozen episodes, then you can do as many as makes sense. For me, coming from a news background, that was very liberating. So in the end we have 12 episodes beginning with reporters who covered the Chinese Civil War from '45 to '49, and ending with the beginning of Xi Jinping's era in 2012-2014.

For example, there's one episode called "China Watching" that looks at the two plus decades when Western journalists were not able to go to China and had to sit in Hong Kong trying to figure out what was happening. The circumstances of being one step removed created its own sort of—what's the right word—it became kind of an art form different from conventional journalism in a lot of ways. A type of "Peking-ology." So part of our project was to track down people who were based in Hong Kong in the '50s and '60s, and early '70s.

Another episode is about the untold backstory of the press and the Nixon trip, which is absolutely fascinating. And then there's an episode at the end of the Mao era dealing with the first generation of reporters who opened bureaus in Beijing after normalization. There is one on the 1980s up to '89. We devoted a whole episode to Tiananmen, partly because the story is extremely dramatic and partly because in terms of the American perceptions of China, it was really this kind of watershed moment that changed the way people looked at China, and in terms of journalism it was really important because it was the first time an upheaval of that scale was shown to American audiences; it was broadcast live on TV. People take it for granted today. You expect to see live reports from anywhere and in fact, you can go live with an iPhone from anywhere. So it's hard to appreciate how revolutionary it was that I, working as the CNN Beijing bureau chief, could stand in the middle of Tiananmen Square with hundreds of thousands of protesting students behind me and do a live broadcast.

Then we look at the 1990s, and there are four episodes examining the period from 2000 to the present day. The final episode called "Follow the Money" tells the story of how David Barbosa of the New York Times did his remarkable investigative reporting about the hidden wealth of the relatives of Premier Wen Jiabao, and Michael Forsythe, then of Bloomberg News, did the same kind of amazing reporting about relatives of Xi Jinping, which brought the story full circle because you ended up with a lot of the reporting for this being done back in Hong Kong. Also as the Chinese got more muscular in their dealings with the international press, people had trouble with visas. For example, Forsythe ended up back in Hong Kong. The irony is you have a different kind of China watching, in which instead of reading the tea leaves of the People's Daily, people are going through public financial documents of companies in which relatives of senior officials have lots of money invested, or going through property records to see multimillion dollar apartments. So it seemed to be a good place to end it. But it's a pretty comprehensive look at the kind of major moments in Chinese history from the end of World War II to today.

The idea as we put this all together is that primarily the goal here is that this material can be used in the classroom, but by no means is it exclusively intended for use in class. The 12 episodes provide a foundation for a course that could be used in journalism education on covering China, but each episode is self-contained and so you can watch one without having to watch the others, although there is a cumulative effect, particularly because a lot of the same characters appear in multiple episodes and you get to know them better and learn more about them. But if you were teaching a course on recent Chinese history or international relations, the episode on the Nixon trip, for example, and the role of the press in the making foreign policy, would fit well. There are also lessons in how the Chinese economy works today, for example with the episode on the hidden wealth of relatives of Chinese leaders, and many other possible lessons embedded in each episode.

**PP: *A theme that runs through the episodes is this relationship of the foreign press with the Chinese government, and it seems like it ebbs and flows. Sometimes it's more open, then it's more closed. Can you comment on that and then on what the current environment is for foreign journalists in China?***

MC: There's a permanent tension between the foreign press and the Chinese government. The Chinese kicked all the Americans out in 1949 and with very few exceptions didn't let any of them back on a regular basis until the late '70s. But what you have here is a permanent tension and it waxes and wanes, depending on the overall climate.

For example, around the time of normalization there was this American love affair with China. Deng Xiaoping was the cuddly Communist who went to Washington and wore a cowboy hat when he met Bush in Texas. As a result, there were friendly stories as the reforms took hold: the first restaurant, the first private store, and so on. And the government was sort of okay with that.

But journalists wanted to go deeper. This theme runs through all of these episodes, going over years and years of how journalists pushed the limits, how hard it was to meet Chinese people, how hard it was to have Chinese friends, how difficult it was to get any authoritative information, being followed, being bugged, being hassled. And to some degree it's always there. When the political climate in China is looser, it's less evident and the limits are broader.

For example, the late 1980s – which is when I first was based in Beijing in '87, up through Tiananmen – was a remarkably open time and everybody who was there then remembers it as a time when you could really meet people, and there was this tremendous lively positive engagement, which the authorities didn't like, but they didn't push back that hard.

And then after Tiananmen, there was a very deep chill; and then in the '90s, again, as the economy began to pick up, it became easier to meet people as the story shifted from political repression to economic growth. But over and over again, it happened where the journalists got in the firing line. Part of what journalists do is to report on issues and tensions in the society and so when journalists went to talk to dissidents, Falun Gong activists, human rights lawyers, etc., they came under all sorts of pressure.

And then there was a period around the Olympics when the atmosphere again relaxed very considerably because the Chinese promised the Olympic committee there'd be a more open China. That was when they changed the rules so that you could travel more freely.

But I would say starting at the end of the Olympics – 2009 onward – the climate got tighter, and I think the key turning point was 2011, which was the so-called Jasmine Spring. I think the Arab Spring really freaked out the Chinese authorities, and there were these calls on the internet for demonstrations in Beijing. Nobody knows whether it was just a few Chinese exiles in a basement on a computer in New Jersey putting this out, but the authorities totally flipped out. When journalists started going to Wangfujing Street to see whether anything was happening, there was a really, really aggressive push. This expanded into a degree of intimidation that we had not seen in a very long time. Journalists got phone calls in the middle of the night, security people were going to their homes at 5:00 in the morning and threatening, "You better not cover this." It is unlikely that anything remotely like what was happening in the Middle East was happening in China, but Chinese officials were nervous, combined with a sense of assertiveness more generally in Chinese behavior that comes from their sense that the economic crisis of '08 and '09 showed the West was in steep decline and China was on the rise, and they have muscles so why not flex them. As a result, there has been an attempt to not only control the narrative of the Chinese press, which has always been there and has gotten much stronger, but they're now trying to extend that to the foreign press. And so you had a very, very difficult period.

The other thing is that even though the rules officially say you can travel anywhere and talk to anybody who's willing to talk to you, the fact is that local authorities either haven't heard of, or don't pay any attention to that. Journalists discover when they go around the country, local thugs paid by the local authorities often go after them, beat them up, take their gear, or intimidate people, prevent them from talking to people, or retaliate against people to whom they try to talk. So for many stories, it's almost like guerrilla war now, where a reporter goes in, gets what they can, and slips out as quickly as possible. And then the investigative reporting I mentioned – Barboza at the Times, and Mike Forsythe at Bloomberg, as well as The Wall Street Journal – around corruption of the Bo Xilai case, I think also contributed to the sense of anger at the foreign press and the determination to try and curb that. So a lot of news organizations have had trouble getting visas. It's eased up slightly compared to 2012, '13, and '14. But it's still a very tough assignment.

On the other hand, I think a lot of journalists feel that it's such an amazing story, and it's such a big complex country that the government can't stop you from doing everything, and there's still a lot of amazing things that one can do. So even today it's much easier to operate as a journalist, and it's a much more open society than it was 30 years ago, but it's tough and you have a government now that if you cross lines, and say things the government doesn't like, you're going to hear about it, and sometimes more. There was a French journalist who wrote a commentary about Xinjiang after the Paris terrorist attacks last fall that challenged the government's narrative that all dissidents in Xinjiang are terrorists, and as a result she was forced to leave.

So it is a very difficult place because the Chinese are much more willing to push back on the foreign press now that they feel "We're a big power; we can throw our weight around."

**PP: *The other change is that now Chinese journalists and media are going all over the world and reporting back in China. This is new and I just wonder: do you have any sense about whether that is influencing the media in China, given that they understand they want to get information too?***

MC: It's a really interesting question because you do now have Chinese foreign correspondents showing up at all the conflict zones, and I think a fair amount of what they do is just straight news reporting, particularly when it's not an issue that is too sensitive to China. But when it is, the reporting either in the original form or once it is edited is shaped to fit the narrative. There was a debate I know among many Chinese journalists about the fact that CCTV now has a big English language service, and some people see this as just an attempt to project soft power, and it is. But I've known Chinese who work there who said, This is a good thing because if we want to be credible, we can't just be party mouthpieces, we have to do more. That pushes things in the right direction.

Maybe four or five years ago there was some hope that that was the case but I think the direction it's going now is not great and so it will be interesting to see how this affects the way Chinese operate internationally. If the media has to be such a loyal tool of the Party, at what point can it still credibly report things internationally? But it is true that the Chinese have put a lot of money into it and they're making these services available like CCTV English for free in many parts of the world, and it's pretty slick. So it's a very interesting trend, although if the ultimate overall situation in China continues to tighten up, it's hard to know how appealing that's going to be or how skillfully that image can be softened in presentation for the rest of the world. I don't honestly know the answer, but it's a very interesting question.

**PP: *Underlying that there is this expectation that journalists want to be professional, and I think that's true across China and across the world, so that's a good trend.***

MC: Many young Chinese now, and I've taught some of them, are studying at journalism schools outside of China in the West and they're absorbing some of the ideas and values of Western journalism. And it raises a very interesting question about what happens to somebody like that when they go back to China with their newly minted master's degree in journalism from a good U.S. journalism school. How can they apply their skills? I think it's difficult, to be honest, and I think a lot of people are going to be quite disillusioned. On the other hand, these are people who have had those influences, and if they stay in the media and communications world, in 15 years they're all going to be significant, influential players, and nothing in China ever stays the same. I do think the tightening we're seeing under Xi Jinping is not another shift back and forth, as we saw on and off from the late '70s on, but this is something more substantial and possibly more enduring. But nothing stays the same forever.

**PP: *Very interesting. Your project is a valuable contribution to the China field, to history, and to journalism. How can people access the episodes?***

MC: All of the episodes are available for free at The U.S.- China Institute website http://china.usc.edu/complete-series-now-available-assignment-china-us-ci-series-american-reporting-china

# An Interview with filmakers
# Adam James Smith and Song Ting

*Penelope B. Prime*
*Vol. 14, No.1*
*2015*

*The new documentary film "The Land of Many Palaces" examines planned urbanization in China from the vantage point of Ordos in Inner Mongolia. Ordos is a vast, newly built city populated by people who have moved by the thousands from surrounding farms. Penelope Prime, Founding Director of the China Research Center, interviewed filmmakers Adam James Smith and Song Ting by email about the film and about doing documentary work in China.*

**Penelope Prime: Tell us about the film, why China, and what motivated you to focus on this subject.**

**Adam James Smith**: I've been going to China for 10 years, and have also been making documentary work for about the same time. As my interest in documentary filmmaking grew alongside my interest in the continued development in China, it seemed appropriate to make my first feature film in China. I'm also very interested in how cities develop and why people move to them. The powers-at-be in Ordos have turned how cities normally organically grow based on voluntary migration to them, on its head, by building an entire city from scratch and them moving a rural population in. I was personally curious as to why this city had been built and who for. This curiosity sustained us through the production of the film.

**PP: *How did you meet, and why did you choose to work together?***

AJS: We were introduced through a mutual friend who knew we both were interested in urbanization and migration issues in China. He also knew Ting and I have quite similar filmic sensibilities, so it seemed like a good match.

**PP: *Why choose Ordos, Inner Mongolia, for the film?  How did you get started there to find people to film for the project?  How did the permissions for filming work?***

AJS: Independent documentary film production is still very much a fringe activity in China, and there really is no official route to go about gaining full permission to shoot a documentary there. We embraced the philosophy that it's better to ask for forgiveness than permission. That said, during our first scouting trip, in which we interviewed hundreds of people in Ordos, we realized we wanted a government worker and also a farmer to be our main characters in the film. In order to film with a government worker, who ends up being Yuan Xiaomei in the film, we had to gain approval from her leaders in the community. This involved building trust with the government body she was attached to over several trips. On the first couple of trips Xiaomei and her leaders were quite suspicious about what we were doing, and so we were only able to secure simple scenes with her to begin with. It wasn't until our fourth or fifth trip that they began to feel comfortable with us filming and we were able to secure scenes deemed more sensitive.

**PP: *What was it like working with the people of Ordos?  Was there one particular poignant moment for you?***

AJS: For me it was realizing on our second trip to the city that farmers were being moved in from the countryside. At that point it became clear what our story would be in the film. There were also many surreal moments in which I found myself witnessing something strange or without explanation. As Ordos is a new city, and its residents are new to the urban experience, there were moments in which we witnessed people trying to figure out how to work things in their new environment. These were poignant moments.

**Song Ting**: In general the people we encountered were nice. Especially the Mongolian friends we made there, who are good at singing and drinking. My poignant moment was when policemen came to our place and asked us to go to police station. We even didn't know how they found us. At that time we stayed at a friend's place and that made her family unwilling to host us anymore. I was worried that they thought we were doing something illegal.

**PP: *Now that you are showing the film, are there permission hurdles? Have you run into any censorship?***

AJS: We specifically made the film with a foreign audience in mind, to help foster a better understanding of China abroad. We are therefore screening it almost exclusively outside China and haven't needed to gain any permissions from the Chinese government for that. We have had a few screenings in Beijing, but they were mostly to expat audiences within expat run institutions. If we did seek a general release in China, I imagine we would need to gain some kind of permission from a government body and perhaps we would encounter censorship. We'll cross this bridge if we decide to distribute the film in China.

**PP: *What did you learn about the incentives that farmers have to move to cities, and what holds them back?***

ST:  Young rural people hope to move to a modern city after being exposed to the "glorious" vision of urban life through mass media. It is easy and natural for the young generation to migrate. But for the older generation, they are concerned about the finances of their family and the dangers of living in a brand new environment they are not used to. For them to move, incentives need to include, satisfying financial compensation, efficient education of the new environment and a promised "brighter" future, all of which the government in Ordos are working hard on.

**PP: *You may not want to give away the ending, but were you happy with how the story unfolded?***

AJS: The film documents a process that is still underway in Ordos, and is just beginning on a national level. The process is instigated by the government, and involves rural people being moved into purpose built urban districts. As this is just the beginning it was hard to decide upon what would be an appropriate ending for the film, so the last scene is quite opened-ended and allows the audience to see that really this is just the beginning and the outcomes of this plan are unknown.

**PP: *How do you view China's urbanization plan now that you have seen it from a community perspective? How does it compare with your experiences***

*elsewhere?*

AJS: It's hard to pass judgment on China's urbanization plans as they're unprecedented, and involve so many people. They're also unfinished, and therefore the outcome of the country's push to urbanize is unknown. All I can do is think about my experience of visiting a variety of Chinese cities, and wonder what all of these new cities might end up being like as the country builds them to accommodate 250 million rural to urban migrants over the next two decades. Most Chinese cities I have visited – with the exception of Hangzhou, Wuxi, Suzhou, and a handful of other cities on the East Coast – are pretty unpleasant places, plagued with air and water pollution, noise pollution, crowds of people and cars, poor quality buildings with ugly facades sheathed in garish neon. I wonder if these urban problems will be remedied and the Chinese urban experience improved, and I also wonder what all of China's new urban residents will do in the cities they arrive in? It's hard to imagine how the Chinese government will educate so many farmers on how to survive and thrive in their new cities. I also wonder about how the plans to implement more of an industrial style of agriculture throughout China, once farmers have vacated their land, will pan out, seen as the country has little experience with anything but traditional modes of farming.

ST: I think the urbanization plan of China is even bigger than what many citizens in remote areas can comprehend. It is somehow rushed and brings a lot of pains. Maybe this is unavoidable for a country that has suffered too much in the 20th century. It just seizes each and every new opportunity to catch up with the rest of the world with not enough time to digest the results. I have traveled and worked in many other countries and none of them can compete with China in terms of vibrancy and complexity. Any social problem that exists in Western countries is enlarged in China.

**PP: What was the work environment like in Ordos—a brand new city but in a relatively remote part of China?**

AJS: The winters are brutal in Ordos, and the lack of buildings that were open for customers during our earlier shoots, made for little respite from the cold conditions. The spring and summer shoots were very enjoyable though. The city itself, at least the downtown, is very pleasant compared to most Chinese cities that really suffer from air and noise pollution, depressing and uninspiring buildings, a lack of green space, and overwhelming numbers of cars and people. The city was only starting to fill up during the time we shot our film there, and therefore was free from the many problems most Chinese cities suffer from, and the city is generally quite well designed and has been built with good quality materials. As there were relatively few people there, it made it hard as a visitor to find restaurants, shops, and places with wifi that were open.

ST: It developed very fast. The city now already differs from the one where we shot the film 2 years ago. As a brand new city, it is clean and is full of big plans. The government is working hard on bringing more manufactures such as an automobile assembling sector. Back when started shooting, there were not many job opportunities and many of them were related to construction. As the construction form expands and new factories are introduced, there should be a growing need for manpower in processing and manufacturing. The Ordos region is extremely rich in natural resources, having one sixth of national coal reserves. The pillars of its economy are textiles (wool), coal mining, petrochemicals, electricity generation and production of building materials. The further development of these industries will underpin the economy of the new city in Ordos.

**PP: *What advice do you have for others working in China—in film or other sectors—about how to be successful?***

AJS: I think before embarking on a film project, or any endeavor in China, one must understand certain unique aspects of Chinese culture that may seem perplexing or frustrating at first. These include the importance of *guanxi* (connections), face (that refers to how people and things are presented), the importance of forging relationships with people, usually over dinner, before asking them to help you, and lastly, being flexible with arrangements: They will always change! Once you have a basic understanding of how relationships work in China, it's then far easier to pursue a project there.

**PP: *Do you have plans for another documentary on other aspects of urbanization or to follow the process as it matures?***

AJS: Yes, I just began work on a new feature documentary project. "Mountain Town" (working title), will be about the replica of the Wyoming town of Jackson Hole, built in Hebei, China, two-hours north of Beijing. Many wealthy Beijing residents have bought second homes there, or have even relocated there. The community that has been created has really embraced every aspect of the Western American lifestyle, down to the attire, celebrations, and ideas about freedom and independence. I think this community has really stemmed out of urban people's desire to not only escape cities in China, but to escape China itself, and acts as an accompaniment to "The Land of Many Palaces" which sees the opposite happening: farmers moving from the countryside and into the city, in an attempt to improve their living standards.

ST: I'm in the middle of making a TV documentary about Chinese architects. I work around several very different architects. This film is set to air on China Central Television's documentary channel later this year. Apart from that, I'm developing a fictional film, which will be a collaboration between China and the U.S.A.

**PP: How can people find more information about this film and your other work?**

AJS: During the filming of "Mountain Town" this summer (2015), I will post regular updates on my blog: www.adamjamessmithfilm.com/blog

ST: People can keep up to date with my work on: www.songtingfilm.com For "The Land of Many Palaces" updates please visit our website: www.theland-ofmanypalaces.com or our Facebook page: www.facebook.com/landofmanyp-alaces

# What China's 'export machine' can teach Trump about globalization

*Penelope B. Prime*
*Vol. 16, No.1*
*2017*

Chinese goods seem to be everywhere these days.

Consider this: At the Olympics in Rio this summer, Chinese companies supplied the mascot dolls, much of the sports equipment, the security surveillance system and the uniforms for the volunteers, technical personnel and even the torch-bearers.

Do you own a personal computer or air conditioner? Or a pair of shoes or set of plates from Wal-Mart? They all almost certainly bear a "Made in China" label.

Put another way, China has become an "export machine," manufacturing an increasing share of the world's products. Its initial success exporting in the 1990s – which surged after it joined the World Trade Organization in 2001 – surprised everyone, including Chinese policymakers. The result was rapid growth of over 9 percent for many years. In 2014, China surpassed the U.S. as the largest economy in the world in terms of purchasing power parity.

How did a country with a national income of just US$155 per capita in the 1970s turn into one of the most economically powerful countries in just 40 years? The answer not only shines light on China's success story but also offers some important lessons for governments considering a turn inward, such as the incoming Trump administration.

I visited China for the first time in the spring of 1976 – just before China's renewed entry into global markets. Research, teaching and taking students to China over the following decades have given me a window to observe the dynamic development that has occurred. And now, as a clinical professor at Georgia State

University and director of the nonprofit China Research Center, I am involved with research and outreach that informs policy and business to strengthen U.S.-China relations.

## The costs of isolation

Historically, China has nurtured strong connections to world commerce.

From the Han Dynasty (206 B.C. – A.D. 220) until the Ming (A.D. 1371-1433), goods, culture and religion flowed among Central Asia, the Middle East and China via the various overland routes of the Silk Road. Sea exploration began in the Ming Dynasty, when the famous Captain Zheng He took seven voyages to establish trading contacts with Africa, Arabia, India and Southeast Asia. In the early 1900s, Shanghai was nicknamed the "Paris of the Orient" based on its role as a center of trade and finance.

But after Mao Zedong led the communists to victory in 1949, China established a planned economic system, withdrawing from global markets, which the communists deemed capitalist and imperialist. Foreign assets were nationalized and companies left the country. Trade increased with the communist Soviet Union and Eastern Europe during the 1950s, but that was sharply curtailed with the Sino-Soviet split in the early 1960s. The U.S. did not even have official trade links with China between 1950 and the early 1970s.

From Mao's point of view, China's goal was to build a strong economy by being self-sufficient in production of all its needs. He believed that self-sufficiency should even extend to each province as well. His "plant grain everywhere" policy, regardless if the geography was ill-suited for it, is an example of how far he implemented this strategy. One consequence was the disastrous Great Leap Forward, in which an estimated 30 million or more died from famine.

This disaster resulted partly from pushing self-reliance in industry in the countryside, as well as setting impossible grain output goals. The idea of specialization of production based on relative efficiency of resources was seen as capitalist and dangerous to communist development. To benefit from specialization, China would need to depend on other countries and deal with competition. As a result of rejecting specialization and trade, China's economy grew slowly, with poor living conditions based on backward technology and little exchange within the country, let alone between China and the world.

Because China had been closed to foreign investment since the early 1950s and exported primarily to pay for essential imports, the value of China's exports in 1978 was less than $7 billion – a mere 0.3 percent of their value today. This isolation contributed to China's low living standard. Its GDP per capita of $155 ranked 131st out of the 133 countries with reported data, just above Guinea-Bissau and Nepal.

When I visited in 1976, I saw men with belts wrapped a couple of times around their waists – because they were very thin, and perhaps because the planned economy did not produce many sizes of belts.

## Renewed global connections

When Mao died in 1976, a group of leaders, including Deng Xiaoping, believed that market reforms would revive the economy through more efficient production and better technology. China's so-called "opening up" officially began with the Third Plenum of the Chinese Communist Party Central Committee in December 1978.

As part of the reform strategy, China's leaders established four special economic zones in southern China near Hong Kong with incentives for foreign companies to invest in production aimed at exporting. The most well-known zone is Shenzhen, located in Guangdong Province.

At the time, U.S., Japanese and European companies were looking for new locations to manufacture their goods cheaply after wages rose in East Asian countries like Hong Kong, South Korea and Taiwan. And few other countries were welcoming to foreign investment. India, for example, remained closed to foreign direct investment for another decade.

In other words, China's policies changed at a fortuitous time.

Companies moved quickly to China, especially across the border from Hong Kong, giving birth to deep manufacturing capacity that became the center of the world's supply chain. By 2006, foreign companies were generating nearly 60 percent of China's exports and even today produce close to 43 percent of them.

## The power of specialization

China's export story is a lesson in the power of globalization for development. Specifically, China's policies leveraged its comparative advantage.

It attracted foreign direct investment with incentives to export, which included an undervalued exchange rate and a large population willing to work for relatively low wages. The returns to this investment were used for infrastructure, education, R&D and institution-building. This focus on domestic capabilities supported growth and rising living standards, avoiding a "middle income trap" where a country is not able to move its production beyond the lower end of the value chain.

Over time, Chinese domestic businesses became increasingly competitive as they developed management skills and market knowledge. Even small domestic firms have grown their exports in recent years as a result of access to international e-commerce platforms such as Alibaba.

China's embrace of global merchandise trade and capital markets has transformed it into a middle-income country with a GDP of almost $8,000 per capita in current U.S. dollars, and the largest producer of manufactured goods in the world.

Chinese families now have enough income to travel the world. Chinese tourists are expected to soon be the biggest spenders on travel. Meanwhile, labor-intensive, low-wage manufacturing is moving to new opportunities in Bangladesh, Vietnam, Cambodia and elsewhere, and the composition of China's exports is changing from textiles, furniture and toys to sophisticated pumps, electronics and engines. China is successfully moving up the value chain.

### The next stage and lessons for the U.S.

Going forward, however, exports are not likely to dominate China's development process. Its outward investments will. Chinese companies are investing worldwide. The value of their investments outside of China reached $1 trillion in 2015, up from just $57 billion a decade ago. Some analysts expect it to double by 2020.

The impact of Chinese companies investing abroad looks likely to be as big, or bigger, than that of its exports. Chinese outward investment is growing very fast both because of industry conditions within China, loosening of constraints on outward investment by its leaders and growing capabilities on the part of business managers.

In just the U.S., already Chinese companies have invested an estimated $64 billion and employ 100,000 people. So while we will continue to buy goods "made in China," we will increasingly work with, and for, these very same companies.

That is, if we are lucky. If the next administration carries out its campaign promises, then the U.S. may miss out on many of the benefits of foreign investment all together from China and elsewhere, such as revitalized towns with new jobs and tax-paying businesses. In recent decades, the U.S. helped China join the global market system through corporate investment and government policy. Both countries benefited tremendously.

The irony is that China has learned its isolation lesson and is now promoting trade agreements that will substitute for the ones that the U.S. may leave on the table, such as NAFTA and the Trans-Pacific Partnership. And if the U.S. begins a trade war with China, then all bets are off. Not only will new jobs not materialize, but the low-cost goods we have enjoyed will be much more expensive, and our growing exports to China will no doubt be hurt by Chinese retaliation.

---

*Penelope B. Prime is Clinical Professor of International Business at Georgia State University and Founding Director, China Research Center. This article was originally published by The Conversation at* http://theconversation.com.

# Employ "Design Thinking with Chinese Characteristics"

*Michael C. Wenderoth*
*Vol. 15, No.2*
*2016*

## Introduction

Western executives are accustomed to long, deliberate planning cycles to research, develop, and launch products in their mature home markets. Many of them find it hard to manage the size, complexity, and speed with which business in China moves. Most multinationals have passed their "market entry" phase and have been forced out of their comfort zones to grow. Business conversations today focus on three topics: 1) scaling the business via geographic, customer segment, product line, or business model expansion (moving beyond established higher-end product positions in Tier I cities)[1], 2) turning around a failing Chinese business, or 3) defending against aggressive Chinese competitors.

The holy grail solution in the West is "innovation:" create a killer product that fits the market to create long-term sustainable advantage. Yet McKinsey's 2015 China CEO survey revealed executives believe the key to success is credibility with headquarters and the local team, followed by people management (finding and retaining talent).[2] Innovation was ranked lowest.

Why the disconnect?

In this article, I argue that innovation (at least the simplified "new product" definition) is overrated in China. Given the pace of the market, innovation should not be viewed as an end-goal, but as a *process* that unlocks profitable business opportunities. Western executives should create an organization, operating mindset, and executional capabilities that enable them to quickly detect customer trends, create valuable solutions, and learn from local competitors. To achieve this aim, I propose companies embrace design thinking ("DT") – a not-so-new methodology to bring innovative products to market. Channeling Deng Xiaoping and the spirit of China's political and economic transformation, I propose Western firms employ "Design Thinking with Chinese Characteristics," to make the approach more suitable and successful in the Middle Kingdom.

Specifically, I recommend companies follow five principles in adapting their DT approach in China: 1) think like an anthropologist – and *maintain that mindset*; 2) embrace and (gasp) copy Chinese competitors; 3) view innovation more broadly, focusing on improving service to the customer; 4) do less market research, do more market; and 5) look beyond the China-U.S. or China-EU framework, deriving ideas from other markets that may be more appropriate to China's context.

To illustrate key points, I draw heavily from my focus in the dental/medical sector, which I believe is broadly applicable because of the diverse range of customer types and challenges present.[3] I also reference the collective experience of InterChina Consulting, a leading M&A and Strategy Advisory in China, where I serve as senior advisor.[4] In the conclusion, I present limitations to the DT approach and suggest areas for further inquiry, acknowledging that there is no "one-size-fits-all" solution in China.

## Background
### From Guanxi to World Class

To win in China, Western firms need to run world-class operations.[5] Gone are the days when companies could offer second-generation products and rely solely on "guanxi" (relationships) to move business. In China, consumers are hard to pin down, competition can arise overnight, the playing field is not always level, and new technology and globalization accelerates the speed of change.[6] In response, companies are demanding more "compressed" consulting engagements, ones that seek rapid understanding of customer segments – an area where design thinking works extremely well.

### Design Thinking 101: Put the Customer First

Design thinking has gained a widespread following the past two decades in the design community, with consumer product companies, and in the field of innovation.[7] DT involves five steps, putting the customer and rapid product iteration and development at the core: 1) empathize with your customer, often through observing them in situ; 2) define (or reframe) the problem/real issue(s); 3) ideate and brainstorm to generate solutions; 4) rapidly prototype concepts; and 5) quickly test those concepts, gain feedback, and iterate.

The most common consulting request I receive is to evaluate potential distributors. Lured by a promise of "contacts" and "guanxi," many executives forget basic business sense and make poor distribution choices. Without a serious understanding of the customer – who they are, how they buy, contexts in which they use or engage the company's products – it's impossible to determine whether a specific distributor makes sense. In fact, the majority of turnarounds InterChina has worked on are the result of poor distributor or partner selections. Many Chinese distributors don't share a company's brand vision, prefer to sell on relationship and price discount, and do not maintain sophisticated records. One European client had no visibility into end-purchases and price and was lucky to receive periodic Excel spread sheet updates. Clearer understanding of what is happening with customers – even if it means doing one's own research or implanting one's own employee in the distributor or with a key customer – has become more important than ever and benefits from thinking like an anthropologist.

**Principle #1: Think like an Anthropologist – and *Maintain that Mindset***

Anthropology distinguishes itself from other social sciences by its emphasis on the examination of context, the importance of participant-observation, experiential observation in research, and making cross-comparisons.

Observation is critical because people don't always do what they say they do. They may not be aware of their actions or may not be able to articulate their needs or desires, particularly in rapidly changing markets like China. To get a true picture of customers, companies need not only to talk to them, but also to observe them in situ, seeing through a customer's eyes how they engage the product, category, or company. By doing so, companies gain a richer sense of their customers' daily lives, specific language they use, and their moments of joy and pain.

Industry reports are a good point of departure but lack the richness of observation. Traditional surveys rely on the fact that customers understand – and can clearly articulate – their own behaviors, attitudes, and needs. Interviewing and focus groups are slightly better, as adept facilitators can read or probe attendees, but they too rely on people accurately reporting what they actually do. Social media has become cost-effective and insightful, but online and offline behavior can vary widely.

Firms like IDEO, Frog Design, and Continuum specialize in DT, but strategy consulting firms such as InterChina left our desks long ago, integrating field work into the approach to see the whole picture. As the Chinese say – 百闻不如一见 (*bai wen4 bu ru yi jian* – asking one hundred times falls short of seeing it once.) Companies with limited budgets can conduct "secret shopper" visits, ask to observe customers (such requests are often honored, and after 15 minutes they often forget they're being observed), or visit customers with sales representatives. In any case, a best practice is to have company employees participate and learn observation techniques so they can later champion and spread the mindset internally, as many companies mistakenly view observation as a one-off conducted at the start of a process, rather than an ongoing process.

One medical company performed observations (with permission) in public and private clinics. They wanted to understand doctor-patient dynamics and differences between the segments. In the public hospitals, industry reports and interviews claimed doctors favored prescribing "the top imported product," but observations revealed doctors prescribed domestic knock-offs more than three-to-one over imports. Digging deeper, they discovered doctors were not conscious of their actual prescription habits, and found that doctors simply excluded imports from consideration because of perceptions ("This one I know won't be able to afford it…" "This one will ask me lots of questions and I can't interrupt my workflow…" "This one I might have to explain to the chair…"). These insights led to a better understanding that public doctors were busy and wanted minimal workflow interruptions, which in turn led the company to focus on correcting doctor and department misconceptions, as well as pre-educating patients.

The Western executive who participated also left with a deeper respect for how the segment worked: "I was told public doctors have massive workloads and don't have any chair-side rapport with patients, but until I saw it, I didn't believe it." He was also shocked to see the amount of data moving around by USB and local competitor reps assisting doctors, a direct response to restricted internet access in the hospital and the needs of doctors to get through patients quickly. The company, which relied on doctors downloading and displaying digital treatments, made it a top priority to figure how to adjust their offering to make it fit into a Chinese public doctor's reality.

Observations in private clinics revealed an opposite problem, one the executive had never experienced in Western markets: lack of patients. Through secret shopper feedback, the company learned private doctors lacked confidence and patients did not trust them. This led to a critical customer insight that drove action: "Private doctors need help building their reputation and patient trust." Attitudes among patients varied heavily by city, complicating but clarifying their efforts. Patients in Beijing believed Beijing University (a public hospital) was the gold standard, so references to Beijing helped build credibility. In Shenzhen, a city of domestic immigrants with fewer State hospitals, patients were swayed by advertising and trends in Hong Kong. In response, the company launched "business education" classes for private clinics and created online forums that elevated the status of doctors in the eyes of consumers in a regionally relevant way. Importantly, none of these initiatives required reconfiguring the company's product.

Two years later, having established a base in 北上广 (*bei shang guang* — Beijing, Shanghai and Guangzhou), the same company considered geographic expansion. Knowing dynamics in Tier II and III cities were different, they maintained the anthropologist mindset. By listening to patients chatting on their cell phones in waiting areas, they discovered that the majority of patients in Shanghai were not from Shanghai, but hailed from affluent cities in the Zhejiang and Jiangsu area. This changed their expansion strategy dramatically. Investigation revealed that patients from Wenzhou came to Shanghai to see the top doctor in the region and to shop – something that would be difficult to replicate in Wenzhou. So instead of entering Wenzhou, they doubled-down to help existing Shanghai customers grow, and reallocated their search engine marketing spend to keywords and geographic pockets outside Shanghai to drive awareness of medical options in Shanghai. Similarly, they found competition among clinics intense, which worked in their favor to focus on Shanghai and open additional accounts there.

For many Western executives, insights like these were counterintuitive. The logic in many Western countries would be "go to new geographies where additional demand lies," but in East China they found they had much more room to grow without expanding. By thinking like an anthropologist and maintaining that mindset, the company dramatically outpaced its competitors. And by deeply studying Chinese competitors and looking for analogies beyond the U.S. and EU, they can tap into even more insights.

### Principle #2: Embrace and (Gasp) Copy Chinese Competitors

Gone are the days of laughing at Chinese companies and products. The debate can rage over how "innovative" Chinese companies are, but in a growing economy with hyper competition and occasional government support, the law of large numbers is in full force. It's hard not to find examples of companies that have become wildly successful, even if serving the domestic market alone.[8] The government's approach the past 30 years has been to build "socialism with Chinese characteristics." Western firms need to wake up and consider what "management with Chinese characteristics" looks like, and how it may help them succeed.

Aside from having "home field advantage" – being more in tune with the culture, rules, and local business environment – Chinese companies exhibit several areas that Western managers can learn from.

First, Chinese companies are keenly aware of the government's role and the shifting regulatory environment, making them attuned to the importance of non-market strategies. A common belief among experienced expatriates is that anything is possible, but you need to understand where the government's interests lie. Inside counsel for a large U.S. machinery maker learned tracking features on their equipment could run afoul of local regulators, so their government relations team took a humble approach and sought ways to shape unclear policy in more favorable ways.

More importantly, Chinese firms – primarily the small, entrepreneurial ones – find ways to strip down products and get them to market quickly, often settling for razor-thin margins. One U.S. dental maker of sophisticated devices was shocked to find multiple competitors in China when they first entered the market.

Rather than dismiss them as copycats, they took a step back and deeply studied how they had been successful. They uncovered many service-related areas where the Chinese firms excelled. To serve public hospital doctors, the Chinese competitor hand-delivered information, taking advantage of cheap and efficient local delivery services (such as one of China's leaders, SF Express)[9], and often accompanied the information with in-person sales rep support. On the consumer side, by studying their Chinese competitors' digital patient education efforts, they were quickly exposed to new areas like using online bulletin boards to reach university students and "instant call" customer support to serve demanding Chinese professionals who wanted immediate answers. One executive, China head of a worldwide healthcare leader, received a constant barrage of requests on what to do with Chinese companies that copied or repurposed his company's logo and brand imagery. His response: "We're never going to shut all these down, so I encourage my team to study what was done. Many times, savvy competitors reconfigure our website so it becomes more appealing. If their format actually is better, I am open to adopting that web format ourselves. It's very easy to run an A/B test!"

Studying what Chinese try can be a shortcut to gaining local knowledge. As one marketing head of a U.S. consumer product giant shared, "I could do a lot of research, but sometimes I need to take off my Western hat and try things in a much more Chinese/local way."

To put this in practice, companies should place more emphasis on competitive analysis and intelligence, making it a dedicated part of an employee's role. One company extends competitive insight across the company by placing their own and their competitors' social media sites on monitors near the tea station so employees can see how customers interact with the local and foreign brand. Additionally, a common practice among top Western firms is to regularly review competition in management meetings. One U.S. tech company's Beijing office huddles 15 minutes daily to discuss what their main Chinese competitor (who owns 75 percent market share to their eight percent) is up to. The marketing head, who is Chinese, says the review sessions prepare them mentally for anything that might happen. Most competitive moves they ignore, but she reported they fold multiple ideas into their own offerings.

### Principle #3: Think about Innovation More Broadly, Focusing on Service to the Customer

"Chinese service" is no longer an oxymoron. Chinese firms are using technology, manpower, and talent to find creative new ways to capture and retain demanding – and less loyal – Chinese customers.

A focus on service addresses a major problem multinational executives face: reconfiguring a physical product takes time, energy, and political will. Most foreign multinationals develop product centrally (outside China), using elaborate stage-gate methods. Getting central corporate resources and approval to develop a product specific to China, to say nothing of local regulatory approval or launch preparation, takes time. And unless the CEO or executive team is fully committed to China, a Chinese business that contributes less than five percent to worldwide corporate revenue rarely will get special consideration. Instead corporate favors focusing on product changes that will increase sales in their larger, existing developed markets (usually the U.S. and Europe). Sadly, by the time changes make it to market, the executive has already rotated into a new position.

So for today's executives – particularly those working for U.S. public companies where pressure to meet quarterly sales targets runs high – "quick wins" that come with service innovations or improvements are highly valued. Speed is everything in China. Repositioning a product, localizing packaging, reconfiguring price or bundling, rethinking sales/marketing/service, working with local partners, can all make a difference, and be done quickly.

The most striking example of translating this principle into a winning go-to-market strategy is how one company up-ended its customer service model. The company, which provided customer service and treatment advice to doctors, started with a very Western approach to customer support: a toll-free phone number. By observing one segment of customers – clinicians in aesthetic plastic surgery centers who had low clinical skills but were strong at marketing and selling to patients – the company realized no one picked up a phone for help. The doctors, they discovered, wanted instant support but found it difficult to describe a patient's condition over the phone, and they were too busy to download and email photos and fill out forms, the company's service approach in the West. Around the same time, the company observed sales reps communicating to doctors with a new app called Wechat. In a semi-annual user insight roundtable, key customers bragged how the company's Chinese competitor was using Wechat to update doctors on their order status in real time.

Seeing the power of Wechat, the company set up a regional pilot that allowed doctors to use the mobile app to submit photos and leave voice messages with their questions. Doctors got rapid responses from the company's support team in written form (doctors did not want their patients to overhear the advice), with links to similar treatment types they could show to patients. Doctors and sales reps loved the immediacy and intimacy. The team went on to win a regional innovation award, and the company began exploring ways to scale the service in China (Wechat has made a push in the B2B/customer service space) as well as take the service innovation to other emerging markets where Wechat is used widely.

Because Chinese traditionally don't expect a lot from China-made products, Chinese firms have had to work harder to differentiate, particularly through service. While Chinese firms don't always nail service, they do try things. Western firms would be wise to do the same.

### Principle #4: Do Less Market Research, Do More Market

The top comment I heard last year came from a European gourmet foods CEO, lamenting his company's uneven success in China. He argued that all their deep research had not taken them very far over five years. Perhaps emboldened by the fact a Chinese company had purchased a stake in his firm, he argued: "Do less market research, do more market." By that, he meant actively testing and trying ideas: essentially the core DT idea of rapidly testing, collecting feedback, and iterating.

Marketers know that the best market research is live testing. One China GM told me that he takes a venture capital approach: every year he allocates at least 20 percent of his budget to five-to-10 new, riskier initiatives. "Every one of my competitors is trying to secure top talent, optimize their sales force, cut costs. We all grow 20-30 percent annually. The question is, 'What are you doing that's different to grow 50 percent and reach a size that makes corporate take notice?"

He sets a few "design guidelines:" ideas cannot violate corporate ethical standards, marketing initiatives should integrate the sales force, and data to measure success must be generated. He gives his team some open rein, and then largely steps out of the way.

A French consumer products marketer echoed that sentiment: "I encourage us to try new things and challenge my assumptions. More often than not, my gut is wrong, but if it drives sales, I am happy to be wrong." She added: "Like the Chinese government, I am pragmatic and I encourage my team to be the same: If it fails, we learn, brush it under the rug, and move on."

None of the western executives admit it, but they actively pursue local initiatives that fall "under the corporate radar," embodying the Chinese saying that the mountains are high and the emperor is far away (山高皇帝远 –*shan gao huangdi yuan*). The key to success with this strategy is having a good relationship with one's regional or corporate boss, and the ability to dramatically execute if the idea is a winner. Fast execution is critical because the window of time on successful ideas is brutally short in China.

An example of this practice at work came from a provider of aesthetic medical solutions. They realized doctors wanted to grow their businesses and consumers were skeptical of private doctor clinical skills (the trust issue alluded to earlier). In response, they created an online forum where doctors, backed by the brand, could provide live "expert" Q&A to consumers nationwide. The forum became a win-win-win for the company, doctors, and consumers, with doctors lining up to use the service.

## Principle #5: Look beyond the China-U.S. or China-EU Framework, Deriving and Feeding Ideas from and to Other Emerging Markets

Most of the companies and executives I work with are of U.S. or Western European origin. The vast majority, however, are global citizens – they speak multiple languages and have taken on postings around the world. The most interesting sea change is that most look beyond the U.S. and EU for inspiration. Like anthropologists, they realize China is at a different stage of development and has a different historical and political-economic underpinning, one that doesn't fit the Western model.

"I find myself trying to tap into our ex-Soviet Bloc country team to understand how to navigate political uncertainty. Americans and Northern Europeans have no appreciation for that," said one GM. Others talk to Latin America GM heads, who must manage a complex region and multiple distributors. Said another, "In many ways I start with the assumption that China is many different markets. This helps me break it down into manageable chunks."

One dental company found China more similar to Spain than any other Western country: customers that operated on lower margins, regional differences and languages, heavier reliance on relationships, considerable grey market activity, and a burgeoning segment of university students seeking treatment that did not show up in the U.S. or Northern Europe. The two general managers opened a direct line and benefited immensely from the conversations, taking strategic advice from one another. Indeed, top managers actively develop the ability to look at analogous areas and build relationships with those who can bring them insight.

There is still plenty to learn from the West, and no country or company has a monopoly on ideas. Silicon Valley's tech environment closely resembles the complex, rapid change in China, and approaches there can work in China. But the tide is shifting, and the hubris and slow corporate decision-making in the West is running its course.

## Conclusions

In this article, I've put forward the notion of "Design Thinking with Chinese Characteristics" and provided examples for how this approach can help Western firms succeed in the complex, rapidly changing mainland marketplace.

No approach fits all. Sectors that are heavily regulated by the Chinese government (banking, energy, telecom, insurance) still exist, where foreign players are more restricted to the fringes. Even in these sectors, a thorough understanding of customers and intermediaries is fundamental to playing the game, and in fact may point to heavy and creative use of nonmarket strategies. Even seasoned "China hands" (expats who speak Mandarin or who worked in China earlier in their careers) need to find ways to let go of outdated models they have about China. More research is needed on Chinese management techniques, how Chinese innovation expresses itself, and differences between sectors.

Anyone who touches Chinese consumers knows how rapidly they are changing. Technology, globalization and the rise of China and its homegrown companies will shape the new business landscape of the future. Executives and companies with experience in the China market gain valuable skills and experience necessary to survive in the new global economy. May a design thinking approach with Chinese characteristics better prepare us all.

## The idea in brief:

| | |
|---|---|
| **The Problem** | Western firms find it difficult to navigate the China market due to its size, complexity, rapid pace of change, local competition, shifting regulatory environment, and cultural differences. The issue is more acute than ever since most hold high-end market positions in Tier I cities – but now need to leave this "comfort zone" to grow. Traditional strategic and product planning cycles, conventional market research approaches and long approval loops with distant corporate decision-makers result in go-to-market strategies that are often obsolete before they reach the marketplace – or miss the mark entirely |
| **The Challenge** | How to rapidly, accurately, and efficiently understand Chinese customers and key business drivers, keep one's finger on the pulse of market changes, and rapidly convert insights into profitable and sustainable go-to-market strategies. |

| The Solution | To be successful, firms should adopt a design thinking approach with Chinese characteristics to unlock critical customer and business insights. They would benefit from applying the following five principles: <br><br> 1. **Think like an anthropologist and maintain that mindset** – Being close to customers and observing them is critical to picking up market insights – not only at the initial discovery stage, but on an ongoing basis, too. <br><br> 2. **Embrace and (gasp) copy Chinese competitors** – Rather than competing head-on or ignoring entirely local competition, following, analyzing, and copying savvy Chinese companies can be a shortcut to gaining local knowledge. <br><br> 3. **Think about innovation more broadly, focusing on service to the customer** – Taking advantage of local insights and conditions to deliver service innovations makes a big impact quickly. <br><br> 4. **"Do less market research, Do more market"** – Staying in close touch with customers, testing and co-creating concepts as they head to market is the best way to succeed in a rapidly changing market like China. <br><br> 5. **Look beyond the China-U.S. or China-EU framework** – deriving ideas from, and feeding ideas to, other emerging markets are often more appropriate and beneficial than looking back to the U.S. and Western Europe. |
| --- | --- |

*Notes*

1  For definitions of Tier I, II, III cities, see for example: http://www.chinabusinessreview.com/reaching-chinas-next-600-cities/

2  McKinsey China CEO Survey 2015. Highlights from the report: http://www.mckinsey.com/business-functions/organization/our-insights/how-china-country-heads-are-coping

3  Lessons from the dental sector are broadly applicable because of the diverse range of customer types and challenges presented. On the B2B side, dental customers range from large State-run companies (hospitals) to privately run owner-operated businesses (clinics) to private chains; on the B2C side, patients range from teens to university students to young professionals and seniors. Geographic diversity prevails and the market spans luxury products that are aspirational to functional products that cover core needs. To sell to hospitals and clinics, western companies use dealer networks or sometimes sell direct; on the consumer side they partner or directly engage in patient education and demand generation.

4  http://www.interchinaconsulting.com/en/index.php

5  http://www.amazon.com/Operation-China-Execution-Jimmy-Hexter/dp/1422116964

6  http://www.mckinsey.com/global-themes/asia-pacific/meet-the-chinese-consumer-of-2020

7   https://hbr.org/2008/06/design-thinking. *For a crash course on design thinking, visit:* http://dschool.stanford.edu *or* http://www.ideo.com

8   *See for example:* https://hbr.org/2014/03/why-china-cant-innovate; https://www.weforum.org/agenda/2015/10/how-innovative-is-china/; http://venturebeat.com/2012/03/26/why-china-doesnt-innovate/

9   https://en.wikipedia.org/wiki/SF_Express

---

*Michael C. Wenderoth is Associate Professor at IE Business School in Madrid, Spain, and Senior Advisor with InterChina Consulting.*

# Responsible Sourcing Standards and Social Accountability: Are They Possible in a Global Supply Chain?

Katherine Peavy
*Vol. 14, No.1*
*2015*

The allegation of child labor did not exactly fit the picture I was looking at — a photo of a toddler sitting next to a box with my client's logo on it. Accompanying the photo, a whistleblowing email from the client's supplier of Christmas ornaments claiming he had visited a factory near Guangdong Province's Dongguan. During the visit, he said he observed children working in the factory. For anyone familiar with toddlers, the chances of one participating in any organized activity, much less labor as detailed as painting Christmas ornaments, would seem highly unlikely.

Still, the picture was taken by the supplier and sent to the client, who forwarded it to me along with the email. The photo and email warranted further examination, particularly since the factory had passed a number of social accountability audits required by the retail brands that bought its products. If the allegation turned out to be true, then all orders bound for the U.S. would be cancelled since U.S. Customs regulations prevent products suspected of originating from factories using child or prison labor from entering the U.S.

The concept of social accountability – sometimes called social responsibility, ethical sourcing, and responsible sourcing among other names – became prominent for manufacturers, brands, and retailers in the early 1990s after it came to light that many factories producing clothing and footwear for brands such as Nike had poor working conditions, even in some cases using child or prison labor. From the late 1990s, brands and retailers got serious about implementing labor standards as identified by the International Labour Organization's Declaration on Fundamental Rights, the United Nation's Universal Declaration of Human Rights, and local labor laws. In 1997, Social Accountability International, a non-governmental organization that works to improve human rights for workers globally, published the SA8000 Standard, a set of guidelines based on the ILO labor conventions and integrating ISO management system principles. The guidelines promote such concepts as fair pay, limitations on overtime, days off, and preventing child and prison labor.

In the late 1990s and early 2000s, hoping to avoid the situation that the garment industry had faced, many multinational corporations began auditing their suppliers and their supply chains for compliance with local labor laws using the SA8000 standard. But, as my client discovered, particularly in developing countries, rural areas, and in certain categories, the supply chain lacks transparency and labor practices still differ from expectations even after more than 20 years of publicity and advancement in the field.

For me, working in China, allegations of child labor were fortunately rare. More common were issues related to falsified records ranging from faked time sheets to doctored payroll records. In an established area like Dongguan, factories have been audited for labor practices and trained in local labor law for a long time. If the child labor allegation were true, it would be a disappointing set back. I had to ask the question: Is it even possible to have a supply chain that is compliant with responsible sourcing standards?

Hong Kong-based Jon White, Managing Director of Omega Compliance Ltd., a firm that conducts social responsibility audits and consults with brands and retailers in the field, told me that in China, child labor is rare now. In the summer months, however, underage workers – those within a year of the legal working age – can be found in factories after they've gotten out of school. They are trying to make some money during the holidays. However, White cautions that "applying a blanket approach to labor law compliance across every category of products is a mistake." He points out that the garment industry has 15 years of exposure to fair labor compliance and auditing, and that their customers have worked very closely with garment suppliers and have long-term relationships with them that enhance communication on labor issues. By contrast, suppliers in other industries, such as furniture or seasonal categories (like my client) may have only five years of exposure to the concepts, training, and auditing.

Closer to home, The Coca-Cola Company's Director of Global Workplace Rights, Ed Potter, outlined for me how an industry sector develops toward their goals of implementing a responsible sourcing framework. Potter says that when he joined the company in 2005 to build a framework around the Supplier Guiding Principles defining company expectations around workplace rights, his team started working with China immediately. The standards were new to the fast-moving consumer goods supply chain. Potter's team discovered that of their 1,600 suppliers and bottlers in China only 29 percent complied strictly with China's labor laws. But by 2008, working with their supply chain in China, he says Coke raised the compliance rate to 63 percent, and by the end of 2014 it hovered around 90 percent. "The company's goal is to improve the score each year in every country we work in," Potter says. But, he counsels that there is still detailed work to do. In his 10 years heading the Workplace Rights team, he feels he has only built a framework, which needs to be filled in now.

Most experts in fair workplace practices agree that monitoring is not the answer; it's just the first step to get factories to start to understand fair workplace practices. Most brands and retailers have the belief that factory management will follow and manage labor policies themselves. However, many factories still follow the retailer or brand's lead. An ideal scenario would be for the purchasing team, the factory, and the workers to all take ownership and control of implementing fair workplace practices.

Craig Moss, an Executive Advisor at NGO Social Accountability International, agrees. "A factory owner once mentioned a Chinese idiom 'he who holds the gold, makes the rules,' and right now the purchase order is gold, and that's the way most manufacturers understand and implement labor practices."

At the factory producing Christmas ornaments, we learned that some workers had brought their children to the factory on a public holiday. The local day care was closed, but the factory was open because of the push to complete purchase orders by the shipping date necessary to meet the all important Christmas shopping season in the U.S. While the few children were looked after by one employee, their parents were able to get overtime pay of three times the normal rate for working on a public holiday. China's labor law requires this overtime calculation on public holidays so technically, the factory was operating within the law.

Typically, the allegations we look into involve situations in which orders to be shipped prior to Chinese New Year or the National Day holiday would involve factories not paying worker's overtime and trying to disguise that by creating fake records or turning security cameras off on sensitive days. At certain times of year, Chinese and U.S. holidays align in a way that causes rush orders and necessary overtime for workers.

Sometimes, the client's purchasing practices are the cause of factories not following local labor laws, and then stepping over the line and falsifying labor records. For some buyers, the bottom line matters more. Factory management would comment they had to require overtime to reach shipping deadlines, in some cases because the buyer changed his mind about the color or the volume at the last minute. Most social accountability experts now agree that educating the supplier and the U.S.-based purchasing teams is key to getting factories to manage compliance to labor laws and standards.

SAI's Moss points out that over the 15-20 years that social accountability has been practiced, a policing approach comprising audits and customer-designated labor codes has been most common. Factories see social accountability as external compliance. But, he added, leading brands are seeking to change this dynamic now, by supplementing audits with more transparent efforts to collaborate and help suppliers improve their internal processes for managing labor standards and performance.

Suppliers and their factories are often caught between the rock of a purchase order deadline and the hard place of complying with labor standards they agreed to when accepting the purchase order. For my client, the allegation was very serious, in the case of child or prison labor, as U.S. Customs will turn away products. Their company policy was to reject the product if child or prison labor were found. Consequences would be serious for the factory too, which would have lost the purchase order and been forced to absorb the expenses for raw materials and labor. A lot of businesses could not survive that kind of financial blow.

Even though the factory had a reason for children being on the property, an allegation of child labor is difficult to put into an acceptable perspective. The factory management saw the situation as a way to give their workers well-paid overtime, but the allegation could have led them to lose the business or any other future purchase orders. It was difficult to believe that the supplier making the allegation had done so knowing the seriousness of the consequences.

SAI's Chief Operation Officer, Jane Hwang says that overtime regulations, rather than child labor, are among the biggest challenges for China because of the government's strict limits conflicting with workers' economic necessities. Hwang says many of the challenges faced in implementing workplace compliance guidelines are more socio-economic than cultural. "A generation of workers are used to certain conditions and opportunities. That changes. But you can never discount economic necessity and lack of access to opportunities."

Omega's White believes that for factories, "the temptation to shortcut is enormous," precisely because of the facts of purchasing like changes in purchase orders, rushing to meet shipping deadlines, and labor shortages. He says that in some areas, factories are still presenting about 80 percent false or doctored records to auditors. White believes that the key to successful social accountability in a supply chain is "trying to get the brand or retailer to encourage transparency in their manufacturing base."

For factories, fair labor practices can be complex. SAI's Moss reports that there are more than 10,000 different labor codes globally. Big brands, industry, local laws, NGO codes, all have different details, language and terminology. A factory such as the one making Christmas ornaments, supplying to five or six different retailers around the world, could have to comply with five or six different labor codes, not to mention local laws.

So how can companies and their business partners in the supply chain avoid unwanted surprises in such a complex environment?

Coke's Potter cites transparency, ethos, and anticipation as helping the company implement its Workplace Rights Program. After 2005, he says transparency became the key for the company's work on human rights, which he calls "open source reporting." This includes publishing all documents and reports on the corporate website, and producing a global workplace rights scorecard accessible to all business units. With huge, complex operations in 207 countries, Coke has "a basic belief that the company cannot be sustainable unless the communities in which it operates are sustainable." And finally, anticipating the next big thing in the fair workplace practices field helps Coke maintain leadership on the issue, such as endorsing the U.N.'s 2011 Guiding Principles on Human Rights and disclosing country due diligence reports by third parties about Coke's progress on Human Rights in the supply chain. Potter cites the publication of Coke's due diligence in Myanmar as one of the benchmarks of transparency in the company's Workplace Rights Program.

Omega's White sees brands and retailers working closely with their supply chain partners as the key to success.

SAI's Moss and Hwang echo the message of partnership. Their teams have seen the most success stories when partnerships in the supply chain encourage open dialogue, transparency, and responsibility. Moss cites one SAI program called Ten Squared, whose approach is to establish worker-management teams in a facility to improve a specific management system issue over 100 days. He says the combination of worker engagement and cross-functional teams helped create "trained, committed people who followed procedures to accomplish goals."

But guidelines, standards, and sometimes lofty goals can get lost in the hustle to competitiveness. Otherwise, I probably would not have had to look into a case in which a questionable allegation was made in an attempt to hamstring a competitor.

SAI's Moss thinks that a different type of competitiveness has improved workplace practices in China over the last two years. "The cost of labor pressures, labor shortages, and mobile technology have contributed to factory owners realizing the efficiency of applying labor standards. The most forward-thinking factory owners are working with productivity experts now," he says. "They want to be competitive in getting and keeping good workers because they realize the cost of turnover and training now."

At the end of our conversation, Potter tells me, "There are lots of good things happening and it all takes time." That was true for the Christmas ornament factory as well. The client committed to working with this factory management, and with a number of seasonal production facilities, to understand how purchase orders and timing could be scheduled so that situations like the one in the whistle-blowing email would not crop up as a surprise again.

**Terms Used in Relation to Fair Labor Practices:**
Social Accountability
Ethical Sourcing
Responsible Sourcing
Social and Environmental Responsibility
Workplace Rights
Labor Compliance
Social Compliance
Labor Relations and Corporate Social Compliance
Corporate Social Responsibility
Ethical Trading
Fair Labor Practices

**Organizations and Related Declarations:**
International Labour Organization (ILO)
Social Accountability International (SAI)
The U.N. Declaration of Human Rights
Global Social Compliance Program (GSCP)
Ethical Trading Initiative (ETI – UK organization)

---

*Katherine Peavy spent 15 years in China working in the risk management field on hundreds of due diligence cases and fraud investigations. She is a founding partner of the consulting firm Cross Pacific Partner (www.crosspacificpartner.com).*

*Economic and Business*

# Fast Fashion and the Pursuit of a Global Market

*Nancy Medcalf*
*Vol. 16, No.2*
*2017*

## Introduction

Metersbonwe is a company with humble beginnings. In true rags-to-riches form, founder Zhou Chengjian created a brand that is now a household name across the country. Now, he is looking outward, and the company faces its greatest challenge yet. In the approximately 22 years since Metersbonwe was founded, the company has been successful in capturing business from the growing Chinese middle class by combining fashionable products with affordable prices through the utilization of the "fast fashion" model. However, over the past few years, the company's fortunes have shifted. Plagued by financial woes and a corruption scandal, a company that was once ripe with opportunity seems to be balking at the prospect of international expansion.

Metersbonwe can attribute its success to an ambitious leader, economic reforms, and a rising middle class. However, the integrity of its leader recently came into question. Last year, Zhou Chengjian became embroiled in a corruption scandal brought to light after his mysterious disappearance. His disappearance turned markets sideways and led to many questions, but few answers were given, and the repercussions of the entire ordeal remain unclear to this day. Furthermore, Metersbonwe is beginning to struggle in the market in which it initially found success. The popularity of foreign fast fashion brands continues to rise in China, and domestic brands are being pushed aside in favor of global chains with prestige and brand recognition. Metersbonwe must find a way to keep these fast fashion brands at bay and reassure Chinese consumers that it is the brand that epitomizes both the quality and upward mobility they so desire. Only then will it be able to support a global campaign with any chance of success.

## A Portrait of a Leader

Metersbonwe (měi tè sī bāng wēi) was founded in 1995 by Zhou Chengjian. A self-made entrepreneur, Zhou was born in 1965 to a family of farmers in the eastern Chinese city of Lishui (Waldemeir 2015). After quitting school at the age of twelve, he began working as a tailor while starting his first clothing business (Waldemeir 2015). This first business was bankrupt by 1985 and went bankrupt again after Zhou restarted it a year later. Neither of these bankruptcies deterred Zhou; he says his ambivalence toward past failures can be explained by the Chinese saying that "ignorant people fear nothing" (Waldemeir 2015). Zhou's purported ignorance paid off, and he found success almost immediately after founding Metersbonwe in 1995. Today, Metersbonwe operates almost 4,000 stores in China, and Zhou is one of the richest men in the country, with an estimated worth of more than $2 billion (FT Confidential Research 2016; Waldemeir 2015).

Metersbonwe entered the Chinese market at a seminal time when privatization in the country was just beginning. To "jump into the sea" and become an entrepreneur was incredibly risky, but Zhou possessed the vision and drive to do just that. He says the shift from a planned economy to a market economy caused a high demand for products, and "If you were brave enough, and your performance wasn't too bad, you could be successful" (Waldemeir 2015). However, Zhou admits that this model of success is no longer viable today. To succeed, entrepreneurs must possess professional skills and a deep knowledge of consumer demands (Waldemeir 2015). Furthermore, Zhou believes that Chinese entrepreneurs will be successful if they are "tireless in starting up, restless in development, and relentless in innovation" (Tan 2011, 97). Zhou's realization that he cannot hope to succeed using the same tactics he used two decades ago is encouraging, and his sentiments mark him as a leader who is willing to adapt to and overcome the challenges that the 21st century business environment presents.

## What is Fast Fashion?

The fast fashion industry is a relatively recent phenomenon characterized by the speed with which clothing goes from runway to retail. The most successful fast fashion brands cultivate streamlined and sophisticated value chains with the ability to bring designs to fruition over the course of only a few weeks. The speed with which styles arrive in stores stokes demand and guarantees quick turnover of products, thus ensuring fewer markdowns (Loeb 2015). Rather than restocking, fast fashion brands replace sold out products with new styles, so consumers must buy a product as soon as they see it because they may not see it again. Some of the most well-known fast fashion brands include Sweden's H&M and Spain's Zara, which are also a few of Metersbonwe's biggest rivals.

Metersbonwe fits the fast fashion niche by constantly churning out new styles at incredibly low prices. Zhou Chengjian estimates that the company releases 3,000 designs each year (Tan 2011, 97). Fast fashion brands also cater to a wide variety of demographics, which is why Metersbonwe not only specializes in men's, women's, and children's apparel, but also in footwear, accessories, home, and beauty (Nelson 2014).

## A Recipe for Success: Institutional Reforms and Favorable Demand Conditions

Economic reforms have played a considerable role in the success of Metersbonwe. Because the company has always been privately held, founder Zhou Chengjian controls all aspects of the company, allowing him to turn his vision for Metersbonwe into reality. Metersbonwe's founding in 1995 coincided with the second phase of economic reform in China. The first phase began in 1978, two years after the death of Mao Zedong, and ended in the mid-1990s (Kroeber 2016, 104-105). During this time, resources were reallocated from the public to the private sector, and private sector activity quickly expanded, but the legal basis for these private businesses was unstable. The second phase of reforms brought with it private property rights, fewer restrictions for corporate organizations, and a diminished role of the state in private business (Kroeber 2016, 105). Firms in the private sector benefited greatly from these reforms, and the number of private businesses continued to increase, as did private companies' share of industrial value added. In 2007, the private sector share of value added was 63 percent of total production (Kroeber 2016, 106). The second phase of reforms concluded in 2008 at the onset of the global financial crisis.

Metersbonwe entered the retail industry at a time when consumer demand in China was just beginning to escalate. Since the beginning of reforms, GDP per capita and purchasing power parity have continuously grown, allowing consumers more freedom than ever in their financial decisions. Despite relatively slower GDP growth over the past several years, China is poised to become the world's largest apparel market in 2017 (Fung Group 2014). This trend is explained by the continued growth of disposable income in both urban and rural households. According to the Fung Group, disposable income grew by seven percent in urban households in 2013 (2014). In rural households the growth was larger, reaching nine-point-three percent in 2013. Clothing purchases made up 10.6 percent and seven-point-two percent of total annual expenditure in urban and rural households, respectively (Fung Group 2014). With a middle class estimated in 2012 at approximately 328 million people and rising, one can be certain that Chinese consumption will only increase (Kroeber 2016, 188). Metersbonwe would not exist without the institutional reforms that occurred in China in the latter half of the 20th century. Put simply, the company was in the right place at the right time.

## Strategy, Criticism, and Changing Consumer Trends

Metersbonwe is a company that subscribes to the belief that there is never a weak market, only weak management (Tan 2011, 97). With this in mind, the company takes great measures to invest in its employees through the Metersbonwe College, which is located at the company's Shanghai headquarters. Students at Metersbonwe College are all store employees. They are exposed to a variety of lecturers from professors to business executives (Tan 2011, 98). The purpose of Metersbonwe College is simple: to train the company's future senior executives. Additionally, founder Zhou Chengjian takes steps to ensure employee morale is high. Employees are granted access to an anonymous company forum, which Zhou often browses to evaluate complaints and suggestions raised by workers (Tan 2011, 98). Employees also are encouraged to share opinions through an internal company newspaper. Each of these aspects of the employee experience showcases Metersbonwe's strategy of effective leadership in building the foundations for a successful business.

Regarding production, Metersbonwe has formulated a strategy in which costs are minimized when they can be, but company executives are willing to spend on technology and intelligence when necessary. Low value-added processes such as manufacturing and sales are outsourced through franchising or the enlistment of consulting firms, respectively (Tan 2011, 97). High value-added processes such as research and development, channels, and logistics are given special attention and greater expenditure.

Metersbonwe often utilizes celebrities and public figures for its ad campaigns. This is a strategic move, as Chinese consumers are very receptive to marketing campaigns featuring influential people. If a popular Chinese entertainer is seen as the face of a brand, consumers are likely to respond by buying the brand's products. Not only does Metersbonwe hire pop stars to act as spokespeople for the brand, but many also serve as fashion consultants (Ying 2011, 97).

One reason Metersbonwe has become so profitable is its focus on entering second- and third-tier cities (Faber 2012). With first-tier cities oversaturated and the brand's losing luster among the big-city young, Metersbonwe made a lucrative push into second- and third-tier urban centers. These markets have yet to be penetrated by global brands such as Zara or H&M, and as a result, Metersbonwe has been able to achieve brand recognition in smaller markets. While successful in building a consumer base in smaller cities, Metersbonwe is not viewed by youth in first-tier cities as prestigious in the same way that international brands are (Faber 2012).

However, it appears that Metersbonwe's recent efforts have not been entirely effective in capturing the consumer base it desires. In the beginning, Metersbonwe appealed to cost- and style-conscious Chinese consumers. Now, as tastes refine and brand image is paramount, consumers' attitudes toward Metersbonwe have begun to sour. In an interview, Xu Weidong, vice president of Metersbonwe, expressed the company's desire to become a "global value brand," and help establish China as a global exporter of style (Faber 2012). However, young consumers in China's top-tier cities do not view Metersbonwe in the same light as Xu would hope. These shoppers are adamant in their distaste for the company and its products, stating that its clothes are cheap, ill-fitting, and more suitable for high schoolers than the 18-25 demographic the stores target (Faber 2012). The young people quoted in Bennett Faber's article for Cargo Collective would prefer to shop at stores such as Zara, H&M, and American Eagle (2012). Clearly, it is a problem when a store's products do not appeal to its target audience. Judging by the reactions of consumers, Metersbonwe must focus more on branding. Recent ad campaigns have sought to update the brand's image by not relying solely on celebrity spokespeople to attract young consumers. For example, in collaboration with Hong Kong label Subcrew, Metersbonwe launched a viral video campaign featuring subculture characteristics such as graffiti, skateboarding, and action sports (Faber 2012). Additionally, the company collaborated with iconic Japanese photographer Yasumasa Yonehara on a t-shirt and has featured underground Chinese talent on other t-shirt lines. Through these attempts to update its image, Metersbonwe appears to make a departure from its original target audience in hopes of wooing label-savvy consumers from first-tier cities such as Shanghai and Beijing (Faber 2012).

## Further Challenges to the Company: The Technology Boom

In 2013, Zhou Chengjian outlined plans to expand beyond China, pledging to open stores in New York, Tokyo, and London within three years (Schuman 2013). These plans were put on hold when the company began to encounter financial problems. Up until 2011, Metersbonwe's profits grew more than 30 percent annually (Nelson 2014). Since the explosion in popularity of e-commerce in China, Metersbonwe has struggled to keep up with online retailers such as Alibaba. As a result, the company lost 95 million yuan ($14.9 million) over the first half of 2015. In attempts to combat this, Metersbonwe declared a private placement plan to raise nine billion yuan ($1.4 billion) to be spent on the construction of an online to offline platform, data support, and industry chain integration (Flannery 2015). However, in December 2016 the company announced it was scrapping the private placement plan in response to "changes in market conditions" (Reuters 2016).

Metersbonwe's online to offline integration initiatives are both extensive and impressive. In addition to developing a website, the company has developed a mobile portal, social media presence, and various in-store initiatives. All stores have free Wi-Fi and support mobile payment, while some store branches have touchscreen devices (Fung Group 2014). Additionally, shoppers have the option to scan a product's QR code with their phones, where they will then be directed to the store's product page on Banggo.com, the store's online platform. From there, shoppers can view full product information and shop online if they choose (Fung Group 2014). Finally, the company has attempted to make the transition from offline to online as seamless as possible by integrating online and offline prices and ensuring there are no discrepancies between the two. Metersbonwe has also learned how to utilize technology to monitor quality control and gauge customer satisfaction. In the company's flagship stores, remote-controlled video-taping allows executives at the company's headquarters to observe sales associates' customer interactions, customers' reactions to products, and the way products are displayed in stores (Tan 2011, 97). While it can be argued that any company hoping to compete in the 21st century must undergo a certain degree of techno-logical innovation, Metersbonwe's extensive efforts have proven the company's ability to adapt and directly confront pressure from competitors.

**Zhou Chengjian's Fall from Grace**

Despite his leadership achievements, Zhou Chengjian's reputation recently took a beating. On January 6, 2016, Zhou was reported missing. His disappear-ance was reportedly related to President Xi Jinping's anticorruption campaign (Waldmeir 2016). In response to Zhou's disappearance, Metersbonwe immedi-ately suspended trading shares on the Shenzhen Stock Exchange. It was later al-leged that Zhou conspired with Xu Xiang, then-manager of Zexi Investment, to manipulate Metersbonwe shares ahead of a 2015 stock market crash (Yang and Zhai 2016). Zhou returned to work a week later, and Metersbonwe officials have given no explanation.

It may seem strange to many that a high-profile businessman would be taken into custody on suspicion of serious criminal charges, only to be released with no explanation given and no apparent punishment. However, these circumstances have become something of a trend, as several other wealthy Chinese businessmen have been arrested in a similar fashion over the past few years. The disappearances cause instability in the Chinese stock markets, but have varying effects on the men who are arrested (Straits Times 2017). The president of China Minsheng Bank-ing Group, Mao Xiaofeng, resigned for "personal reasons," after a January 2015 stint in custody, where it was reported that he was assisting with an investigation (Straits Times 2017). In Zhou's case, the aftermath was subtle, and there have been no further reports about his disappearance.

While it does not appear that there will be any further ramifications for Zhou's behavior, the entire ordeal undermined both his credibility and integrity. For someone who built his empire through determination and hard work, it comes as a disappointment that he might take advantage of his arduously won power to manipulate his company's stock price. His humble beginnings seem forgotten, and the entire controversy has tarnished his image as a visionary leader. Although additional repercussions do not appear to be evident, the controversy should not be ignored, as it also underscores the tenacity with which President Xi has conducted his anticorruption campaign.

### Conclusions: Global Market Entry and the Future

Per a statement by Metersbonwe, 2016 was a year for product innovation, brand upgrade, good governance, and bravery (Metersbonwe Official 2016). Despite strong competition from online retailers and other fast fashion brands such as Zara and H&M, Metersbonwe experienced a sharp increase in online sales and opened 235 stores in 2016 alone (RLI 2016). It appears that the fall from grace of the company's leader will not spell the end of the company; rather, 2017 will be a return to business as usual as Metersbonwe hopes to build on the success it experienced in 2016.

It is unclear whether Metersbonwe still plans on expanding into Western markets. However, if it wishes to do so, it might be best if it first expanded into Southeast Asian markets where tastes are similar and labor remains inexpensive. If the company does this, it will likely be able to replicate the success that it has continuously found in smaller Chinese cities where few international brands have established a presence. By introducing themselves into markets with limited penetration, Metersbonwe will cultivate brand recognition and loyalty before other brands begin to consider those markets.

In conclusion, Metersbonwe is a company that has achieved success through considerable drive and determination, and a certain degree of luck. Zhou Chengjian was fortunate to found the company when he did, and economic reforms in China allowed him to leverage favorable demand conditions to his advantage. Popularity and a prominent presence in second- and third-tier cities have proven strong enough to counteract Metersbonwe's dwindling popularity in first-tier cities, and as a result, the company remains the most popular Chinese casual wear brand (FT Confidential Research 2016). Though faced with setbacks, the company has displayed the tenacity to bounce back as well as the desire to remain successful. In this way, Metersbonwe truly epitomizes the modern-day Chinese brand.

## References

Faber, Bennett. "The Sufferings of Metersbonwe." The Cargo Collective. March 2012. Web. http://cargocollective.com/bennettfaber/The-Sufferings-of-Metersbonwe

Flannery, Russell. "China Retail Billionaire's Metersbonwe Posts Loss as E-Commerce Squeeze Continues." Forbes. August 27th, 2015. Web. http://www.forbes.com/sites/russellflannery/2015/08/27/china-retail-billionaires-metersbonwe-posts-loss-as-e-commerce-squeeze-continues/#7a872a876ac0

FT Confidential Research. "Fast-fashion brands defy slowdown in China's apparel market." Nikkei Asian Review. December 20th, 2016. Web. http://asia.nikkei.com/Features/FT-Confidential-Research/Fast-fashion-brands-defy-slowdown-in-China-s-apparel-market?page=2

Fung Group. "China's Apparel Market, 2014." Fung Business Intelligence Center. December 2014. Web. http://www.funggroup.com/eng/knowledge/research/industry_series25.pdf

Kroeber, Arthur. China's Economy: What Everyone Needs to Know. Oxford University Press, 2016: 104-106, 188. Print.

Loeb, Walter. "Who Are the Fast Fashion Leaders and Why Does It Matter?" Forbes. 2015. Web. https://www.forbes.com/sites/walterloeb/2015/10/23/who-are-the-fast-fashion-leaders-and-why-does-it-matter/#259e91cf1555

Metersbonwe Official. "Metersbonwe brand presents a multi-style upgrade fission into a consumer to open a variety of lifestyle experience a new chapter (translation)." 2016. Web. http://corp.metersbonwe.com/Index/ArticleInfo?aid=557

Nelson, Christina. "Fast Fashion in China: Revved Retail." China Business Review. February 24th, 2014. Web. https://www.chinabusinessreview.com/fast-fashion-in-china-revved-retail/

Reuters. "BRIEF-Shanghai Metersbonwe Fashion and Accessories to scrap private placement plan." Reuters. December 25th, 2016. Web. http://www.reuters.com/article/idUSL-4N1EL15M

RLI. "Current Features – Issue 120." RLI Magazine. 2016. Web. http://www.rli.uk.com/features/current-features/metersbonwe/

Schuman, Michael. "Never Heard of Metersbonwe? Well, You Will Soon." Time Magazine. November 13th, 2013. Web. http://business.time.com/2013/11/15/never-heard-of-metersbonwe-well-you-will-soon/

The Straits Times. "String of disappearances in recent years." The Straits Times. February 2nd, 2017. http://www.straitstimes.com/asia/east-asia/string-of-disappearances-in-recent-years

Tan Yinglan. Chinnovation: How Chinese Innovators are Changing the World. John Wiley and Sons, 2011: 97-98. Print. https://books.google.com/books?id=Q5WWpqxHEb0C&pg=PA97&lpg=PA97&dq=metersbonwe+market+share&source=bl&ots=RV2y3q4iwfD&sig=JOpFfVIAwDEJ3P62T5Ugi4XbPFY&hl=en&sa=X&ved=0ahUKEwjfxeeEr6nTAhWF64MKHR1jC7kQ6AEIWDAL#v=onepage&q&f=false

Waldmeir, Patti. "Living the Chinese Dream." Financial Times. September 10, 2015. Web. https://www.ft.com/content/9ddb3ffc-5734-11e5-9846-de406ccb37f2

Waldmeir, Patti. "Missing Chinese billionaire Zhou Chengjian returns to work." Financial Times. January 28th, 2016. Web. https://www.ft.com/content/a2a3567a-bdcb-11e5-9fdb-87b8d15baec2

Yang, Steven and Zhai, Keith. "Probe of Top China Hedge Fund Boss Said Linked to Apparel Maker." Business of Fashion. February 25th, 2016. Web. https://www.businessoffashion.com/articles/news-analysis/probe-of-top-china-hedge-fund-boss-said-linked-to-apparel-maker

---

*Nancy Jennings Medcalf is a student in the Georgia State University College of Arts and Sciences studying for a B.I.S. in International Studies with plans to earn her Masters in International Business.*

*Economic and Business*

# Mobile Technology in China: A Transformation of the Payments Industry

*Vijaya Subrahmanyam*
*Juan Feng*
*Murthy Nyayapati*
Vol. 14, No.1
2015

## Introduction

Alibaba, the Chinese e-commerce firm, raised $25 billion from its initial U.S. public offering (IPO) in September 2014 putting China on the e-commerce world map. This exemplified China's ongoing transformation from a low-skilled, cheap labor manufacturing assembly economy to a higher-skilled, innovation-based service economy. China's 12th five-year plan defined the communications sector as a central tenet in its new economic developmental model with the Financial Industry Reform Plan sharing center stage.[1] At the same time, the adoption of mobile technology within China has been remarkable in acting as a catalyst in changing consumer behavior, creating access to goods and services and targeting marketing and expansion of the consumer base for businesses. With the promise of inclusiveness, mobile technology is increasingly permeating various sectors covering financial inclusion of banking the unbanked; assisting farmers in rural areas by providing market information regarding price, demand, and information on weather, fertilizers and pesticides; creating virtual classrooms in the education sector; spurring online commerce in retail and wholesale; and expanding delivery of health care services.

Our specific focus in this article is how mobile technology is transforming the landscape of the payments industry in China. This research has been motivated by a confluence of several recent events:

1. In 2011, the China Banking Regulatory Commission (CBRC) planned to increase the number of rural commercial banks and has been encouraging banks, both domestic and foreign, to establish tangible links across the nation and meet the financial service needs in the rural areas.

2. The 12th five-year plan outlines financial inclusion programs that deliver full financial services with a greater emphasis on the finance industry serving the real economy, as well as support for technological innovation, economic restructuring, manufacturing, and above-average growth rates in lending in rural areas, specifically to small and micro enterprises (in rural and urban areas).

3. The number of subscribers to mobile phones in China has grown from seven percent of the population in 2000 to almost 90 percent in 2013.[2] We argue that mobile technology's ubiquitous nature, as well as its capacities in the financial services sector, make it a perfect mechanism to align commerce and payments. In China, where consumers often lack access to other noncash forms of payments, such as checks or credit cards, and where e-commerce is rapidly on the rise, mobile payments (mPayment[3]) and mobile commerce (mCommerce) are gaining traction and are rapidly transforming the payments industry.

Banks, given their experience in the industry and governmental support, have a distinct advantage. However, the financial service sector is expanding to offer both traditional payment and settlement services alongside non-financial services.[4] Thus the financial sector is increasingly faced with competition from technology companies in the areas of remote account access; online commercial transactions such as people to people, business to business and business to consumer (P2P, B2B, and B2C); and outreach to remote rural areas in mCommerce and mPayment arenas. In addition, banks are heavily regulated compared to the technology companies, limiting their easy transition to mobility.

## Mobile Technology in China – a brief background

Although limited, recent literature has shown evidence of relationships between mobile penetration and economic growth in both developing and developed nations.[5] While the pervasive nature of mobility has helped include the disenfranchised in developing countries, the focus has largely been in communications and information-gathering. Researchers have noted that increases in mobility result in increased productivity thus creating a competitive advantage in nations with large investments in technology infrastructure.[6]

Up until 2004, the Chinese mobile communication market was dominated by two large companies, China Mobile and China Unicom. The dynamics of this changed in 2007 when China joined the World Trade Organization (WTO), opening this market for foreign companies to compete thus changing the mobile landscape. With a large number of Chinese companies entering the mobile eco-system to support the increasing mobile subscriber base (expected at 700 million smartphone subscribers by 2018[7]), the market for mobile holds great promise in China. It is estimated that by the end of 2018, the population of smartphone us-ers will increase from 38 percent to 51 percent. Companies in China are increas-ingly able to penetrate the rural and urban markets simultaneously, using mobile technology innovations.

The payments industry is at a tipping point around the world largely due to mobile technology. New non-banking players such as PayPal, Apple, Alipay, and Google have entered the payments arena, changing the financial services land-scape. The radical changes in this industry in China have been thrust forward largely because of two events: the Chongqing Rural Commercial Bank (CRCB) IPO in 2011 and Alibaba's IPO in 2014.

In July 2011, CRCB introduced the first mobile banking product in western China to expand mobile financial services and products for corporate customers.[8] CRCB raised US$1.48 billion in an IPO in Hong Kong. This company is one of China's largest lenders to farmers and small businesses, and is expected to be the first in a wave of listings by smaller rural-focused Chinese banks. With the mis-sion of being financially inclusive of agricultural and rural areas and supportive of small, medium and micro businesses, CRCB centered its innovative efforts on developing mobile payment services.

Simultaneously, Alibaba – through its platforms, Taobao (similar to eBay for C2C) and Tmall (similar to Amazon for B2C), with payments facilitated by Ali-pay – has dominated the development of e-commerce in China. With its recent IPO, Alibaba is now a global contender in e-commerce around the world. Morgan Stanley estimates that while still in its initial phase, China's e-commerce industry will be about 18 percent of the country's retail sales by 2018, up from eight per-cent in 2013.[9] The Morgan Stanley study also purports smartphone penetration will increase online shopping, especially in the lower-tier cities in China where a majority of the active mobile devices are registered and where most internet ac-cess is via mobile usage. Furthermore, the internet provides a level playing field for small entrepreneurs, who make up a majority of Chinese firms, since they can compete better in the online market compared to offline commerce. Concurring, the Boston Consulting Group notes that small and medium-sized companies in emerging markets are largely leapfrogging older generations of technology used in developed nations.[10]

In many ways, e-commerce has stimulated the growth of the e-payment arena in China. Because of rapid growth of internet users, improved online services coupled with lifestyle change due to rising incomes, China lends itself to creating a huge market for ePayment services outpacing even the United States.[11] A new industry of mobile operators and technology companies are entering into the payments industry once monopolized by the financial services industry, which is rapidly expanding from ePayment to mPayment.

## Examples of mobile payment system in China

*Tencent's WeChat's e-red envelope and mobile payments[12]*

Distributing "red envelopes" is a famous tradition in the Chinese New Year. In 2014, the popular application WeChat promoted the WeChat Red Envelope [Weixin hongbao 微信红包 ]. Users only needed to link their bank cards to WeChat to be able to distribute or claim an e-red envelope that then could be used to send money to friends, or to pay bills, hail taxis, pay for parking, buy movie tickets and book flights. Even though Tencent did not reveal how many new bank cards had been linked with WeChat, it announced that from December 30th, 2013, until January 8th, 2014, more than eight million Tencent WeChat users participated in e-red envelope distribution. More than 40 million e-red envelopes have been claimed, and on average, each user claimed four to five e-red envelopes. WeChat's success with its e-red envelope largely depends on the social network built by Tencent. Despite the surge in the use of WeChat e-red envelope, ZhiFuBao, the liaison payment company (similar to PayPal for eBay) from Alibaba, remains the market leader for online payment, especially in the mobile payment market. Alipay has become increasingly used to pay for theater tickets and is also used more recently to invest in money market funds called Yu'e Bao. By the end of 2013, ZhiFuBao had three billion users and more than one billion of these users paid over 900 billion RMB through their mobile devices.

These micro-payment businesses are increasingly being used in online markets, the sales of insurance products, stock exchanges, P2P lending, and have become some of the greatest competitors for traditional banks in China.

*Taxi booking and mobile payment[13]*

Consumers in China can now book or hire taxis through smartphone apps in real time. The two biggest apps, KuaiDi and DiDi, claim 97 percent of the taxi booking app market in China. By the first quarter of 2014, KuaiDi had as many as 6.23 million orders a day, covering 261 cities. DiDi had 5.21 million orders a day, covering 178 cities. To be able to cultivate and sustain a large market base for mobile payments, marketing strategies of such apps often focus on discounts in payment schemes such as consumers bundling their bank cards into their mobile devices.

Perhaps due to the novelty, these applications have raised concerns. First, the apps allow consumers to raise prices of hiring a taxi, or tip the driver in real time, creating concerns about illegal and irregular competition. Second, it excludes the elderly who seldom use mobile devices, and creates increasing difficulty for the elderly to hire a taxi. Third, it lures away consumers from the government's official taxi booking platform. This latter concern resulted in the government quickly launching new regulations covering pricing and information sharing between different platforms, among other restrictions.

## Sustainability

Mobile technology in China has created a value chain that includes financial institutions, operators, third party providers (TPP), device vendors and technology providers, with increasing collaboration among these participants. Alongside competition, there are also concurrent alliances being created among the various participants in the mobile technology network. The biggest breakthrough is seen in the online banking platforms. Banks have a relationship advantage with their customers, as well as trust due to the in-built capacity of data security centers. Because of infrastructure limitations in offering physical wired banking services to remote and rural locations, banks can work closely with application and solution providers to deliver integrated technology and security in the mobile banking space. Given the wide coverage of mobile networks and the high penetration of mobile phones in the countryside, banks in China are now able to circumvent geographic barriers and expand business coverage by offering mobile payment and financial services to remote rural locations. These services include money transfers to credit card management to wealth management and other online banking services. In addition, non-financial services are increasingly becoming commonplace, ranging from payments of utilities to business travel and hospital registrations, to managing phone accounts, among others. Many national commercial banks have introduced various financial IC (integrated circuit) cards with special features in 30 provinces and there is a push for alliances with public service departments such as transportation, health, and education.

The growth of the mPayment sector in China holds tremendous promise due to strong program support from the central and local governments, who have developed policies to support and advance e-commerce and mobile technology. The 12th five year plan places emphasis on expanding the scope of e-commerce to industries such as heavy industry, logistics and tourism, improving online sourcing and retailing capability, boosting cross-border and mobile e-commerce, and creating a more secure online e-commerce system (Xin, Chen, 2011).[14], Chinadaily. com.cn, Available from: http://www.chinadaily.com.cn/bizchina/2011-07/13/content_12893796.htm, (Accessed 22 October 2011).] In addition, the People's Bank of China (PBC) in 2006 published the *China Payment System Development Report*, which for the first time publicly disclosed the data and policy leanings of the payment system. Weighing in, Su Ning, Deputy Governor of the PBC stated, "The payment system was an important component of a country's economic and financial system, and the foundation of economic and financial operation. The development of the payment system and the improvement of the payment efficiency could boost the economic, financial, and social developments, influence peoples' lifestyle, and enhance the quality of life."[15] The PBC has also developed the *Measures for the Management of Payment and Settlement Organizations*, which created a licensing regime for ePayment service providers. Hence this sector is becoming regularized and institutionalized.

## Limitations

Penetration of technology in the countryside is a boon to financial inclusion. Yet the daunting task of investment in mobile networks and the viability of the mobile value chain remain a bane to the adoption and diffusion of mCommerce and mPayment. As China shows signs of an economic slowdown, one concern is that this may cause the government to rethink some its investment priorities, possibly impeding some of the mobile growth initiatives.

mPayment is primarily used to mitigate transactions' costs by offering a gamut of services for a lower average cost by bundling goods or services. From the business standpoint, this allows for cost savings via increases in scale and scope. From the consumers vantage point however, in order to achieve these economies, the consumer may need to increase his/her purchase size and limit choices to a few goods/services to take advantage of the economies of scale.

Many challenges remain, and policies and legal infrastructure are still being refined and promoted. Banks and non-bank operators are separately regulated, and the expansion of mobile financial services is still a work-in-progress. Technology companies are threatening the banking turf in the areas of remote account access, online commercial transactions such as P2P, B2B, B2C and outreach to remote rural areas in mCommerce and mPayment arenas promoting financial inclusion. Given their unique accessibility to their client information, banks have the advantage of offering a multitude of services including brokerage, insurance, real estate services, and trust services, among others, while remaining leaders in the mobile financial services industry. The development of mCommerce and mPayment appears to be the next frontier for banks with an established mobile internet presence. However, while banks are protected by the government and are relatively safe from bankruptcy – unlike technology companies – the latter face less regulatory scrutiny and have a freer rein in developing products and offering innovative solutions.

Regulators have to walk a thin line between fostering innovation and promoting self-regulation while protecting the safety and soundness of the financial system. This causes them to limit banks' strategic choices in transitioning to mobility. One such example is seen in the highly restrictive bank technology rules that were recently announced by PRC banking regulators wherein all banks are required to prove that their computer technology and software are "secure and controllable." The extreme measures taken in this regard require banks to provide all sensitive intellectual property, such as their source code for all software to government regulators in China. In trying to address cyber-security issues, China has announced plans to become more self-reliant in its lagging chip and server industries. China has also tightened restrictions for internet companies in the past year, as it seeks to secure control over its online environment. These restrictions may negatively affect the mPayment industry that includes several foreign players in the banking and non-banking sectors.

## Conclusions

Given that financial inclusion has increasingly become a policy priority and is seen as a complement to financial stability goals, the outreach capacity of mobile payment services, combined with the rapid growth of e-commerce, is becoming more commonplace in China. The Chinese government has aided in the development of mobile technology and is working to correct issues with poor infrastructure, logistical limitations and government restrictions.

Concurrently participants in China have enthusiastically invested in technology, capital and human resources needed to gain competitive advantage in the mPayment industry. However, investors should also be aware that the e-commerce business model for China has been tweaked and the internet sector regulated, enabling domestic incumbents to grow without much foreign competition. Potential deregulation of the internet industry in the long term could also change the competitive dynamic over time. In addition, mobile devices cause ongoing concern for security as sensitive information can be easily stolen or lost. In this regard, the Chinese government has been imposing regulations regarding online transactions as noted in the recent bank technology rules. With recent concerns around the world about data security issues in some large firms, this may limit the growth of the mCommerce and mPayment industry. Thus the future landscape of the payments industry in China, while transforming, remains uncertain at this juncture.

## Notes

1   See the 12th Five-Year plan for the Development and Reform of the Financial Industry. *http://www.csrc.gov.cn/pub/csrc_en/newsfacts/release/201210/W020121010631355001488.pdf*

2   Gary Coleman, Ira Kalish, Dan Konigsburg and Xu Sitao, *Competitiveness: Catching the next wave: China*, Deloitte, September, 2014, *http://www2.deloitte.com/content/dam/Deloitte/global/Documents/About-Deloitte/gx-china-competitiveness-report-web.pdf*

3    *ePayment (electronic payment) is largely used in e-commerce transactions for buying and selling goods or services offered through the Internet. mPayment (mobile payment) is a point-of-sale payment made through a mobile device, such as a cellular telephone, a smartphone, or a personal digital assistant (PDA). Mobile payments can be funded in a variety of ways: (1) directly from a bank account (through automated clearinghouse (ACH)), a system for direct electronic transfers between bank accounts or an account at a non-bank payment provider; (2) with a traditional credit, debit, or prepaid card; (3) through a mobile carrier, either by drawing on a prepaid account with the carrier or adding the purchase to the monthly phone bill. A consumer could also consolidate multiple funding options on a mobile device, through an application known as a "mobile wallet." (Mobile Payments: What's in it for Consumers? F. Hayasho, Economic Review, Federal Reserve Bank of Kansas City, 2012).*

4    *Financial services include account inquiries, remittance and transfer, wealth management services (bonds, funds, insurance), foreign exchange management, financial information inquiry, etc. Non-financial services include payment services (payment of utilities, lottery tickets, hospital registration, hotel travels), account top-up, game cards, business travel services, payments collection, etc. Non-financial services are delivered by banks in partnership with third parties on the banks' platforms.*

5    *Economic Impact of Broadband: An Empirical Study," LECG Ltd (2009),* http://www.connectivityscorecard.org/images/uploads/media/Report_BroadbandStudy_LECG_March6.pdf. *Kpodar, Kangni and Andrianaivo, Mihasonirina, ICT, Financial Inclusion, and Growth Evidence from African Countries (April 2011). IMF Working Papers, Vol., pp. 1-45, 2011. Available at SSRN:* http://ssrn.com/abstract=1808446; *Williams, Chris, Davide Strusani, David Vincent, and David Kovo, Deloitte LLP. The Economic Impact of Next-Generation Mobile Services: How 3G Connections and the Use of Mobile Data Impact GDP Growth, Chapter 1.6 in The Global Information Technology Report 2013, World Economic Forum.* http://www3.weforum.org/docs/WEF_GITR_Report_2013.pdf; *What is the impact of mobile telephony on economic growth?* http://www.gsma.com/publicpolicy/wp-content/uploads/2012/11/gsma-deloitte-impact-mobile-telephony-economic-growth.pdf

6    *The 32nd China Internet Development Statistics Report, CNNIC, June,* http://www.cnnic.net.cn/hlwfzyj/hlwxzbg/hlwtjbg/201307/t20130717_40664.htm.; *The Mobile Economy 2013 A. T. Kearney,* http://www.atkearney.com/documents/10192/760890/The_Mobile_Economy_2013.pdf

7    http://www.chinainternetwatch.com/11769/china-smartphone-users-to-be-574-2-mln-2015/

8    *Trends and Prospects of Mobile Payment Industry in China 2012-2015- Creating Innovative Models, Boosting Mobile Financial Services, Deloitte, 2012.*

9    *eCommerce: China's Consumption Growth Engine, Morgan Stanley, Nov 7, 2014.* http://online.barrons.com/articles/ecommerce-chinas-consumption-growth-engine-1415323378?autologin=y

10    *Ahead of the Curve – Lessons on Technology and Growth from Small Business leader, Boston Consulting group, Oct. 2013.* http://www.bcg.com.cn/en/files/publications/reports_pdf/BCG_Ahead_of_the_Curve_Oct_2013.pdf

11    http://www.forbes.com/sites/russellflannery/2013/09/02/lifestyle-changes-are-driving-big-growth-in-china-e-commerce-spending/

12    *Online Finance Report, No. 12, Feb 10, 2014. Sohu Finance.* http://stock.sohu.com/s2014/olfin12/

13    *"KuaiDi and DiDi Occupies 97% Market in Taxi Booking Apps." 15/5/2014, People.cn.* http://auto.people.com.cn/n/2014/0515/c1005-25022304.html; *"Ministry of Industry and Information Technology Discusses the Market for Taxi Booking Apps." From Sina Finance, June 5th, 2014.* http://finance.sina.com.cn/chanjing/cyxw/20140605/165619325858.shtml

14    *Xin, Chen. (2011) "E-Commerce to quadruple by 2015, official says," [Internet]*

15    http://www.pbc.gov.cn/publish/english/955/2022/20225/20225_.html

*Vijaya Subrahmanyam is Professor of Finance, Stetson School of Business and Economics, Mercer University-Atlanta; Juan Feng is Associate Professor, Department of Information Systems, City University of Hong Kong, Hong Kong; and Murthy Nyayapati is former director and co-organizer of GMIC, one of the largest mobile internet conferences in China and Silicon Valley.*

# Advertising in China

*Hongmei Li*
*Vol. 16, No.1*
*2017*

The history of Chinese advertising in the broad sense can be traced back to the Song dynasty when stores used signs and words to advertise services (Wang, 2008). In the 1920s and 1930s, advertising in Shanghai was already a dynamic industry, with foreign advertising agencies and brands competing with the Chinese counterparts prior to World War II.

After the Chinese Communist Party takeover in 1949, the government gradually eliminated commercial advertising in the belief that a centralized socialist economy did not need advertising. During the Cultural Revolution (1966-1976), almost no commercial ads existed, except for limited commercial information about exports to foreign countries (Chen, 1991).

China officially announced a resumption of commercial advertising in 1978 after the Third Plenary Session of the Eleventh Central Committee of the Chinese Communist Party. At this meeting, China's paramount leader, Deng Xiaoping, declared that China would shift from a political orientation – focusing on class struggle – to a more pragmatic approach – centered on economic reforms and the opening of the economy to global capital. Since then, advertising has gained strategic and symbolic importance in opening up society and developing the economy in China.

In the past few decades, Chinese advertising experienced exponential development. Foreign advertising agencies urged their global clients to enter China in 1979, right after the country opened its door to the outside world. Now foreign brands and advertisements have become an inherent part of the daily lives of Chinese consumers.

### Convergence between foreign and Chinese advertising practices

The Shanghai TV Station aired China's first foreign commercial for the Swiss Rado wristwatch in 1979. The one-minute English commercial, focusing on product information, was broadcast only twice, but it produced a huge impact in China. Hundreds of people went to state-run local stores to inquire about the product in the next few days. Interestingly, the product was not sold in China until four years later, suggesting that the advertiser was initially more interested in image advertising than selling products since China had not yet developed a consumer market.

Coca-Cola entered China in 1979, and it was the first foreign brand that was sold in the Chinese market. The first foreign commercial that China Central Television (CCTV) – the only national TV network in China – aired was for Coca-Cola. It caused criticism because the product was viewed as not aimed at ordinary Chinese consumers.

During the 1980s, Japanese brands and advertising achieved wide recognition. Brands such as National, Panasonic, Sony, Toshiba, and Toyota became household names among urban Chinese. Similarly, Japanese advertising agencies also achieved prominence in the Chinese market largely because Dentsu and a few other Japanese agencies collaborated closely with Chinese advertising professionals and academics. However, since the 1990s, American advertising agencies have obtained a more prominent position in China.

In the 1980s Chinese advertisers used hard-sell advertising strategies, focusing on product information and production processes (gates of factories, machinery, diligent workers, their awards, etc.). With increasing influence of foreign advertising practices, Chinese advertisers later adopted soft-sell strategies that catered to a variety of values such as family bonding, individualism, romance, adventure, love, beauty, modernity, newness, masculinity, and femininity.

Chinese ad professionals also demonstrated a strong desire to learn from their Japanese and American counterparts. Many exchange programs were established for Chinese ad professionals to learn the newest advertising practices. Professionals working at foreign ad agencies were constantly invited to give talks about foreign advertising. With various efforts to professionalize advertising, including the establishment of professional associations, the opening of degree programs in prominent universities, and the publication of advertising books, advertising gradually became an attractive profession that elevated its lowly image of puffery to a career that ambitious young Chinese were interested in pursuing.

Initially, Chinese professionals were more interested in working at foreign advertising agencies since they provided better salaries, benefits, and training. Chinese advertising agencies were generally viewed as having a lower status. In the last decade, foreign and Chinese advertising practices have converged, largely because of the constant exchange of advertising personnel, ideas, and practices. While Chinese advertising agencies in the past offered lower pay to employees, starting in the mid-2000s Chinese ad agencies offered even higher salaries to professionals who already had experience in foreign advertising practices. Now ads in the Chinese market featuring foreign and Chinese brands look very similar. Both types of ads stress affective connections with consumers in order to generate demand.

### Swinging between nationalism and cosmopolitanism

A prominent theme in Chinese advertising is the selling of nationalism and cosmopolitanism. Both foreign and Chinese brands resort to the promotion of these concepts in their ads. However, there are some subtle differences given their different origins, perceptions, and relationships with modernity. One obvious difference is that Chinese brands are more likely to resort to patriotism or nationalism as a selling strategy. Chinese brands such as Li Ning (a Chinese sportswear brand) and Hai'er (a home appliance brand) have long been selling national pride in marketing their products. Li Ning, in particular, has been inherently associated with China's Olympic glory and "Chinese-ness." Hai'er, on many occasions, has sold its foreign expansion as a successful story in the Chinese market not only to endorse the quality of its products, but also to claim itself as a pioneer in increasing China's global influence. The selling of nationalism is about the reconstruction and reinforcement of traditional images, symbols, rituals, myths, and customs in the context of China's search for national identity and modernity in an increasingly globalized world. Advertisers appropriate and reinterpret Chinese symbols, images, rituals, historical heroes, and China's anti-imperialist history to create a narrative of patriotism, loyalty, and national glory.

The promotion of Chinese-ness is particularly seen when China hosts global events such as the Beijing Olympics, the WorldExpo, and the Asian Games. During the Beijing Olympics, foreign brands also celebrated their connections to China. For example, McDonald's asserted "I'm lovin' it when China wins." Coca-Cola had a record marketing blitz with theme music "China is red" and "China is hot." The Olympic sponsor Adidas tried everything to establish its connection with Chinese culture and national pride. Non-official sponsors such as Pepsi and Nike also made efforts to connect their products and brands to China's rising patriotism. Such endorsements of nationalism often met with consumer approval.

Given that foreign brands already had established their cosmopolitan identity, the appropriation of nationalism made them powerful rivals of Chinese brands, which could not claim to own nationalism in China any more. To compete with foreign brands in the Chinese market, Chinese brands also aimed to balance nationalism and cosmopolitanism.

Chinese advertisers use various strategies to make global connections and sell

the globalized images to Chinese consumers. Oftentimes, such global position-
ing is seen as contrived "Western-ness," either by appropriating Western symbols
– including Western languages, Western models, European-style architecture,
sculpture, and famous tourist sites (such as the Seine River, the Arc de Triomphe,
the Louvre, the Château de Versailles, the Eiffel Tower, Cambridge, Paris and
Rome) – or by selling values associated with Western modernity (such as individualism, freedom, newness, and the pursuit of pleasure). In China, Western-
ness is often associated with product quality and prestige. Products with foreign
sounding names are many times sold at higher prices than brands with Chinese
names. As a result, many clothing brands use foreign-sounding names. And some
products also make false claims about their foreign origin.

Chinese ads often juxtapose foreign and Chinese cultural symbols, project-
ing the celebration of universal humanity through the meeting between East and
West. Chinese advertising also sells dreams of common humanity and the desire
for Chinese people to be recognized in the global market. The combination of
foreign and Chinese elements means that Chinese brands aim to target the growing middle class in China, which often harbors a strong desire to have more global
connections, while simultaneously treasuring their roots in Chinese culture.

However, global brands often enjoy more advantages in constructing such a
convergent identity. After all, their cosmopolitan identity has been established in
their origins and global success. Chinese brands instead are often viewed as having
contrived cosmopolitan identities.

In other words, when Chinese brands compete with global brands, they are
somehow at a disadvantage because foreign brands are inherently viewed as having higher quality and prestige. Considering the product scandals in China involving contaminated baby milk, poisonous rice, and other goods of questionable
quality, foreign brands are often chosen because they are considered safer and of
a higher quality. Chinese consumers now use foreign agents to buy directly from
Western countries, and they purchase products when traveling to Europe, the
United States, Hong Kong, Japan, and South Korea.

**Digital advertising**

Since China joined the World Trade Organization, Chinese advertising has
not only been shaped by loosening regulations, but also by digital technologies.
Now companies allocate more money to digital advertising in response to rising
TV advertising prices and declining readership of print media.

The rapid development of digital and mobile advertising has seriously challenged traditional advertisers. For example, Baidu—on online portal–has already
surpassed CCTV to become the largest advertiser in China, forcing CCTV to
collaborate with new players.

Digital advertising focuses more on consumer participation, branded entertainment, and fan-centered advertising strategies. The pervasive use of digital advertising also means that it is becoming more difficult for Chinese regulators to administer advertising, thus leading to an increasing number of illegal, offensive, and controversial ads in China. Controversial advertising not only includes problematic products, but also the problematic use of questionable symbols, images, and words.

While there is hope that digital advertising will flatten the advertising gaps between Chinese and foreign advertisers and between Chinese and foreign advertising agencies, foreign brands and their agencies still enjoy some advantages because of their extensive networking, know-how, and capital. A vast number of Chinese ad agencies and brands still compete at the lower end. The global economic recession of 2008 has increased the Chinese market, which may lead to different dynamics in China's advertising market in the future.

## Conclusion

Chinese advertising is a dynamic industry and profession, which is closely related to China's economic development in general. China's rapid economic development amid the global recession makes the Chinese more significant. However, the Chinese economy is now slowing down, as Europe and the U.S. are recovering, which may further shape how China is perceived. Nevertheless, a sense of national pride among the Chinese consumer-citizens has strengthened, which influences advertisers and will shape advertising strategies in the future.

---

*Hongmei Li is an associate professor of strategic communication at Miami University, Oxford, Ohio.*

*Economic and Business*

## Macau: New challenges test the city's prospects

*Clifton W. Pannell*
*Vol. 15, No.1*
*2016*

Macau, first established in 1557 and the oldest former European colony in East Asia, is again facing challenges to its recently established status as the world's largest gambling center. Enormous revenues derived from gaming activity – a key driver of Macau's prosperity – have suddenly diminished. In 2014, monthly casino revenue peaked at almost $5 billion per month, and a year later the figure had fallen by almost half to a level last seen in 2010, according to the New York Times.

A number of forces have coalesced to prompt this decline. Perhaps most challenging for Macau has been President Xi Jinping's vigorous campaign to eliminate corruption by officials, including those who gamble and move money through Macau and its casinos. Thousands of officials have been charged with corruption, and the fear of punishment in China has spread. Authorities have focused on "VIP rooms," where many of China's elites had been doing their gambling. Large junket operators – who loan incentive funds to gamblers from China – also have been hurt because of a growing failure of gamers to repay large debts. In addition, the courts in China will not enforce rules on repaying gambling debts.

At the same time, China's economy has been slowing for several years, undercutting the wealth and affluence that had been fueling gambling and reckless spending among officials and elites.

Local government and political forces in Macau also have tightened regulations on the hotel/casinos and limited the number of gambling tables. Unlike in Las Vegas where much of the revenue is generated from lower-return slot machines, the big money in Macau has come from gaming tables and VIP rooms where high rollers wage huge sums on games such as baccarat. Casino executives including Steve Wynn have been highly critical of these restrictions.

Another indication of the seriousness of the crackdown is a proposal to ban smoking in casinos and hotels. Smoking is common in China, and it is prevalent among casino goers.

The declines have taken place just as new gaming facilities have come on line. In May 2015, the first of several new billion-dollar-plus hotel/casinos opened, the Galaxy Macau, Phase II. In October, another great hotel complex opened, the $3.2 billion Studio City with its Gotham City design features.

More are promised. Six casino operators are slated to invest more than $20 billion in new resorts in the Cotai zone, the landfill area that is the Macau equivalent of the Las Vegas strip. This zone was created between the two islands, Coloane and Taipa, just south of the Macau peninsula and linked by bridges and causeways.

## Evoking Macau's History

The current challenges evoke the territory's long history as colonial entrepôt and former role as a gateway for the early China trade. Once the British developed Hong Kong after the Opium War and Treaty of Nanjing (1842), Macau went into a steady decline as Hong Kong captured the China trade and became the main entry portal to south China and the Pearl River Delta. Such were the vagaries of Portuguese colonial administration that for more than a century after the arrival of the British in Hong Kong, Macau struggled to find new sources of revenue to maintain its viability. Sadly, for most of its history prior to the last few decades, it was a sleepy backwater, neglected by its Portuguese colonial administration and visited by a modest tourist trade for gambling or other salacious activities.

In the early 1960s a new authority was installed over the poorly organized gambling houses, as a monopoly license was awarded to a new syndicate, *Sociedade de Turismo e Diversoes de Macau* (Macau Tourist and Amusement Company, or STDM). This finally brought in new investment capital to create casinos and hotels such as the original Grande Lisboa. The STDM also brought much-needed revenue to the government to create new infrastructure to support more and better facilities and arrival terminals for tourists coming by high-speed hydrofoils from Hong Kong. One of the very special opportunities for Macau was that it is the only place in China that allowed casino gambling, adjacent to a country with more than a billion people, many of whom enjoyed gambling.

The creation of VIP rooms for high-stakes players encouraged the tourist and gambling trades. These private rooms were designed for anonymity. Once economic reforms began to take hold in China in the 1980s and 1990s, the VIP rooms, supported and funded by junket operators, began to attract high rollers from China who were provided funds that could later be repaid in China with Chinese *yuan*. In this way, gamblers could avoid currency controls that limited the amount of cash Chinese visitors were allowed on each exit from China.

Major changes for Macau followed the return to Chinese sovereignty in December 1999. Macau became a Special Administrative Territory (SAR), and more new licenses were granted. Two were awarded to Las Vegas casino operators, Sheldon Adelson (Sands and Venetian) and Steve Wynn, and another went to Galaxy. The reason was because criminals were operating more openly in the last years of Portuguese control in the run-up leading to the handover, and the Chinese government desired to modernize and upgrade the quality and number of casinos and hotels with some other goals in mind for Macau.

## Communist Takeover and New Directions for Macau as SAR

Granting new licenses for casinos and hotels signaled that the new SAR government (and implicitly the Chinese government in Beijing) had new plans for Macau. The broad and bold goal was for Macau to become the key recreation and tourist center for the Pearl River Delta city-region and south China.

China first introduced four special economic zones in the 1980s, three of which were in the Pearl River Delta city-region. These were linked to Hong Kong and were to be used as tips of an economic spear to drive China's economic growth with new innovations and trade links to the global marketplace as well as sources of capital from Hong Kong, Taiwan, and Southeast Asia. This became especially prominent in the mid-1990s following the storied southern tour by China's aging paramount leader, Deng Xiaoping.

The Pearl River Delta was then a densely populated region of roughly 40 million people with a network of cities and towns increasingly linked through new transport arteries. Factories producing consumer goods for the world marketplace attracted huge inflows of transient laborers to the area from the interior of China.

Guangzhou (formerly called Canton) at the head of the Pearl River in the north was the apex of a great triangle of which Hong Kong was the anchor point on the southeast leg of the Pearl River estuary and Macau was the anchor point on the west leg. All three cities were given key roles in an evolving regional urban plan for the long-term development of the Pearl River Delta city-region.

A 2009 Guangdong provincial document laid out a plan for the development of the greater Pearl River Delta region, and Macau was given a key role with high expectations as the leading recreation and tourist center. While gambling was not identified as the centerpiece for Macau, any knowledgeable person would understand the subtext: the desire to develop Macau as a hub for gaming as well as for other tourist activities.

All of the recent prosperity and funds for Macau's infrastructure were drawn from gambling revenues. The Macau government levied a 35 percent tax on gross gambling revenues and levied other special fees on casinos. The remarkable growth of the casino and hotel industry provided employment for many Macau citizens and attracted additional workers from the adjacent mainland.

Despite the best ambitions and aspirations for Macau to become a tourist destination with a multiplicity of activities, its key attraction has been gambling, and this has been the basis for the territory's financial success and growth.

The numbers tell the story. The first of the new Las Vegas-style casinos opened in 2004; by 2009 there were 32 casinos overall, while there had been only 11 in 2002. The Macau government reports that gross gaming revenues grew during the period 2003 to 2008 from $3.6 billion to $13.7 billion, while the number of visitors almost doubled in the same period. More than half of these came from mainland China.

Pannell and Loughlin found in a 2015 paper that increasing numbers of the recent visitors were from China and many were one-day visitors who came specifically for gambling. This contrasts with the typical visitor to Las Vegas, who stays two or three nights and who may seek a variety of entertainment activities other than gambling. Consequently, the goal of transforming Macau into a tourist center for families does not appear to be working.

Hotel complexes in Macau are seeking to offset gambling revenue declines by becoming recreation centers for affluent tourists from China with Disney World-like attractions such as a Ferris wheel, a fake Eiffel Tower and gondolas on an ersatz Venetian Grand Canal. With these huge investments, and the reality of a diminution in gaming, can these hotels and their corporations survive?

The latest reports from Macau suggest that the government is beginning to feel pressure from hotel and casino operators to loosen up and allow more gaming tables. Such a relaxation also would ease a threat to jobs so critical to the social welfare and economic health of Macau. Of the territory's 600,000 residents, 100,000 work in the casinos and hotels.

Macau, as it has done many times over the centuries, is again facing new threats to its well-being after a brief period in which it enjoyed unparalleled prosperity and wealth. The Macau SAR must walk a tightrope between local administrators and investors and the political forces in mainland China.

China wants Macau to be an attractive and wholesome recreation center for the Pearl River Delta region and south China: gambling would be allowed, but it would be done in a restrained and controlled manner. China's citizens would enjoy the pleasures of a big entertainment center without the corrupting influence of excessive gambling as seen in the capitalist West.

Casino operators, meanwhile, seek the enormous returns that are so tantalizing in the gaming industry. Yet they must face the vicissitudes of policy-making and competing political factions in a Leninist state. Will the anti-corruption campaign fizzle out after a couple of years, allowing high rollers to return to Macau and its VIP rooms? Or will a more modest and restrained atmosphere evolve that reduces the opulence and wealth, while recent investors lick their wounds and accept lower rewards? The bets are on the table, and the roulette wheel is spinning.

## References

Boehler, Patrick, 2015. *With new resorts, Macau places its bets on the Chinese middle class,* New York Times, May 27.

Gaming, Inspection and Coordination Bureau, Macao SAR (2015) *Macao gaming history.* Direcção de Inspecção e Coordenação de Jogos (DICJ) http://www.dicj/gpv.mo/web/en/history/index/html

Gough, Neil, 2015. *Macau gambling industry faces challenges on multiple fronts.* Nov. 26. New York Times. November 26.

Government of Macao, Special Administrative Region, Statistics and Census Service. www://dsec.gov.mo

Guangdong Province, Hong Kong SAR & Macau SAR (2009). *Building coordinated and sustainable world-class city region. Planning study on the co-ordinated development of the greater Pearl River Delta townships. Consolidated final report.* Hong Kong: retrieved June 5, 2010 from http://www.pland.hk/pland_en/misc/great_prd/news/report-e.htm

Loughlin, Philip H. and Clifton W. Pannell, 2010. *Gambling in Macau: A brief history and glance at today's modern casinos.* Focus on Geography. Vol. 53, no. 1, 1-9.

Pannell, Clifton W. and Philip H. Loughlin, 2015, *Macau's role as a recreation/tourist center in the Pearl River Delta city-region.* Urban Geography. Vol. 36, no. 6, 883-904.

---

*Clifton W. Pannell is emeritus professor of geography at the Franklin College of Arts and Sciences at the University of Georgia and an associate of the China Research Center.*

## Shanghai FTZ: Expectations Have Never
## Been Aligned With Reality

*David Risman*
*Vol. 14, No.1*
*2015*

**"Unrealistic Expectations"**

On September 29, 2013, China officially opened the Shanghai Free Trade Zone, or FTZ, an outwardly ambitious project to bring a new wave of foreign investment and reduction in restrictions that have plagued foreign businesses in China for years. The Chinese Communist Party promised sweeping reforms that would both reduce administrative burdens and create a generally more business friendly environment in the Zone, located in Shanghai's Pudong District. Foreign investors, in anticipation of reform, purchased surrounding property immediately causing home prices in the area to surge 30 percent. Stock prices of logistics and shipping firms also climbed dramatically.[1] The announced framework in the FTZ was geared towards broad administrative reforms to simplify the burdensome processes that often impede or delay foreign direct investment in China's economy. The announcement was bold and expectations even bolder. Han Zheng, Shanghai's CCP Leader, and leader of the FTZ implementation, stated upon launch that the Shanghai FTZ would "transform the government's role in business," and that the "FTZ is part of a national strategy, a key decision that deepens reform, a breakthrough that overcomes the main obstacles of reforms. With this breakthrough, the government's role can undergo changes. It can also boost scientific development and increase China's competitiveness."[2]

Foreigners who had done business in the Chinese market often shared the same frustrations; slow, unpredictable administrative approval processes, a largely unreliable legal system, highly limiting restrictions on sectors of capital investment, interest rate volatility, and the inability to convert currency in an expeditious manner. The Shanghai FTZ promised to fix many of these issues, initially in Shanghai but with an eye towards nationwide reform. In mainland China, sectors for foreign investment are controlled through a series of classifications such as "encouraged," "restricted," and "prohibited."[3] In what was the most anticipated reform, the FTZ announced the use of a "negative list," allowing wholly foreign capital investment in any industries not on the list. When initially released, the list covered 16 service sectors including: agriculture; mining; manufacturing; production of power; gas and water; construction; wholesale and retail; transportation; computer information services; finance; real estate; scientific research; environmental; education; health; and sports and entertainment.[4] The foreign expectation was for the release of the list to be a historical moment, opening foreign investment to markets never previously allowed. In reality, it was a similar set of restrictions dressed up to look like reform. While the negative list does not ban foreign investment in these industries, it does limit investment in joint ventures largely to small equity ownership stakes and requires a burdensome administrative process, leaving sectors of foreign investment in a similar place as it was prior.

Immediately upon release of the list, Chinese leadership began backtracking to quell foreign investor's concerns by promising that the negative list would become less restrictive. Han Zheng stated "This is the 2013 version, and we will start garnering consensus for how to manage the negative list. Then we will have the 2014, 2015, and 2016 version. The NPC (National People's Congress) gave us three years. We will make progress every year, making gradual improvements." He also stated: "Even with the restrictive nature of the negative list, the reforms are progress. This is a major innovative reform. It frees companies from reviews. Companies used to register with the local bureau of industry and commerce in several different categories. But now there is only one category. We have realized the value of a 'register first, approve later' process in the FTZ, which means companies can start operating after registration, and applies to government licensing or approvals only when they deal with the businesses required under these procedures."[5] It's a bold promise that as of yet, does not seem to be delivered.

Now entering the FTZ's second year, Westerners are beginning to lower their expectations. While the 2014 "negative list" has been reduced from 190 items to 139, China has seen little actual change in this area. The negative list, offered as the most sweeping of political reforms in Shanghai, has made little difference in opening up Chinese markets to foreign capital, with criticisms by even the state-run media that the zone has been too conservative in reforms.[6] Experts in Chinese business policies feel that there has been no significant change. The managing director of the China Market Research Group in Shanghai states: "It's great talk by Premier Li Keqiang and a lot of senior government officials, but there's no execution. Nobody knows what you can do."[7] In the areas of currency convertibility and interest rate volatility, there has been less movement than promised.[8] What was expected to quickly become a hub for Western banking has seen very little growth. Only one offshore bank has opened a free trade account available to clients in China: HSBC, which had been negotiating with the Zone prior to the initial announcement.[9] Xinhua, the state-run news agency, has touted that there has been growth over the past year from 8,000 businesses in the zone to almost 20,000; however this seems to be below expectations.[10]

### "It's not you, it's me"

This is not China's first time utilizing localized experiments to develop nation-wide reforms. Isolated experimentation in economic reform is an integral part of China's success in the world economy. Beginning with the central government allowing businesses to lease land long-term in the late 1970s, China has seen a rapid transformation in domestic economic policy. Between 1981 and 2001, the proportion of the population living in poverty in China fell from 53 percent to just eight percent. Late in 1979, the first Special Economic Zones (SEZ) were commissioned in Shenzhen, Shantou, Zhuhai, and Xiamen, with the goal of testing progressive domestic economic policies for implementation on a national scale. The development of the SEZs were based on four underlying objectives: (1) utilizing incremental experimentation and workforce education through trade, supported by government policies, (2) attracting of foreign capital to promote export growth and generate domestic employment, (3) overcoming the common problem of limited resources by supporting large scale investment with outside capital, and (4) facilitating economic liberalization through policy measures and private innovation. The SEZs initially saw great success in meeting these objectives. In 1981, the four SEZs accounted for almost 60 percent of Foreign Direct Investment (FDI) in China, with Shenzhen accounting for the most. By the end of 1985, realized FDI in the four zones totaled US$1.17 billion. From 1980 to 1984, Shenzhen grew at a 58 percent annual rate, while the national average for GDP growth was only estimated to be 10 percent.[11] Foreign capital, technology, and management techniques drove economic modernization. The foreign capital enabled the country to acquire the needed technology and skills without draining the limited public revenue that existed after the Cultural Revolution. At the time of its designation as an SEZ, Shenzhen was a fishing village of no more than 30,000 people. It was no bigger than three square kilometers and lacked even a traffic light.[12] By the end of 2011, Shenzhen had 10.47 million permanent residents, ranked fourth in economic power on the Chinese mainland, and placed second in global rankings of economic strength compiled by the U.K. Economist Intelligence Unit in 2012.

Shenzhen's success can be attributed to attracting FDI through favorable legal policies and reduced administrative and tax burdens on businesses. Shenzhen streamlined administrative processes, allowing foreign investors to have direct access to provincial and central level planning authorities through the local Shenzhen authority. As a result of these successful reforms at the local and provincial level, many of these practices were put into place nationally. However, despite Shenzhen's 58 percent growth rate from 1980 to 1984, it was not until 1987 that land utilization for business became common throughout China. Even when it was most needed, change was predictably slow in China.

The China of today is not the China led by Deng Xiaoping, in need of rapid change to adapt to the world economy. In that sense, Shanghai is not Shenzhen. Western expectations are based on the success of prior localized reforms operating with a very different goal. Shenzhen was the first of its kind. The framework under Deng Xiaoping was to begin to experiment with economic policies that were unfamiliar in China's system of governance. China is no longer a stranger to capitalism. Thus the focus of the Shanghai FTZ is not to experiment with new ideologies but to tweak existing ones. Where the SEZs were designed to focus on generating domestic growth through foreign direct investment, the FTZ is built with an eye towards opening borders to become a larger part of the international community. For a political class afraid of fallout and familiar with effective domestic economic policies, there is more to lose in Shanghai by rushing reforms. As such, the implementation of true change in Shanghai is predictably more gradual than that of the SEZs of the 1980s.

**"Not a Dud"**

Despite disappointment from foreign investors, the Shanghai FTZ is starting to see some progress. If the FTZ is the more predictable marathon, rather than the anticipated sprint, it is on pace to serve its purpose. Prior to January of 2015, Chinese regulations had heavily restricted technology related industries to limited joint ventures with local partners. A wholly foreign owned technology company had been unheard of in China. An announcement in January 2015 from the Ministry of Industry and Information Technology stated that it will now permit wholly foreign-owned "online data processing" and "transaction handling" industries, geared toward e-commerce industries. While it will likely take considerable time before corresponding rules and regulations are released, this move could allow Western companies to compete with Chinese e-commerce behemoths such as Alibaba on their home turf.[13]

In regard to currency convertibility, while reforms have moved dramatically slower than initially announced, there have been significant changes in the FTZ. In February of 2014, FTZ-based businesses were granted the ability to create a two-way cash pool of yuan, now the fifth most traded currency in the world.[14] The cash pool allows individuals at these companies to engage in cross-border trade settlements using the yuan, making capital flows much easier in and out of China. Prior to this change, currency often had to be converted into a foreign currency before leaving China's borders. The policies were largely successful and have been implemented on a national scale in a short period of time.[15] Whether as a result of these policies or otherwise, the yuan has overtaken the Canadian and Australian dollar in world trade.[16]

Another aspect of the FTZ that has benefited small and middle-market foreign investors entering the Chinese market is the rise of serviced offices. Serviced offices are rentable office spaces that come with technology infrastructure, fully furnished work spaces, and secretarial services. These services have allowed foreign businesses to maintain a presence in China without having to deal with skyrocketing commercial real estate prices in an unpredictable Chinese business environment.[17] These offices are a part of the reforms allowing a presence in China with minimal upfront capital. In addition to serviced offices, the authorities are correcting a major disadvantage of the FTZ: it was far away from the central business district. The FTZ was geographically isolated from the ports and airport, making many of its liberalized policies difficult to take advantage of for businesses operating in the main business zones in Shanghai.[18] The expansion of the FTZ will move into the Shanghai city center where large multinational companies and banks already have their headquarters.[19]

Small businesses are not the only ones assisted by these reforms. Amazon.com, which already has significant operations in China, is opening a new logistics warehouse to try to lower shipping charges and speed delivery in and out of the zone.[20] Relaxation in tariffs, as well as import/export regulations, has made for increased ease in logistics and transportation. Amazon.com intends to capitalize on these reforms with its new warehouse. Microsoft Corp. announced in September that it would release its signature game console, the Xbox One, in the FTZ after the country lifted a more than decade-long ban on gaming.[21] Even Victoria's Secret is opening a store in the FTZ. Although limited to a $1.1 million capital investment, it is the firm's first move into the Chinese market. The lingerie brand was attracted to the ease in logistics and warehouse services, allowing it to reduce wait times for product delivery from months to weeks.[22]

After early success in the zones, China has announced there will be three new FTZs, each experimenting with its own economic reforms. The zones will be located in Guangzhou, Tianjin, and Fujian, focusing on specific geographic areas within those cities.[23] While the reforms are likely to be slow, China is determined to make FTZs part of the future, in the way Shenzhen was a part of the past.

## "No Surprises"

It is hardly surprising that the FTZ has not lived up to Western expectations. It was, however, the Western expectations that were unrealistic, not the rate of reforms in the FTZ. China's appetite for radical reforms has slowed dramatically since the early 1980s, as China has adapted to a new economic status quo. What was once an economy based almost exclusively on providing cheap labor has now developed a thriving service sector, a domestic luxury goods market, and a banking sector that is beginning to rival any modern nation. As the level of reform required to transform the landscape of China slows down, its rate of experimentation does too. This is not to say that experimentation as a result of policies in the FTZ could not have dramatic change on the way the Chinese do business, it is just that it will not happen at the pace Westerners would like. Chinese authorities are being slow and methodical in their rate of reform. The pace of change is as much about mitigating the risk of moving backward as it is about moving forward. In the words of Deng Xiaoping: "Keep a cool head and maintain a low profile. Never take the lead but aim to do something big."

### Notes

1   Heather Timmons & Ivy Chen, *The updated knowns and unknowns of Shanghai's soon-to-launch Free Trade Zone*, Quartz (Sept. 26, 2013), http://qz.com/128580/psst-did-you-hear-whats-happening-in-the-shanghai-free-trade-zone/

2   Hu Shuli, Han Zheng: *How Shanghai's Free Trade Zone Works*, Caixin Online (Nov. 14, 2013 3:33 PM), http://english.caixin.com/2013-11-14/100604877.html

3   Chuck Comey et. al, *Breakthrough Reform? Shanghai Free Trade Zone*, Morrison Forrester (Oct. 8, 2013), http://www.mofo.com/files/Uploads/Images/131008-Shanghai-Free-Trade-Zone.pdf

4   Hu Shuli, Han Zheng: *How Shanghai's Free Trade Zone Works*, Caixin Online (Nov. 14, 2013 3:33 PM), http://english.caixin.com/2013-11-14/100604877.html

5   Hu Shuli, Han Zheng: *How Shanghai's Free Trade Zone Works*, Caixin Online (Nov. 14, 2013 3:33 PM), http://english.caixin.com/2013-11-14/100604877.html

6   http://www.nytimes.com/2014/07/02/business/international/shanghai-trims-list-of-restrictions-on-foreign-investment.html?_r=1

7   http://money.cnn.com/2014/10/06/news/economy/shanghai-free-trade-zone/

8   http://knowledge.ckgsb.edu.cn/2015/01/20/finance-and-investment/has-the-shanghai-free-trade-zone-lived-up-to-its-promise/

9   http://english.cri.cn/12394/2015/01/22/3685s862868.html, http://www.bloomberg.com/news/2013-10-12/hsbc-bea-win-approval-for-outlet-in-shanghai-trade-zone.html

10   http://knowledge.ckgsb.edu.cn/2015/01/20/finance-and-investment/has-the-shanghai-free-trade-zone-lived-up-to-its-promise/

11   Douglas Z. Zeng, *China's Special Economic Zones and Industrial Clusters: The Engines for Growth*, 3 J. Int'l Com., Econ. & Pol'y 1, 2 (2012)

12   Yue-man Yeung et. al, *China's Special Economic Zones at 30*, 50 Eurasian Geog. & Econ. 222, 223 (2009)

13   https://www.techinasia.com/china-wholly-foreignowned-ecommerce-companies-shanghai-free-trade-zone/

14   http://www.wsj.com/articles/yuan-is-worlds-fifth-payments-currency-1422431603

15  http://knowledge.ckgsb.edu.cn/2015/01/20/finance-and-investment/has-the-shanghai-free-trade-zone-lived-up-to-its-promise/

16  http://www.wsj.com/articles/yuan-is-worlds-fifth-payments-currency-1422431603

17  http://www.nzcta.co.nz/advice/1727/using-serviced-offices-to-support-your-china-growth-strategy/

18  http://www.china-briefing.com/news/2015/01/06/china-rolls-new-ftzs-expands-current-one.html

19  http://www.reuters.com/article/2014/12/27/china-economy-ftz-idUSL3N0UB04I20141227

20  http://fortune.com/2014/08/21/amazon-to-launch-in-shanghai-free-trade-zone/

21  http://www.wsj.com/articles/one-year-on-shanghai-free-trade-zone-disappoints-1411928668

22  http://www.wantchinatimes.com/news-subclass-cnt.aspx?id=20150114000164&cid=1202

23  http://www.china-briefing.com/news/2015/01/06/china-rolls-new-ftzs-expands-current-one.html

---

*David Risman is an international tax professional with a JD from Georgia State College of Law.*

*Economic and Business*

# Intellectual Property Right Challenges and Opportunities in China and U.S.: An Interview with Dr. Lei Fang

*Penelope B. Prime*
*Vol. 16, No. 1*
*2017*

*Penelope Prime, Founding Director of the China Research Center, interviewed Dr. Lei Fang on October 18, 2016, about intellectual property right (IPR) protection in China, and the new trend of Chinese companies investing in intellectual property (IP) and technologies in the U.S. The text has been edited for clarity and length.*

*As a partner and founder of Jin & Fang LLP, Dr. Lei Fang practices U.S. IP law and counsels clients on IP protection and enforcement strategies in domestic and global markets. She represents multinational clients ranging from start-up companies to large corporations, universities, and research institutes in various technology fields, particularly in pharmaceutical biotechnology, medical device, and life sciences. She helps clients seeking patent, trademark, and copyright protections; IP due diligence; technology transfer; and licensing on various transactional IP matters. She also assists in the Hatch-Waxman ANDA (Paragraph IV) patent litigation involving generic pharmaceuticals, and managing International Trade Commission Section 337 investigations and related district and appellate court cases involving Chinese companies. She is currently an adjunct professor at the Emory University School of Law, where she teaches a contract-drafting course.*

**Penelope Prime: Dr. Fang, thank you for sharing your expertise in IPR protection with the China Research Center. We know that many companies investing in China have faced serious challenges with IPR issues because**

*of weak enforcement. As an attorney who has worked a long time on IPR issues, how do you assess the situation in China today, and going forward? What kind of changes are you seeing?*

Lei Fang: In general, both IPR protection and enforcement in China have been improved dramatically. Intellectual property refers mainly to patent, trademark, and copyright. China has fully developed laws governing these three types of intellectual properties, and Chinese patent laws, trademark laws, and copyright laws have all been amended several times since they were enacted. The latest amendment for the Chinese trademark laws was in 2014. I believe between 2014 and 2015, the Chinese copyright laws were amended, too. Since last year, China is preparing to amend its patent laws for the fourth time. The latest draft was prepared by the State Intellectual Property Office (SIPO) and was submitted to the State Council Legislative Affairs Office for review. A new draft of the fourth amendment may be available for public comments by early 2017. So we can see that Chinese policymakers are continuously trying to change their laws and make them more compliant with international standards.

With respect to the protection side, China continuously increases its patent application filings both inside China and in other countries through international PCT or Paris Convention filings. In 2015, Chinese innovators filed over a million patent applications for the first time ever within a single year.

With respect to the enforcement side, I actually just discussed this issue with a few Chinese IP attorneys in China the other day. I was informed that China has set up special IP courts to deal with patent and complicated trademark infringement cases in three major cities: Beijing, Shanghai, and Guangzhou. These IP special courts are equivalent to the appellate court level in the U.S., but any patent infringement cases or complicated trademark infringement cases can be filed in these IP courts directly. There are about 20 highly experienced judges in these IP special courts. Each of them must have more than 10 years working experiences in dealing with IP issues. Therefore, the decisions rendered by these judges in the IP special courts should be reasonable and fair, I hope.

Furthermore, the statutory damage for IP infringement cases has been increased, and punitive damages for willful infringement are acceptable, too. For instance, for the trademark infringement cases, the statutory damage increased from 500,000 to three million RMB; For the patent infringement cases, the current statutory damage is about one million RMB, but the draft fourth amendment proposes to increase statutory damages for patent infringement, as well.

With respect to the national/local protectionism, the recent survey indicates "foreign plaintiffs notched a 100 percent win rate in civil cases heard by the Beijing IP court last year."[1] This is very encouraging and good news for U.S. and foreign companies that are doing and/or will do business in China.

**PP: *Are those IP courts for foreign companies or both Chinese and foreign companies?***

LF: These IP special courts handle all the patent infringement and complicated trademark infringement cases in China, regardless of the nationality of the companies or individuals. Basically, all the patent infringement cases can be filed directly before the IP special courts, but for the simple trademark and copyright cases, they would start with the local court first, and then can appeal to the IP special court, if needed. Although right now, there are only three such IP special courts in the three cities, eventually more IP special courts will be set up in other jurisdictions.

**PP: *So, if you have a problem in Sichuan you can't go to one of the three courts?***

LF: You can, if you (or the company) can show you are doing business in any of those three cities. It's the same concept as in the U.S.: one must show a "personal jurisdiction" in the selected court.

**PP: *Do you see these rule and enforcement changes creating less infringement because people who might infringe see that they will get in trouble or more likely get in trouble so there's more respect for IP today?***

LF: Absolutely. Increasing damage awards and acknowledging punitive damages would certainly send more serious messages and imposing more serious punishment to the infringer, as well as more respect for the value of owners' IPR.

**PP: *It is making a big difference, then?***

LF: Yes. China is really trying to switch from "made in China" to "created in China". The Central government is strongly emphasizing innovations and cre-

1   *http://www.iam-media.com/blog/Detail.aspx?g=8dc59dc8-6405-4b86-b241-27e89afc6089*

ative inventions.  Many new policies have been implemented to encourage innovations and technology transfer and licensing.

For a foreign company that is entering the Chinese market as part of its global business, actively seeking IP protections and diligently enforcing its IPRs in China are very critical. Remember, all IPs are territory, meaning you must have IPR protections in each and every nation/country in which you are doing business. Having only a U.S. patent does not prevent an infringer from copying or infringing your products or technologies in China. You've got to have a corresponding Chinese patent that covers your products and/or technologies, and can be asserted in a patent infringement suit, if an infringement arises. Further, you've got to think about all types of IPR protections in China. For instance, a Chinese invention patent to protect your products and technologies, a Chinese design patent to protect your products' designs, a Chinese trademark to protect your brand names, a Chinese copyright to protect your source code, etc.

Many U.S. companies now realize the importance and necessity of obtaining Chinese IPs, and have started to seek Chinese IPR protections, as well as enforcing these IPRs in China diligently. That's good news. Moreover, for any U.S. foreign companies, before entering the Chinese market, conducting due diligence and product clearance are equally important.  One should know potential competitors, their products and technologies, and whether you have "freedom-to-operate" (FTO) in China.

**PP: Do you mean compliance issues?**

LF: No, not just compliance issues. It is the same for a Chinese company thinking about investing or operating in the U.S. Due diligence and FTO assessment of the market are very important. It is very common and good practice for a U.S. company to conduct due diligence and FTO assessment when they develop a new product or technology. Due diligence and FTO assessment would help the company learn whether its product or technology is patentable: whether there are any blocking patents that the company's product or technology may fall into, and if so, how to design around such blocking patent, if possible. In other words, whether the company has a freedom-to-operate its product or technology in the U.S. market.

In the recent years, due to global collaborations, more and more Chinese companies realize the importance of due diligence and FTO assessment, and have started to consider and conduct such assessments, too.

**PP: *A lot of Chinese companies are starting to invest in the U.S. Many of them are interested in developing their own technology, buying new technology, and learning so that they can conduct R&D themselves. What trends do you see in that regard?***

LF: As I said before, China now really focuses on innovations and advanced technologies. Although many Chinese companies are still very interested in merger with, or acquiring, U.S. companies, due to the lack of management and U.S. operating skills in running the company, Chinese companies are more interesting in investing in the U.S. company's technologies, rather than the whole company. Both the central Chinese government and local province level governments are encouraging and providing many incentives for Chinese companies to invest overseas.

For instance, lately there are many China-U.S. innovation and entrepreneurship competitions and forums in the U.S. These competitions are organized and initiated by Chinese investors and government agencies, and the main purpose is to foster communication and facilitate China-U.S. technology innovation and investment.

I just participated the first 2016 U.S.-Southeast China U.S. Innovation and Entrepreneurship competition in August. Surprisingly, more than 400 people attended this competition. The technologies presented related to biomedical, IT electronic, and other advanced technologies. Several Chinese investment groups attended and evaluated these technologies. The selected technologies will go to China to compete there. Even though this is the first of this kind of technology competition in the Southeast, I was told that Silicon Valley hosts such technology competitions almost every month.

**PP: *And these are Chinese companies in the competition?***

LF: No, most of the technologies presented in the competition are from U.S. companies, research institutes, or universities. The Chinese local government on the province or city level sponsors the competition, and could possibly participate in developing the selected "winning" technology.

**PP: *In China?***

LF: Either one, in China or in the U.S.; it doesn't matter. In China, almost every province has, on the government level, set up innovation technology incubation and development centers for companies, particularly start-up companies.

Same here, too. For example, in the U.S. Silicon Valley, there are several incubation centers providing incentive packages for start-up companies to grow up and develop. Same here in Georgia. In Peachtree Corners, for example, there is a new technology park particularly set up for start-up companies and small business owners, including Chinese-owned companies.

China is also working on facilitating university technology transfer and licensing. Anyhow, China is really focusing on developing and acquiring innovations and advanced technologies in the next five to 10 years.

PP: *What kind of areas are priorities?*

LF: Technologies related to life sciences are certainly a big interest. China's pharmaceutical and advanced medical development are behind – not like the IT field.  Others, such as artificial intelligence (AI) technologies, and material sciences – e.g., biomaterials, energy control materials, etc. – are also a focus of China's interest.

PP: *Do you have an example of a Chinese company investing in technology here that you could share with us?  Or is that client privilege that you can't really share?*

LF: I am aware of several Chinese investment companies constantly investing in U.S. companies, and Chinese pharmaceutical companies that are very active in merging with and acquiring U.S. companies.  WuXi AppTec is a good example.

PP: *So the company is acquiring that technology here and taking it back to China?*

LF: Not necessary, and it depends on many factors dealing with business and market strategies. The focus is licensing the technology for further development and commercialization.

Of course, we have been talking about investing in technologies, but there are many Chinese companies interested in investing in real estate and services like

AMC.[2]

**PP: Entertainment.**

LF: Yes, entertainment and more. I just saw the news this morning that a Chinese company is thinking about buying GNC, which sells vitamins and supplements. They are talking about buying a branch of GNC for $100 million.

**PP: Because a company develops a technology or buys a technology or licenses a technology doesn't mean that they can be successful using that technology or selling the products and service—**

LF: No, it's still a long way to go.

**PP: What is it about firms that tend to be more successful in that regard, especially Chinese firms, or is it too early to say?**

LF: I think when a company decides to license a technology, they must conduct due diligence on the technology and the market. Technology development and commercialization, particularly in the life sciences and biopharmaceutical fields, is a very complicated, long process and involves many players in various stages. Of course, the earlier stage, less investment, but higher risk; the later stage, higher investment, but less risk. Even after the development stage, there are animal studies, clinical trials for FDA regulatory approvals, because whatever you make in the lab is different from what can be used in the market.

So, it's very hard to predict, and it depends on many factors. Nothing is guaranteed during the technology development process, particularly in the life sciences. However, if the technology is good and has potential market value, and the company engages the right people to work on it in different stages, then there's a high probability of success.

**PP: In terms of the Chinese companies investing in technology here, what is the breakdown, just a rough estimate, of how many of those companies would be state-owned companies versus private companies?**

LF: I think most of them are private companies. Even if the company is state-owned, it's probably semi-state-owned.

---

2   *AMC Networks provides movie and TV content; http://www.amcnetworks.com*

*PP: Is that in life sciences or in general?*

LF: In general, I believe 80 to 90 percent are private companies, not state-owned companies.

*PP: Thank you so much.*

# New Challenges for Xi Jinping's
# Anti-corruption Crackdown?

*Andy Wedeman*
*Vol. 16, No. 1*
*2017*

*This piece was originally published by the China Policy Institute: Analysis (cpianalysis.org), based at the School of Politics and International Relations, the University of Nottingham.*

As the anti-corruption campaign launched by CCP General Secretary Xi Jinping approaches its fourth anniversary, the question ought to be asked: where is it going? When the drive was first announced in the winter of 2012-2014, it appeared that it would prove a repeat of crackdowns launched by Xi's predecessors – a burst of sound and fury in which a swarm of rank-and file-officials – known popularly in China as "flies" – would be detained by the party's Discipline Inspection Commission, some of whom would then end up being prosecuted by the Procuratorate, and ultimately be packed off to prison by the People's Courts. In the process, a few senior officials – known as "tigers" – would be "bagged." Based on past precedent, Xi's crackdown should have ceased being front-page news after a few months and quietly faded away – until some new scandal prodded the leadership to again declare that the party must fight corruption to the death.

As it developed in the spring of 2013 and onward, Xi's crackdown wrought havoc on such assumptions. As in the past, tens of thousands of flies were investigated (upwards of 500,000 by rough estimates) by the party and indicted (more than 120,000) by the judiciary. The annual rates of increase were impressive. The total number of economic and official malfeasance cases "filed" by the Procuratorate increased nine percent in 2013 and a further 10 percent in 2014, followed by a slight two percent decrease in 2015 compared to 2014. The number of officials at the county and department leadership levels indicted increased nine percent in 2013, 32 percent in 2014, and a further 11 percent in 2015, with the result that the number indicted rose from 2,610 in 2012 to 3,821 in 2015. The number of more senior officials at the prefectural and bureau levels jumped 46 percent in 2013, 126 percent in 2014, and 27 percent in 2015, thus increasing indictments from 179 in 2012 to 747 in 2015. Between 2012 and 2015, the courts convicted 100,200 individuals on corruption-related charges. As of November 2016, 116 civilian tigers – defined as state officials, party cadres, and state-owned enterprise (SOE) managers holding bureaucratic ranks equal to or above that vice minister – and 82 military tigers – officers holding ranks of major general or above – had been implicated, including one former member of the Politburo Standing Committee (Zhou Yongkang); three former members of the Politburo, Bo Xilai (former Party Secretary Chongqing), General Xu Caihou (former Vice Chairman of the Central Military Commission), and General Guo Boxiong (former Vice Chairman of the Central Military Commission); and the former Director of the CCP Central Committee General Office (Ling Jihua).

Far from another short-lived political drama, Xi's anti-corruption drive has thus proven to be more intense and protracted than its predecessors. Moreover, unlike its predecessors, it does not yet seem to have a discernable end. On the contrary, observers have suggested that Xi's intensified drive against corruption is not a finite "campaign," but is rather part of a "new normal" (新常态). It is true that in the past six months or so the drive has become less visible and dramatic. The "heyday" of the tiger hunting when senior officials and generals seem to be falling right and left (roughly from December 2014 to March 2015) appears to have passed. The drive nevertheless continues to claim victims, the most recent (September 2016) being the Acting Party Secretary of Tianjin Huang Xingguo. Flies also continue to fall at an unrelenting pace, as evidenced by terse reports posted daily on the Ministry of Supervisor and Central Discipline Inspection Commission's shared website (http://www.ccdi.gov.cn/) and the party's "anti-corruption" website (http://fanfu.people.com.cn/). As such, the blitzkrieg attacks of the earlier phases of the drive have now apparently given way to a less dramatic but perhaps no less intense war of attrition as Xi and his primary ally in the fight against corruption, Wang Qishan, continue to press onward.

At the Sixth Plenum of the 18th Party Congress in late October 2016, Xi in fact made it clear that the drive would continue, and vowed to continue to attack high-level corruption. But little in terms of concrete regulations was new. For example, the plenum promulgated a new set of guidelines on corruption that included warnings against tolerating corrupt behavior by members of officials' families, but it did not adopt a policy mandating that officials disclose family assets that would have served as a significant new hedge against such corruption. Similarly, talk arose of centralizing the discipline inspection system by pooling the resources of the party's Discipline Inspection Commission, the state Ministry of Supervision, and the judicial Procuratorate, a change that would have helped make its local organs more independent of the corresponding party committees, and therefore less apt to protect local officials from scrutiny and more aggressive in pursuing evidence of corruption. In the end, however, the plenum approved a modest pilot program limited to a few provinces. Shortly afterward, the Central Discipline Inspection Commission also announced that it would dispatch inspection teams to Beijing, Chongqing, Guangxi, and Gansu plus 15 other major state agencies. This new round of inspections, however, replicates a pattern of periodic central intervention put in place back in 2013, not a major new escalation of the drive. In sum, the results of the plenum suggest that Xi intends to continue the drive, but that his basic tactic will likely remain much the same.

It would seem the drive is now approaching a critical juncture. Xi and Wang have bagged a lot of tigers, some of whom also happen to have been Xi's potential or perceived political rivals. Xi has thus clearly used the crackdown on corruption to consolidate his grip on power and to at least partially re-establish the primacy of the central leadership over the sprawling party-state apparatus. In the process, he has perhaps made inroads against the extensive high-level corruption that apparently spread during the Hu Jintao era. He has certainly not, however, dramatically reduced the overall level of corruption. At best, he has perhaps brought the problem closer to some sort of "controlled" level.

Having made some inroads, Xi and Wang now face the difficult task of figuring out how to back off the anti-corruption fires they set during the more intense phases of the drive. Many observers report the ongoing drive has produced a pervasive atmosphere of fear among officials, and has left many paralyzed. Such fear is hardly unexpected. A broad reading of the past three years of revelations suggests many illegal and questionable behaviors and practices on which Xi and Wang have "dropped the hammer" since the 18th Party Congress had become essentially "standard operating procedure" during later Jiang Zemin and Hu Jintao years. Some of those convicted of accepting bribes have, for example, confessed that they thought little of pocketing "red envelopes" (or briefcases or suitcases) stuffed with cash. In some cases, they claimed they felt pressured to accept bribes because to not do so would have violated prevailing informal norms of official behavior, and would have offended and angered those who offered bribes.

Given the apparent extent of corrupt practices among officials, cadres, and managers, Xi and Wang now face four daunting tasks. First, they need to continue to tighten administrative procedures and curb the autonomy of decision-makers and hence reduce the opportunities for corruption. Second, they need to reduce the gap between the pay officials, cadres, and managers receive and the income of private-sector actors with whom they interact. Higher official pay will not eliminate temptation, but so long as poorly paid officials control valuable assets and opportunities, resisting temptation will be difficult.

Third, Xi, and the party more broadly, has to address the reality that since the 1990s rapid economic development has spawned a new economic elite that is linked by blood and marriage to the older political elite. Power and wealth overlap in all advanced economies and political systems, including both authoritarian and democratic systems. Although Jiang Zemin embraced and legitimated China's new economic elite with the Three Represents in 2002, China still lacks a system of ethics to regulate and regularize how power and money interrelate. As a result, a "culture of corruption" has grown and festered. Although the negative economic consequences of such loose ethics and shady officials might have been endurable during the days of rapid economic growth, as China's economy slows, a culture of corruption will prove an increasing drag if it is not replaced by a new set of elite ethics.

Fourth, Xi and Wang have to devise some sort of "amnesty" that would allow corrupt officials, cadres, and manager to make a clean breast of their past transgressions and become part of new "less corrupt" way of doing official business. If corruption has become a near ubiquitous pathology among officialdom, continuing to aggressively combat corruption indefinitely could wreak significant damage to the party-state and could potentially destabilize China's political superstructure. Having bagged more than 200 civilian and military tigers, taken down thousands of mid-level "cats," and swatted upwards of 100,000 flies, Xi and Wang need to figure out how to declare "victory" and let the current anti-corruption drive transition to a true "new normal" of intensified anti-corruption work that deters corruption while also ensuring that the party-state can function.

De-escalating the anti-corruption drive and seeking to transition to a new normal could, however, confront Xi with two major challenges. First, even limited amnesty and marginal pay raises for officials and SOE managers could be seen as rewarding past corruption rather than a means to disincentivize future corruption. After almost three-and-a-half decades of China's war on corruption, many ordinary Chinese have grown cynical and believe that corruption is a pervasive pathology. As a result, Xi is apt to find it difficult to convince the public at large that his crackdown has significantly reduced corruption.

Second, although Xi's crackdown has bagged more than 200 senior party cadres, state officials, senior SOE managers, and military officers, as well as a number of China's brash new tycoons, Xi's critics grumble that his "friends" have escaped unscathed. They argue that the real goal of the tiger hunt has always been to take down Xi's political enemies and thereby enable him to secure a grip on political power akin to that of Chairman Mao Zedong. To an extent, there can be little question that the crackdown has enabled Xi to consolidate power. It also likely true that, like the "dead tigers," others among China's political and economic elite have become wealthy by playing loose with the formal "rules" and using their access to power and connections to gain advantages from the economic boom that accompanied China's transition from the plan to the market. Absent a dramatic takedown of some member of Xi's inner circle, such talk is not likely to die down. On the contrary, if the intensity of the crackdown begins to fade, rumors that Xi allowed other tigers to remain free are likely to continue. Xi thus faces the risk that ramping down the crackdown could be seen as a self-serving attempt to legitimate a political system that remains dirty.

Finally, Xi may be facing a new and potentially serious challenge from China's business elite. In December 2013, 56 delegates to the Hunan Provincial People's Congress from the city of Hengyang were expelled after it was found that they had paid a combined Y110 million to 518 members of the Hengyang Municipal People's Congress and 68 staffers to secure their seats. In September 2016, 45 delegates to the National People's Congress (NPC) from Liaoning province were expelled after it was revealed that they had paid Y40 million in bribes to 523 of the 619 members of the Liaoning Provincial People's Congress. Thirty-eight of the 62 members of the congress's standing committee were axed. Twenty of the 85 members of the Liaoning Provincial Party Committee were among the expelled delegates. Among the 40-odd members of the province's leadership,[1] the congress's chair Wang Min, the former secretary of the Liaoning Provincial Party Committee and a member of the 18th Central Committee; congress vice chair Wang Yang; congress vice chair Zheng Yuchao; congress vice chair Fan Feng; congress vice chair Zhu Shaoyi; Vice Governor Gang Rui; Vice Governor Liu Qiang; and Su Hongzhang, secretary of the party's powerful provincial Politics and Law Committee and Deputy Secretary of the Liaoning Provincial Party Committee, were expelled and in some cases charged with criminal bribery and election fraud.

Although the National People's Congress and its local counterparts nominally exercise substantial legislative authority, they are often described as "rubber stamp" bodies that provide mere window dressing for China's communist party dominated "people's democracy." If the congresses are functionally powerless, why would want-to-be delegates in Liaoning be willing to pay an average of Y900,000 (US$136,000) for worthless seats in the national legislature? Even more perplexing, why would want-to-be delegates in Hunan be willing to pay an average of Y1.96 million (US$295,000) for a seat in the even less influential provincial legislature?

According to Hong Kong-based scholar Suzanne Pepper, even though having a seat in a people's congress may seem bestow no political power, "membership in any honorary body is coveted by people who see it as a mark of social status."[2] The people's congresses, journalist Michael Forsythe writes, have become a "club for some of China's wealthiest executives, keen to rub elbows with government officials." Being a delegate, he continues, "… brings prestige, much like peerage or knighthood in Britain."[3] A deputy's "red hat," Professor Zhang Ming argues, gives its wearer access to powerful officials and nefarious insider deals.[4]

Members of the business community have, in fact, become part of China's political establishment since former General Secretary Jiang Zemin first introduced his "Three Represents" theory in 2000 and announced that the communist party was not only the vanguard of the proletariat but also the representative of the "advanced productive forces." Private capitalists, industrialist, investors, real estate speculators, and white collar professional thus joined workers, peasants, cadres, soldiers, and the managers of state-owned enterprises as part of the China's "socialist" coalition. Preliminary data suggest, in fact, that not only have members of the non-state business sector become part of that coalition, the vast majority of those buying votes were members of the business community. The weight of the business community was particularly great in Liaoning and Hunan where managers and other business professionals made up more than 40 percent of the elected delegates. Among the 45 delegates expelled from the Liaoning Provincial People's Congress, upwards of 40 had business connections. The available data also suggest that the many vote "sellers" were also members of the business community. But they were not alone in taking money for their votes. Delegates from a variety of other sectors – including the party apparatus, officialdom, education, and, perhaps most notably the police and military – were implicated and expelled from the Liaoning PPC. Eighteen of the 25 delegates from the PLA's Liaoning garrison were expelled for selling their votes.

Whether the Liaoning and Hengyang vote-buying scandals are anomalies or indicative of a more widespread problem is not clear. But in light of evidence that vote buying is common at the village level where candidates reportedly often curry favor with voters by handing out relative small sums of cash, free dinners, and gifts such as cigarettes and cheap alcohol, it is possible that vote buying has become an integral part of the "electoral process" at the local and provincial levels in contemporary China. While local business elites may have begun to try to buy their way into the political superstructure from the bottom up, China's new super rich also have been penetrating it from the top down through both the NPC and the Chinese People's Political Consultative Conference (CPPCC). Close to one in 20 members of the 11th National People's Congress (2007 to 2012) and the 11th CPPCC were listed among China's super rich by Hurun, a Hong Kong-based magazine.

Formed in 1949, the CPPCC wrote the organic laws of the People's Republic of China, and transferred its national legislative authority to the NPC in 1954. Relegated thereafter to an amorphous advisory role in a political system dominated by the Communist Party and largely defunct for a decade beginning in the mid-1960s, the national CPPCC, the provincial CPPCCs, and their local affiliates have been described as "useless flowerpots" whose main function was to give delegates from the provinces an opportunity to spend a week wining, dining, and basking in the media spotlight during the annual "double meeting" when the NPC and CPPCC simultaneously convene in Beijing, as well as providing retired cadres and officials with honorary sinecures for the golden years. The CPPCC's apparent lack of any meaningful power notwithstanding, close to two dozen chairs and vice chairs of provincial political consultative conferences and dozens of senior members of local political consultative conferences have been implicated in corruption during Xi's crackdown. Even though it appears that in many cases those implicated were involved in corruption before retiring from their party and state posts, evidence also exists that corrupt monies continued to flow to others after they relinquished their official posts.

If China's growing business elite, with its hybrid mix of private entrepreneurs and SOE managers, is trying to buy its way into China's institutions of power, it is possible that while Xi has been cracking down on corruption among the party and official ranks, corruption has been spreading among the ranks of the broader "united front" that the party has historically relied on for its political legitimacy. Xi may now be facing a new "second front" in the war with corruption. Rather than seeing the gradual de-escalation of Xi's four-year-old tiger hunt, the anti-corruption crackdown could gain new momentum as Xi shifts from fighting corrupt party cadres and state officials to fight a new threat from the business sector.

## Notes

1    *The provincial leadership is defined herein as the secretary and deputy secretaries of the Provincial Party Committee, the provincial governor and vice governors; the chair, vice chairs, and general secretary of the Provincial People's Congress (PPC), and the chair, vice chairs, and secretary general of the Provincial Political Consultative Conference (PPCC).*

2    *Quoted in Michael Forsythe, "An Unlikely Crime in One-Party China: Election Fraud," New York Times, 9/4/2016.*

3    *Forsythe, "An Unlikely Crime in One-Party China."*

4    *Quoted in Michael Forsythe, "China Expels 45 Legislators Over Fraud in Election," New York Times, 9/15/2016.*

*Andrew Wedeman is a Professor of Political Science at Georgia State University and an associate of the China Research Center.*

# Xi Jinping's Soft Power Martial Arts Cultural Trope

*Paul Foster*
*Vol. 15, No.2*
*2016*

Rap propaganda is the latest manifestation of Chinese President Xi Jinping's campaign to consolidate power using soft culture tropes to massage his image with audiences in China. Early in 2016, an official rap cartoon was circulated extolling the virtues of the "Four Comprehensives.[1] The effect of such subtle propaganda, if it can be called subtle, is confirmed in further reports:

> ... a propaganda official from China's Inner Mongolia region offered dubious praise [for the rap propaganda], calling the song "bewitching and brainwashing." What pleased him most, Li said, was that final sentiment, when commenters say they could not get the song out of their heads, or that they sometimes found themselves involuntarily humming it.[2]

The same article cites statistics asserting the video "has attracted 70 million views and appeared on thousands of online accounts." Involuntarily humming the song demonstrates the power of an "ear worm," a song you can't get out of your head, and is an example of the power of culture to captivate people's minds, and maybe even hearts, for better or worse.

Soft power exercised through such cultural tropes provides straightforward, but simultaneously ironic and humorous opportunities for cultural and political analysis. An earlier example of this is President Xi Jinping's state visit to Mongolia from August 21-22, 2014, during which he and Mongolian President Tsakhiagiin Elbegdorj are pictured with bows and arrows in hand (see below):

*"Mongolia treats Chinese president with traditional pageant"*[3]

This weapon-laden photo op is the third of three pictures accompanying the English report — the picture was also circulated in Chinese media — which describes the occasion as a Nadam Fair specially arranged for the visiting dignitaries. Events included "performances of wrestling, horse racing, archery, and dancing." This was the "cultural" dimension of the summit, which had other serious business. The Xinhua report accompanying the slide states:

During the visit, the leaders of the two countries announced the upgrading of their relations to a comprehensive strategic partnership, and pledged to almost double their annual trade to 10 billion U.S. dollars by 2020.[4]

This amounts to the promotion of China's sphere of influence as a "comprehensive strategic partnership" involving mutually beneficial business, couched within the engagement of leaders in seemingly less serious "cultural" exchange. Such cultural trappings may be interpreted as the froth of more serious diplomatic engagement, but on a deeper semiotic level, it functions to key readers to a narrative latent with symbolic importance.

In the current context of Xi Jinping's recent drive to use pop culture to promote his "Four Comprehensives," the secondary objective of the campaign is to raise the president's profile and thus contribute to his accumulation of cultural capital. The archery picture at the Sino-Mongolian summit in August 2014 was taken a year-and-a-half before the current Spring 2016 campaign. Looking back, it appears the soft power campaign started long before the current employment of rap propaganda. The archery picture can be read as a metaphor, a reenactment of a symbol of ethnic nationalism and inter-ethnic cooperation and brotherhood, reprising the myth of martial arts hero Guo Jing, the main character in Jin Yong's famous epic novel, *The Eagle-Shooting Heroes* [*She diao yingxiong zhuan*] 射雕英雄传 (English title from the 1987 Yuanliu Publishing collected works edition, Taiwan).

Compare the picture of Xi Jinping with bow and arrow in hand to the DVD and television series covers below (or in the web links):

The various English titles of the novel and multiple television series adapta-

**The Brave Archer**
*(Shaw Brothers, 1977)*

**The Legend of the Condor Heroes**
*(TVB, 1983)*

**The Eagle Shooting Heroes**
*(Tai Seng, 2008)*

**The Legend of the Condor Heroes**
*(Tai Seng, 1994)*

tions laud the shooter as "hero" or refer to "bravery," a reasonable translation of the Chinese, in which "hero" appears in the title and "bravery" applies to the protagonist's character. The cultural symbolism of the "eagle shooting pose" that Xi adopted for the Sino-Mongolian Summit camera can be read as directly referring to the famous scene from the novel and film/television depictions where protagonist Guo Jing proves himself worthy of Genghis Khan's notice through his archery by shooting eagles (or condors, depending on the choice of translation) out of the sky on a hunting trip. A short list of television and film adaptations of this novel includes: *The Legend of the Condor Heroes* (TVB 1983), *The Brave Archer* (Shaw Brothers 1977), *The Legend of the Condor Heroes* (Tai Seng 1994), *The Eagle-Shooting Heroes* (2008).

Why might Xi Jinping want to identify himself with Guo Jing? The answer may be found in Guo's character, specifically the kind of hero he is:

[Guo Jing's] most outstanding trait is his constant strife for moral rectitude, as seen when he faces a dilemma after Genghis Khan attempts to force him to lead the Mongol army to attack his native land. Although he was born and raised in Mongolia, he is unwilling to side with the Mongols to attack the Song Empire.[5]

"Moral rectitude" is the first order of identification that could benefit Xi Jinping's image, particularly since he has been fighting corruption on many fronts since the fall of Bo Xilai. In this view, President Xi's pose consciously (or unconsciously) mirrors that of Guo Jing, depicted in these four cover photos. Xi Jinping cleverly positions himself as a symbol with which his pop culturally informed Chinese audience may identify. He is a Han national hero, like Guo Jing. What kind of identification is this?

First consider the power of the pop culture icon. The degree of identification hinges on the cultural penetration of the image Guo Jing, whose character is propagated first through the popular novel, then by way of television and film adaptations, and finally by virtue of the stature of the novel's author, Jin Yong. For those Western readers not familiar with this dimension of Chinese culture, author Jin Yong and his character Guo Jing are comparable to J.K. Rowling and Harry Potter. Virtually everyone alive in the last two decades can conjure a picture of Harry Potter. Guo Jing's existence and cultural penetration are equally well established. Although Guo Jing's martial arts/swordsman dimension might be more akin in Western terms to Alexandre Dumas' The Three Musketeers and his protagonist d'Artagnan, the temporal immediacy of Harry Potter fits the pop culture analogy closer. So who is Guo Jing?

As the story goes, he was raised in Mongol society, became the adopted son of Genghis Khan, the blood brother of the Khan's son, and engaged to his daughter. Guo Jing is the kind of hero who is famous not merely for his martial ability, but also because his prime character virtues are uprightness, honesty, and loyalty. Throughout Jin Yong's narrative, Guo Jing relies on these virtues while negotiating difficult terrain in his coming of age, learning kung fu arts, falling in love with the clever Huang Rong, also of Han heritage (and breaking off his engagement with Khan's daughter), and eventually defending the Song against both the Jurchens 女真人 and the Mongols 蒙古人. Guo's upright, straightforward, hardworking, loyal nature simultaneously facilitates close fraternal (albeit adoptive) ties with the Mongol clan that raised him and ethnic allegiance to his Chinese roots. Eventually (it is a long story of 1,600 pages), Guo Jing defends the Song against foreign incursion, but maintains his integrity in all his relationships despite significant interior and exterior conflict.

The novel The Eagle-Shooting Heroes was written in installments and serialized in the Hong Kong newspaper Hong Kong Commercial Daily 香港商報

from 1957 to 1959, and its sequel was continued in Ming Pao 明報, which was founded by Louis Cha (Zha Liangyong 查良鏞). The author and newsman are one in the same – Cha's pen name is Jin Yong. The first film version in Hong Kong was made in 1958, and later film adaptations were made in the 1970s, 1980s, and 1990s.[6] The 1983 TVB television adaptation, titled in English The Legend of the Condor Heroes, was made in Hong Kong and starred Huang Rihua (Felix Wong) and Weng Meiling (Barbara Yung). It spanned 59 episodes, and was a social phenomenon at the time, garnering an incredible 99 percent viewership in Hong Kong, and was rebroadcast in 1985, 1990, 1995, 2012, and 2013 (in Taiwan). This adaptation continues to hold its own in pop cultural consciousness.[7] Jin Yong's books were not available in Maoist mainland China, where politics tightly controlled cultural production, especially during the Cultural Revolution of the 1960s and 1970s. The TVB production time frame of 1983 is coincidental with the early years – shortly after Deng Xiaoping opened up China to the outside world – which were characterized by the massive importation of "Gang-Tai (Hong Kong and Taiwanese) popular culture in the 1980s."[8] This "pop culture craze" was specifically marked by a trio of cultural producers and their products: Jin Yong and Qiong Yao's novels and Deng Lijun's songs. While Jin Yong had become enormously wealthy and influential as a Hong Kong newspaper publisher, his pop cultural impact was most deeply felt through serial publication of his 12 major novels, the revision and publication of those installments as books, and three collected works editions, as well as the multiple adaptations of each of his stories for television and film. He was so widely read in China that "the head of the National Publishing Bureau is reported to have told Jin Yong that in 1985 alone 40 million volumes of his fiction were sold in the Chinese mainland."[9] In fact, the breadth and penetration of Jin Yong's novels and characters in the cultural consciousness are so deep that there are a handful of other characters who are equally recognizable as Guo Jing to the Chinese readership.

The 1983 adaptation of The Legend of the Condor Heroes in 59 episodes is considered the definitive classic version by the generation of Chinese currently in their 50s and 60s, both inside and outside of China. This adaptation is listed variously as the ninth most popular TV series in the Chinese diaspora according to one source,[10] as well as the number five television series in mainland China, with a viewership rate of 90 percent.[11] Given that there have been four other major adaptations of this work, and a 2017 version is currently in production, it is not surprising that there is a stark generational difference in terms of which edition is preferred. This holds for the multiple adaptations of Jin Yong's other works, too. For example, my informal discussion with Chinese graduate students at Georgia Tech reveals that students in their late 20s favor more recent adaptations.

Guo Jing is simple and plain, even slow as a child, but loyal, upright and honest. Hard work accounts for his attainments. In addition to archery, a skill at which Guo Jing excels, his martial prowess is famed. He learned kung fu moves through a lifetime of diligent practice from a wide variety of upright practitioners, including masters from a virtuous Daoist sect as well as the leader of the largest gang in the martial world, the Beggar Band. The photo of President Xi posing like the hero Guo Jing, may be read as a reference to both the President's forthright nature and his commitment as the defender of the nation. Here is the picture of a simple, but hard-working, upright and loyal hero, identifying with virtuous ideology (Daoist sect) as well as identification with the common people (Beggar Band), whose martial skills can protect the nation and whose diplomatic prowess as a leader can facilitate cooperation and harmony with China's external neighbors and domestic ethnic minorities.

Unpacking the image is appropriately complex. Guo Jing straddles ethnic boundaries and belongs to both worlds. Indeed, the official media surrounding the China-Mongolia summit emphasized President Xi describing the closeness of the two nations using the expression, "a visit in the style of calling on relatives" (*yici zouqinqi shi de fangwen* 一次走亲戚式的访问), noting that "calling on relatives" is part of the "comprehensive strategic partnership relationship" (*quanmian zhanlüe huoban guanxi* 全面战略伙伴关系) and deepening China-Mongolia friendship.[12]

The archery image documents the closeness of the Sino-Mongolian relationship and echoes Guo Jing as friend and "relative" of the great Genghis Khan. Did President Xi understand the potential pop cultural significance of paying homage through a picture that imbues himself with Guo Jing's highly laudable virtues?

Is there any indication that President Xi is, or could be, aware of such a connection? A search of official media does not reveal any mention of author Jin Yong or his novel and protagonist Guo Jing in relation to this state visit. However, there is evidence of President Xi's general consciousness of the novel at least. A Sina News article from May 26, 2015 is titled: "The Peach Blossom Island [depicted by] Jin Yong's Pen Attracts Uncle Xi's Visit, Where is It?"[13] This article cites "Uncle Xi" (*Xi Dada* 习大大) directly referring Peach Blossom Island, the childhood home of Guo Jing's sweetheart and eventual wife Huang Rong. Second, a February 27, 2016 article from China News titled "Deng Xiaoping, Jiang Zemin and Xi Jinping All Loved to Read Jin Yong" cites that article and explains:

Actually, among those who have in succession been China's leaders, many are fans of the books of the "great martial knight" Jin Yong, and Jin Yong also had intersections with many leaders.[14]

This article was written in preparation for Jin Yong's 92nd birthday on March 10, 2016, and describes Deng Xiaoping's invitation to Jin Yong to visit in 1981, which "caused a sensation in Chinese society around the world" [*yinqi le quanqiu huaren shehui de hongdong* 引起了全球华人社会的轰动] and eventually led to unbanning his books. Subsequently, Jin Yong also met with leaders Hu Yaobang in 1984 and Jiang Zemin in 1993. Since the article doesn't mention current President Xi Jinping, beyond the Peach Blossom Island citation above, the title of the article may serve two purposes: first, to align President Xi with his predecessors, and second, to associate him with the eminent Jin Yong, who possesses cultural credentials of which any politicians could only dream.

A century of Chinese leadership on the world stage, from Sun Yatsen to Chiang Kaishek, to Mao Zedong to Deng Xiaoping, and up to the present, demonstrates the skill and aptitude of Chinese leaders over at least a hundred years and longer, if one includes the millennia of bureaucratic and educational dominance of China's elite. Furthermore, Shanghai was the business hub of Asia in the early 20th century and is well on its way to regaining that status; China's military leadership helped defeat the Japanese in World War II; some non-state-owned businesses survived even during the Cultural Revolution of the 1960s and 1970s; and of course the phenomenal rise of China as an industrial and export power over the last three decades.[15]

On the global stage, the "rise" of China may be cast as a zero-sum gain, incurring the question whether "rising" China implies "falling" of other world powers, particularly the U.S. Is supplanting U.S. global leadership a prerequisite implied by the word "leadership?" Will China's growing economic and military competitiveness result in enhanced international political competitiveness? In my reading, President Xi's projection of the image of a Chinese leader situated to protect the nation from outside threats through his identification with Jin Yong's martial arts hero demonstrates Xi's cultural savvy: he identifies himself with the upright, honest, loyal defender of the Chinese people, and by extension, their domestic and international interests.

This is soft (cultural) power subtly buttressing the president's image for the domestic audience. Is this is an astute appropriation of pop culture in service of the discourse of nationalism? It is hard to say definitively. Analyzing the archery picture closely, one might note the dignity and spirit of friendship between the two leaders and their wives participating in this activity. They actually look like they are having fun, and the series of photos that accompanies the activity appear to show the Mongolian president politely correcting President Xi's bow-handling, as the arrow will only fly true (for a right-handed person shooting Mongolian style) if it is mounted on the right side of the bow. President Xi will have a chance at hitting the "eagle," so to speak, if he shoots "right."

Can savvy soft power symbolic acts prove useful on the world stage? Employing rap music to promote President Xi's signature objectives and the "brave archer" trope may be seen as steps to engage the discourse of soft power, somewhat akin to the attempt to use the linguistic appellation "Uncle Xi" to infer identification with the common folk.[16] How this is received, especially outside China, is another matter. A Washington Post article by Emily Rauhala from September 23, 2015 discusses the use of video to promote the image of President Xi. This article is titled "China's President Xi is 'so cute,' says world's creepiest propaganda video."[17] The headline may not be fair to Xi Jinping and may indicate a lack of objectivity. Given that the word "propaganda" is a pejorative in English, is it really necessary to use both the adjectives "creepiest" and "propaganda" in the same headline?

Nevertheless, the appellation "Uncle Xi" used to refer to the President is a clear example of image management. Is it a coincidence, as one report puts it:

He owes another portion of his popularity to his wife, a famous singer in China who adds to his popularity. One might not quite believe it, but the people like to call him "Uncle Xi"?[18]

It is logical to think that the spouse of a famous singer with particularly close connections to pop culture may influence the production and management of her husband's popular image. Appropriation of symbolism inherent in pictures like the "archery photo" could be helpful as small building blocks in solidifying Xi's domestic image.

Many questions remain. Since both soft and hard power operate on cultural consciousness, can we prioritize one over the other? Could soft power prove "stronger" than hard military power through its influence over the audiences (think of a Hollywood analogy)? Will overt hard power of nationalism, military or business technocracy dominate the cultural and international discourse? China has many resources and experiences (read "competitive advantages"). And this brings us back to the photo of Xi Jinping shooting the arrow. Is his target, like Guo Jing's eagle in Jin Yong's novel, a metaphor for the U.S.? As the second-largest economy on the global stage, China can make a case that its leadership position should be commensurate with its economic position? Will China attempt to displace the U.S. as the world's leading superpower? Genghis Khan and his descendants established the largest global empire in history in the 13th Century, extending from China to Europe. How will a "comprehensive strategic partnership" between China and its friends unfold in the 21st century?

### Notes

1   Vanesse Piao & Patrick Boehler, *"Video Extols China's Party Slogans, Turning to Rap and Beethoven," The New York Times, Feb. 2, 2016, accessed May 10, 2016, http://www.nytimes. com/2016/02/03/world/asia/china-four-comprehensives-song-xinhua.html. The "Four Comprehensives" are: build a moderately prosperous society, deepen reform, govern according to law, and govern the party strictly.*

2   Gerry Shih & Aritz Parra, *"Chinese Propaganda Machine Places Hopes in Cartoon Rappers,"* Associated Press, Mar. 6, 2016, accessed May 10, 2016. http://bigstory.ap.org/article/ba9fe2fca5f54bbf999e92366881921e/chinese-propaganda-machine-places-hopes-cartoon-rappers.

3   Huang Jingwen, *"Mongolia treats Chinese president with traditional pageant,"* Xinhua, August 22, 2014, accessed Feb. 26, 2016. http://english.cntv.cn/2014/08/22/ARTI1408717310950124.shtml

4   Ibid.

5   *"Guo Jing,"* accessed March 4, 2016, https://en.wikipedia.org/wiki/Guo_Jing.

6   *The Legend of the Condor Heroes,* accessed March 5, 2016, https://en.wikipedia.org/wiki/The_Legend_of_the_Condor_Heroes.

7   *She diao yingxiong zhuan (1983 nian dianshiju)* 射鵰英雄傳 (1983年電視劇) *Legend of the Condor Heroes (1983 television series),* accessed March 30, 2016. https://zh.wikipedia.org/wiki/%E5%B0%84%E9%B5%B0%E8%8B%B1%E9%9B%84%E5%82%B3_(1983%E5%B9%B4%E9%9B%BB%E8%A6%96%E5%8A%87).

8   John Christopher Hamm, *The Paper Swordsman: Jin Yong and the Modern Chinese Martial Arts Novel (Honolulu: University of Hawaii Press, 2005),* p. 227.

9   Ibid., 231.

10   Qin Mei, ed., *"Top 10 Popular Chinese TV Dramas Overseas,"* China Daily, October 16, 2014, accessed March 4, 2016. http://english.cri.cn/12514/2014/10/16/2001s848110_8.htm.

11   *"Zhongguo lishi shang shoushilü zuigao de dianshiju top10"* 中国历史上收视率最高的电视剧 *top10 (The top ten television series with the highest historical viewership rates),* accessed March 4, 2016. http://www.phb123.com/xinwen/rd/3956.html.

12   *"'Zou qinqi shi' de fangwen"* 走亲戚式'的访问 *Visiting in the style of calling on relatives,* ifeng.com 凤凰网资讯, August 23, 2014, accessed February 27, 2016. http://news.ifeng.com/a/20140823/41703057_0.shtml.

13   *"Jin Yong bixia de Taohuadao, xiyin Xi Dada fangwen, ta zai na?"* 金庸笔下的桃花岛，吸引习大大到访，它在哪？*Xinlang-xinwen* 新浪新闻, May 26, 2015, accessed February 27, 2016. http://news.sina.com.cn/c/2015-05-26/175031878476.shtml.

14   *"Deng Xiaoping Jiang Zemin Xi Jinping dou ai du Jin Yong"* 邓小平江泽民 习近平 都爱读金庸. *China News* 中国嘹望, accessed February 29, 2016. http://news.creaders.net/china/2016/02/27/1644887.html.

15   Bill Kirby, *"Can China Lead?"* Harvard Business School Podcast and transcript, April 8, 2014, accessed April 4, 2016. http://www.hbs.edu/news/articles/Pages/can-china-lead-bill-kirby.aspx. Also noted at the China Research Center annual lecture, Georgia Tech on February 25, 2016.

16   Interpretation of the term *dada* 大大 varies from dialects, many which translate as *"uncle"* or *"papa,"* etc. See http://zhidao.baidu.com/question/1495314787679569979.html, accessed 3/5/16.

17   Emily Rauhala, *"China's President Xi is 'so cute,' says world's creepiest propaganda video. The Washington Post,* September 23, 2015. Accessed March 5, 2016. https://www.washingtonpost.com/news/worldviews/wp/2015/09/23/chinas-president-xi-is-so-cute-says-worlds-creepiest-propaganda-video/.

18   Frank Sieren, *"Xi, China's powerful uncle,"* DW, January 4, 2015, accessed March 5, 2016. http://www.dw.com/en/xi-chinas-powerful-uncle/a-18153535.

*Paul Foster is Associate Professor of Chinese at the Georgia Institute of Technology and an associate of the China Research Center.*

# Will All Roads Lead to Beijing? Risks and Challenges in China's "Belt" and "Road" Plan

*Yawei Liu*
*Vol. 16, No.2*
*2017*

China's "One Belt, One Road" initiative is perhaps the most ambitious development plan ever devised by any nation-state. Plans call for trillions of dollars to be invested in roads, railways, and ports to create land corridors across the vast reaches of Asia and sea lanes that link China to markets in Europe, the Middle East, Africa, and beyond. The "Belt and Road" project – as it is now called – is President Xi Jinping's signature foreign policy instrument, and is the cornerstone of China's ambition to transform itself from a mere player and benefactor of globalization to a reformer and leader of the international order.

But the questions and potential pitfalls to the Belt and Road initiative are easily as large as its ambitions.

The overriding question is this: does the Chinese government have the will, willingness, and wherewithal to overcome all difficulties and accomplish the mission? To succeed, China must negotiate with governments of scores of host countries and international institutions to design, build, and maintain projects. The Belt and Road initiative envisions mammoth Chinese government loans to Chinese companies and foreign governments to finance projects. Will projects become financially viable? Will loans be repaid, or will the initiative devolve into a massive boondoggle? Lack of transparency on the sources of project design and funding means these crucial questions cannot be answered fully.[1] In fact, available evidence suggests there is reason for major concern.

**The Origins of the Initiative**

The "One Belt, One Road" initiative was first announced by President Xi in September and October in 2013 in Kazakhstan and Indonesia respectively.[2] At the time, it was simply a concept and an idea. In March 2015, the Chinese government issued a paper that began to turn the concept into a plan.[3]

On April 20, 2017, the spokesperson of the Chinese Ministry of Transportation said during a press conference that China has signed more than 130 bilateral and regional transport agreements with countries involved in the Belt and Road. He said that China had opened 356 international road routes for both passengers and goods, while maritime transportation services now cover all countries along the Belt and Road. Every week, some 4,200 direct flights connect China with 43 Belt and Road countries, and 39 China-Europe freight train routes operate.[4]

Before the Beijing Belt and Road Forum for International Cooperation was held on May 14-15, 2017, the Chinese government issued another paper entitled "Building 'One Belt, One Road': Concept, Practice, and China's Contribution."[5] The paper mentioned six corridors and six means of communication: a New Eurasian Land Bridge Economic Corridor, a China-Mongolia-Russia Economic Corridor, a China-Central Asia-West Asia Economic Corridor, a China-Indochina Peninsula Economic Corridor, a China-Pakistan Economic Corridor, and a Bangladesh-China-India-Myanmar Economic Corridor. The means of communication are rail, highways, seagoing transport, aviation, pipelines, and aerospace.[6]

Xi himself touted the progress already made at the May forum, saying building had accelerated on a number of projects: a Jakarta-Bandung high-speed railway, a China-Laos railway, an Addis Ababa-Djibouti railway and a Hungary-Serbia railway. Ports at Gwadar and Piraeus had been upgraded, and other projects were "in the pipeline.[7] Xi pledged to avoid "outdated geopolitical manoeuvering" and said China hoped for "win-win" relationships. "We have no intention to form a small group detrimental to stability. What we hope to create is a big family of harmonious co-existence."[8]

International think tanks and news organization have taken note. The Center for International and Strategic Studies published a research paper saying the Belt and Road project could span 65 countries, comprising roughly 70 percent of the world's population. Economically, it could include Chinese investments approaching $4 trillion.[9]

The New York Times reported that the initiative was designed to open new markets and export China's state-led development model "in a quest to create deep economic connections and strong diplomatic relationships." The Times highlighted some of the projects:

- Africa's first transnational electric railway, which opened this year and runs 466 miles from Djibouti to Addis Ababa, the capital of Ethiopia.

China financed most of the $4 billion price tag. Chinese companies designed the systems, supplied train cars and engineers who built the line over a six-year period.

- A 260-mile rail line from northern Laos to the capital, Vientiane. China is leading the $6 billion investment. Mountainous terrain means bridges and tunnels will account for more than 60 percent of the line, and construction is further complicated by the need to clear unexploded land mines left from American bombing of the country during the Vietnam War.
- The deep-water port at Gwadar, Pakistan. The facility, on the Arabian Sea, will be linked by new roads and rail to western China's Xinjiang region, creating a shortcut for trade with Europe. The port is part of the $46 billion China says it is spending on infrastructure and power plants in the China-Pakistan Economic Corridor.[10]

## Geopolitical Risks Will Not Go Away

For all the hoopla about the Belt and Road initiative, there are signs that all is not well when it comes to international cooperation needed to make the initiative work. The Belt and Road "summit" in May was attended by only 29 heads of state. Germany, Great Britain, the United States, and Japan sent only government ministers or lower ranking officials to the meeting. India, one of the most important countries for the initiative, chose not to send any representative to the summit because its government believes that China harbors an ulterior motive in establishing the China-Pakistan Economic Corridor, a signature component of the Belt and Road program. "No country can accept a project that ignores its core concerns on sovereignty and territorial integrity," said Gopal Baglay, spokesperson of India's External Affairs Ministry.[11]

Other countries, including the United States, also expressed concerns about Chinese motives. To them, "new international order," "new security framework," "new economic model," "new civilization exchange," and "new ecological order" are synonymous with China's domination first in Asia and eventually in the whole world.[12]

Western press reports reflected the skepticism. "Neighbors Japan and India have stayed away from the summit, suspicious that China's development agenda masks a bid for strategic assets and geopolitical ambitions," wrote Carrie Gracie of the BBC.[13] CNN's James Griffiths reflected similar sentiment in his reporting on the Beijing meeting. "Its boosters tout its massive economic promise and claim it could benefit the entire world and lift millions out of poverty. But no one can say for sure what exactly the plan encompasses, and detractors warn it could be an expensive boondoggle at best or a massive expansion of Chinese imperial power at worst."[14]

Russia appears to be increasingly wary of the Belt and Road initiative. President Vladimir Putin attended the summit, but proposed linking the program to the Eurasian Economic Union, Moscow's own regional economic project. It is common knowledge that Moscow has reservations because Russia is loath to cede influence over Central Asian countries, a main focus of the Belt and Road initiative.[15] A New York Times report quoted a senior associate of Carnegie Center in Moscow saying, "Russia's elites' high expectations regarding Belt and Road have gone through a severe reality check, and now oligarchs and officials are skeptical about practical results."[16]

The Belt and Road initiative faces serious geopolitical risks. Many countries involved in the initiative are situated in the most complicated geopolitical regions pressured by political, religious, and ethnic conflicts. Some are proxies of rival major powers. Pakistan and Afghanistan, key countries for Belt and Road, confront tribal political power that refuses to yield to central control, radicalism, terrorism, and secessionism.[17]

Countries like these can easily derail any connectivity projects in place. The China-Pakistan Economic Corridor is a case in point. The corridor is home to an unprecedented estimated Chinese investment of $48-$57 billion dollars, and the expansion of Pakistan's Gwadar port would provide China with a much-needed access to the Indian Ocean. But this corridor goes through the province of Baluchistan, where "separatist militants have waged a campaign against the central government for decades, demanding a greater share of the gas-rich region's resources." Since 2014, militants trying to disrupt construction on the "economic corridor" have killed 44 Pakistani workers.[18]

**Financing Can Be a Challenge**

The initiative faces challenges attracting Chinese capital in both the state and private sectors. To be sure, the Chinese state is marshaling significant investment resources: a $40 billion Silk Road Fund was created in 2014; the Asian Infrastructure Investment Bank was launched in 2015 with $100 billion of initial capital that is expected to be spent chiefly in Belt and Road countries; three Chinese state-owned banks received $82 billion in state funds in 2015 for Belt and Road projects.[19]

Yet only a small portion of available investment funds appears to be going toward Belt and Road projects. Capital leaving China is largely going to markets that are safer, richer, and better-developed than those under the Belt and Road framework, according to David Dollar, an economist at the Brookings Institution in Washington. Aside from Hong Kong, the top destinations for Chinese overseas direct investment at the end of 2016 were: the Cayman Islands, the Virgin Islands, the United States, Singapore, Australia, the Netherlands, the United Kingdom, Russia, Canada, and Indonesia. "Of these, only Russia and Indonesia are along the Belt and Road," Dollar writes.[20] China's two policy banks, the China Development Bank and the China Export & Import Bank report Belt and Road-related lending totaled $101.8 billion at the end of 2016, or 15 percent of their total overseas lending.[21] Data cited in the *Wall Street Journal* says Chinese companies have invested more in the United States since 2014 than the 60-plus countries touched by the initiative combined. In other words, Xi's regional investment priorities have not translated into a shift in private investors' decision-making.[22]

Jonathan E. Hillman of the Center for International and Strategic Studies, writes that OBOR could include Chinese investments approaching $4 trillion.[23] But Nicholas R. Lardy, a China specialist at the Peterson Institute for International Economics, told *New York Times* reporter Jane Perlez, "China's outlays for the plan so far have been modest: only $50 billion has been spent, an 'extremely small' amount relative to China's domestic investment program."[24] The funding gap is obvious, and the lack of market appeal to capital will certainly become a huge obstacle.

### Lending Perilous for Borrowers

Countries involved in Belt and Road projects often take on crushing debt burdens. Laos, a country with a total output of $12 billion annually, has borrowed $800 million from China's EXIM Bank, in part to finance a rail line from the northern part of the nation to the capital, Vientiane. According to the *New York Times*, Laos still faces a huge debt burden. The International Monetary Fund warned this year that the country's reserves stood at two months of prospective imports of goods and services. It also expressed concerns that public debt could rise to around 70 percent of the economy.[25]

It is reported that Sri Lanka is already overburdened by debt resulting from accepting Chinese concessional loans. As a result of Sri Lanka being unable to keep up with its payments, the Sri Lankan government has converted some of this debt into equity, allowing Chinese firms to control 80 percent of the Hambantota port for a period of 99 years.[26]

The Pakistan corridor is projected to result in $50 billion of debt that will take Pakistan 40 years to pay off. Just like in Sri Lanka, Pakistan's debt contract could ultimately result in a transfer of local assets to Chinese ownership. Some Pakistani critics refer to the corridor as "the new East India Company."[27] Jane Golley of the Australian National University told a *Financial Times* reporter: "The lack of commercial imperatives behind OBOR projects means that it is highly uncertain whether future project returns will be sufficient to fully cover repayments to Chinese creditors."[28]

Many projects are in Central Asian countries. It is clear some of these countries are suffering from "from weak and unstable economies, poor public governance, political stability, and corruption." Chinese lenders are not always blind to risks but many "are being pressed to lend to projects that they find less than desirable.[29] An Economist article indicates that Chinese government sources expect "to lose 80 percent of the money they invest in Pakistan, 50 percent in Myanmar, and 30 percent in Central Asia." This is not just speculation. China has recently lost $60 billion in Venezuela as it descended into chaos.[30]

In addition to this, the Chinese foreign currency reserve is rapidly declining as many companies and individuals are moving their money out of China due to an unprecedented anticorruption campaign and political uncertainty. Thus, Beijing has erected new barriers designed to stem the exodus of capital outflow. In this context, there are two channels through which capital is fleeting from China: first, state-driven, politically motivated, and commercially dubious deals that have backfired on Beijing in the past; second, capital that is going to safer places in the name of the OBOR initiative.[31] One result of the state driven overseas investment will add to China's fast-growing debt burden, "now standing at more than 250 percent of GDP."[32]

**Not All Roads Will Make Economic Sense**

Building major railway lines, one of the primary goals of the initiative, may not make economic sense, even though rail transport is faster and greener than shipping by sea. Turloch Mooney, senior editor of *Global Ports* writes, "The cost of shipping a 20 foot-equivalent unit by rail to Europe still averages around five times more than by ocean, and the capacity constraints of trains and rail infrastructure compared with ocean-going vessels mean that, while rail services have the potential to create a significant dent in air cargo volumes, they will most likely never account for more than one to two percent of ocean volumes." To ship cargo from Suzhou to Warsaw, ocean freight takes 40 days and creates 2.1t of carbon emissions.[33] Now, more and more Chinese companies are shipping goods to Europe via rail but for every five containers going to Europe, only one comes back filled with goods. The other four, unfortunately, come back via ships.[34]

Tom Holland published an article on April 24, 2017 in the *South China Morning Post* declaring, "The idea of a 'Belt and Road' rail cargo route between Europe and China remains nothing more than a fanciful curiosity."[35] The online magazine *Quartz* elaborates:

> "There is really no need to use trains to increase commerce between Europe and China. Sea cargo transportation is much cheaper, and companies already rely on it. More than 19,000 containers can be

placed on a single cargo ship, and they only take 30 days from Europe to reach China. The railway is faster than a shipping container, but is also riskier because it goes through a few unstable countries and can be interrupted by extreme weather, terrorist attacks, and politics. China is trying to justify its domestic overproduction by creating the One Belt, One Road, and framing it as a business strategy that is also beneficial for other nations, but the actual benefit for some trading partners and the long-term global economy is still to be seen.[36]

### There Are More Important Things than Roads

In the name of investing overseas, state-owned Chinese companies have experienced spectacular failures, costing the Chinese government an astronomic amount of money. The unexpected decision by the Myanmar government to suspend the Myitsone Project may have cost the Chinese government $3 billion.[37] The Chinese company involved in the deal firmly believed its agreement with the military-controlled government of Myanmar was ironclad.

The toppling of Gadhafi in Libya led to at least $6 billion in losses as Chinese companies all had to abandon their projects.[38] One of the leading investors in Libya, the Sinohydro Group, said it had never imagined a strong leader like Gadhafi could be overthrown.

The China Railroad Group signed a high-speed train deal with the Venezuelan government worth $7.5 billion although it was clear that country did not have money, electric power, and density of population to sustain such a project. It launched a project even after the Venezuelan government defaulted on repaying a loan of $18 billion from China. The project is now worth nothing.[39] The Belt and Road initiative is only about three years old and there have already been failures and losses of immense proportions. More will certainly come.

Failures are bound recur in the coming years and the Belt and Road initiative surely will be littered with projects that are costly and unsustainable white elephants. In fact, this is already happening. A Chinese scholar recently came back from Ethiopia and said the electric railroad built by the Chinese from Addis Ababa to Djibouti – hailed as one of the first landmark accomplishments – in fact made only one run with a diesel locomotive, and has been idle since completion. When asked why, the scholar said, "Well, there is no electricity to power the trains. The hydraulic power plant is yet to be built."[40]

### Conclusion

Any of the factors discussed above could prevent the Belt and Road initiative from achieving its lofty goals and lead China into a financial abyss. It cannot be China's exclusive endeavor and needs to enlist support from all countries in the world to make it a success. To do that, China needs to be transparent about its geopolitical considerations, decision-making processes, and financial arrangements.

Market forces and not just state investment must be employed. Social dynamics and political uncertainties in each country where a project is launched must be carefully scrutinized. The Chinese government cannot blindly force state enterprises to delve into projects and by the same token, state enterprises must not obediently do what they are asked without due diligence on projects.

Signs are emerging that silent resistance against reckless and mindless Belt and Road projects may be shaping up. China's overall investment in such projects has dipped despite the central government's recent demand for more and larger investments in related projects. China's decision to be part of a globalized market and to follow rules and laws required by this market has enabled China to launch the Belt and Road initiative in the first place. To ignore global market rules is short-sighted and suicidal in the long term.

The initiative is not just about development and prosperity. It is also about China transforming itself from a mere player and benefactor of globalization to a reformer and leader of the international order. Beijing must be aware that before all roads lead to Beijing, it must study past development failures and avoid strategic arrogance and national selfishness; it has to learn that the new roads will go nowhere if they are paved with national glory and supremacy and not common destiny and co-prosperity. Without a broad view, few roads will lead to Beijing.

## Notes

1    *Lack of transparency will be a significant hurdle for many European countries to fully participate in the OBOR. A Guardian report dated May 15, 2017 said, "The EU has dealt a blow to Chinese president Xi Jinping's bid to lead a global infrastructure revolution, after its members refused to endorse part of the multibillion-dollar plan because it did not include commitments to social and environmental sustainability and transparency." See Tom Philipps, "EU backs away from trade statement in blow to China's 'modern Silk Road' plan", Guardian, May 15, 2017, at* https://www.theguardian.com/world/2017/may/15/eu-china-summit-bejing-xi-jinping-belt-and-road.

2    *Xi Jinping, "Work Together to Build the Silk Road Economic Belt and The 21st Century Maritime Silk Road", May 14, 2017, at* http://news.xinhuanet.com/english/2017-05/14/c_136282982.htm *and "Building 'One Belt, One Road': Concept, Practice and China's Contribution," May 10, 2017, at* https://eng.yidaiyilu.gov.cn/zchj/qwfb/12731.htm.

3    *"Vision and Actions on Jointly Building Silk Road Economic Belt and 21st-Century Maritime Silk Road," at* https://eng.yidaiyilu.gov.cn/qwyw/qwfb/1084.htm.

4    *"China signs over 130 transport pacts with Belt and Road countries," Xinhua, April 21, 2017, at* http://news.xinhuanet.com/english/2017-04/20/c_136224127.htm

5    *"Building 'One Belt, One Road': Concept, Practice, and China's Contribution," May 10, 2017.*

6    *Ibid.*

7    Xi Jinping, "Work Together to Build the Silk Road Economic Belt and The 21st Century Maritime Silk Road"

8    *Ibid.*

9    Jonathan E. Hillman, "OBOR on the Ground: Evaluating China's 'One Belt, One Road' Initiative at the Project Level," at https://www.csis.org/analysis/obor-ground-evaluating-chinas-one-belt-one-road-initiative-project-level.

10   Jan Perlez and Yufan Huang, "Behind China's $1 Trillion Plan to Shake Up the Economic Order," May 13, 2017, at https://www.nytimes.com/2017/05/13/business/china-railway-one-belt-one-road-1-trillion-plan.html?_r=0.

11   "India refuses to be part of China's Belt-Road initiative," at http://www.business-standard.com/article/news-ians/india-refuses-to-be-part-of-china-s-belt-road-initiative-117051300941_1.html

12   For the five "new's", check out the Center for China and Globalization, "Paths to Win-Win Cooperation Along the B&R: A Proposal to Enlist Global Partners", at http://www.ccg.org.cn/Research/View.aspx?Id=6593.

13   BBC, "China invests $124bn in Belt and Road global trade project," May 14, 2017, at http://www.bbc.com/news/world-asia-39912671.

14   James Griffiths, "Just What Is This One Belt, One Road Thing Anyway?," May 11, 2017, at http://www.cnn.com/2017/05/11/asia/china-one-belt-one-road-explainer/.

15   Nikkei Asian Review, "Asian neighbors still leery of China's Belt and Road initiative," May 16, 2017, at http://asia.nikkei.com/Spotlight/New-Silk-Road-summit-in-Beijing/Asian-neighbors-still-leery-of-China-s-Belt-and-Road-initiative.

16   Perlez and Huang, "Behind China's $1 Trillion Plan to Shake Up the Economic Order"

17   *Ibid.*

18   REUTERS/Asahi, "Ten gunned down near China "Belt and Road" projects in Pakistan," May 13, 2017, at http://www.asahi.com/ajw/articles/AJ201705130043.html.

19   Tom Hancock, "China encircles the world with One Belt, One Road strategy," May 3, 2017, FT, at https://www.ft.com/content/0714074a-0334-11e7-aa5b-6bb07f5c8e12.

20   David Dollar, "Yes, China is investing globally—but not so much in its belt and road initiative," May 8, 2017, at https://www.brookings.edu/blog/order-from-chaos/2017/05/08/yes-china-is-investing-globally-but-not-so-much-in-its-belt-and-road-initiative/.

21   *Ibid.*

22   The American Interest, "One Belt, One Road, One Boondoggle?," May 11, 2017, at https://www.the-american-interest.com/2017/05/11/one-belt-one-road-one-boondoggle/.

23   Hillman, "OBOR on the Ground: Evaluating China's 'One Belt, One Road' Initiative at the Project Level"

24   Perlez and Huang, "Behind China's $1 Trillion Plan to Shake Up the Economic Order"

25   Ibid

26   Dipanjan Roy Chaudhury, "China may put South Asia on road to debt trap," The Times of India, May 2, 2017, at http://timesofindia.indiatimes.com/world/south-asia/china-may-put-south-asia-on-road-to-debt-trap/articleshow/58470014.cms.

27   Syed Irfan Raza, "CPEC could become another East India Company," October 18, 2016, at https://www.dawn.com/news/1290677.

28   Hancock, "China encircles the world with One Belt, One Road strategy"

29   Ibid.

30   Douglas Bulloch, "As China's Belt & Road Forum Approaches, the Initiative Itself Remains a Distant Dream," Forbes, May 12, 2017, at https://www.forbes.com/sites/douglasbulloch/2017/05/12/chinas-belt-and-road-initiative-remains-a-distant-dream/#607489c32d8a.

31    Hancock, "China encircles the world with One Belt, One Road strategy." According to Jörg Wuttke, president of the European Chamber of Commerce in China, In the face of downward pressure on the renminbi, the initiative has been hijacked by Chinese companies, which have used it as an excuse to evade capital controls, smuggling money out of the country by disguising it as international investments and partnerships. OBOR has also "provided cover for the acquisition of less productive and often trophy assets, such as European football clubs. Chinese tycoons have acquired about 100 of these to date." See Jörg Wuttke, "Xi Jinping's Silk Road is under threat from one-way traffic," May 11, 2017, at https://www.ft.com/content/61c08c22-3403-11e7-99bd-13beb0903fa3.

32    Perlez and Huang, "Behind China's $1 Trillion Plan to Shake Up the Economic Order." According to Oxford University scholars, "For over three decades, China has experienced a staggering public investment boom. In 2014, China spent US$4.6 trillion on fixed assets, accounting for 24.8 percent of total worldwide investments and more than double the entire GDP of India. But China's investment boom has coincided with a rapid buildup of debt. Between 2000 and 2014, China's total debt grew from US$2.1 trillion to US$28.2 trillion, an increase of US$26.1 trillion — greater than the GDP of the United States, Japan, and Germany combined." See Atif Ansar and Bent Flyvbjerg: "China's Great Wall of Debt," November 28, 2016, at http://www.eastasiaforum.org/2016/11/28/chinas-great-wall-of-debt/.

33    "East Wind: a new era of freight between the UK and China," February 20, 2017, at http://www.railway-technology.com/features/featureeast-wind-a-new-era-of-freight-between-the-uk-and-china-5740643/. The author of this article writes, "For that niche section of import-exporters who cannot afford to wait months for product delivery, but are also concerned about their carbon footprint, the rail service is bound to be a great new alternative."

34    "Empty Containers on Sino-Euro Trains Signifies the Tragic Future of OBOR," May 17, 2017, at http://mp.weixin.qq.com/s/pqhq8SykbjoTRP80bln3Cg.

35    Tom Holland, "Puffing across the One Belt, One Road rail route to nowhere," This Week In Asia, South China Morning Post, April 24, 2017.

36    "It costs twice as much to export olive oil from Spain using China's 'One Belt, One Road' railway," at https://qz.com/686816/the-view-from-spain-chinas-one-belt-one-road-railway-is-an-unnecessary-folly/.

37    Mike Ivesmarch, "A Chinese-Backed Dam Project Leaves Myanmar in a Bind," New York Times, March 31, 2017, at https://www.nytimes.com/2017/03/31/world/asia/myanmar-china-myitsone-dam-project.html

38    Asianew.it, "Heavy losses for Chinese companies operating in Libya," February 26, 2011, at http://www.asianews.it/news-en/Heavy-losses-for-Chinese-companies-operating-in-Libya-20887.html.

39    "High Speed Train Project in Ruins and 7.5 Billion USD Wasted," December 25, 2016, at http://cj.sina.com.cn/article/detail/1680937367/132128.

40    Interview with a scholar from the Chinese Academy of Social Science, Beijing Conference Center, May 24, 2017.

*Yawei Liu is the director of the China Program at The Carter Center and the associate director of the China Research Center.*

# Dealing with China: An Indian Perspective

*K.S. Kalha*
*Vol. 16, No.2*
*2017*

Three issues bedevil Sino-Indian relations at present. These are the long-pending boundary dispute, the huge trade deficit in favor of China, and the Chinese initiated "One Belt, One Road" proposal, which – while giving the veneer of advancing economic cooperation – actually has significant geo-political and geo-strategic implications. Recently the Chinese Ambassador to India, Luo Zhaohui, while speaking in Mumbai, said that to improve relations between India and China, "We should negotiate a bilateral Treaty of Friendship and Cooperation, a Free Trade Agreement and gather early harvest related to border issues." Luo also raised the rhetorical question of how to "synergize" China's "One Belt, One Road" project with India's "Act East" policy. It is not in the public domain whether Ambassador Luo has officially proposed these initiatives to the Indian Foreign Office in Delhi or whether he was simply raising these publicly to elicit and test public opinion. Be that as it may, let us assume that these are official Chinese initiatives.

Consider the first offer. Whenever the Chinese take such initiatives, the most important aspect to note is that such initiatives must be examined in the context of the prevailing international situation, for rarely are they bereft of such linkages. In the current uncertain times, any Chinese strategic analyst based in Beijing would aver that the principal security threat to China would emanate from its eastern seaboard, in tandem with the deep anxiety and uncertainties the new Trump Administration engenders. This would also suggest that the Chinese, well versed in the art of strategic manoeuver, would be keen to cover their flanks so as to fully concentrate on the gathering storm that they perceive might come from the Asia-Pacific region.

The Trump-Xi Jinping Summit in Florida was designed for both sides to assess the relationship at the highest level. While China has continued to prevaricate on the North Korean nuclear issue, the U.S. realizes that its options for unilateral action are strictly limited, and therefore reliance on China becomes even more enduring. The outcome of the recent trade deal indicates the final burial of Trump's anti-China campaign rhetoric branding China as a currency manipulator, etc. In some aspects, the announced trade deal is nothing but China implementing what it had already promised. Yet Trump's persistence seems to have paid off. The decision to participate in the Belt and Road meeting in Beijing, however, surprised many in that this was a Chinese initiative designed primarily to challenge U.S. trading and military power in the Asia-Pacific region. This challenge remains and it would be extremely shortsighted for the U.S. to believe that a new equilibrium with China has been established. China's ultimate goal of ousting U.S. power from the Asia-Pacific is unchanged.

## Past as Prologue

Sometimes a review of historical events offers vital and interesting clues on future developments. A near similar situation to the current one arose in the late 1950s when the Chinese were bombarding the two Taiwan-held islands of Quemoy and Matsu just off mainland China, but were deterred from further military action when the U.S. warned that it would use "all means" (a clear reference to nuclear weapons) to defend Taiwan (not including Quemoy and Matsu). This was a bitter period in Sino-U.S. relations that coincided with the final break in Sino-Soviet relations after Soviet leader Khrushchev refused to back China against a U.S. nuclear strike. On March 19, 1959, a revolt also broke out in Tibet that led to the flight of the Dalai Lama from Lhasa to India for personal safety. On May 6, 1959, the People's Daily published a scathing article entitled "The Revolution in Tibet and Nehru's Philosophy." It was popularly believed that the article carried Mao's personal imprimatur and contained a nasty personal attack on Nehru for the first time since the signing of the 1954 Agreement between India and China on Trade and Intercourse between Tibet and India, under which India recognized Chinese sovereignty over Tibet for the first time ever. Nehru was devastated by the viciousness of the personal attack.

Despite extreme Chinese unhappiness at what had happened in Tibet and their unflinching belief that Nehru was involved in the events leading to the Tibetan uprising and the subsequent flight of the Dalai Lama to India, the Chinese never lost sight of the greater strategic threat that was gathering in the shape of U.S. military deployments in the Taiwan Strait and the Soviet refusal to back them in case the U.S. used nuclear weapons. It was a grave threat that they could not ignore. Mao had earlier referred to it in his conversation with Nehru during the latter's visit to Beijing in October 1954. This is what Mao told Nehru:

Between friends, there are times when there are differences; there are also times when there are fights—even fights till we become red in the face. But this type of fight is different in character from the sort of fight we have with Dulles. We are a new country. Although we are counted as a large country, our strength is still weak. Confronting us is a larger power, America.... Therefore we need friends. PM Nehru can feel this. I think India also needs friends.

Therefore, it was not surprising that the then-Chinese ambassador arrived at South Block (the Indian Foreign Office) on May 16, 1959 and handed over a written démarche. It contained a long rambling litany of complaints against India and was reportedly drafted by Mao himself. Toward the end, it contained a most interesting proposal:

The enemy of the Chinese people lies in the east—the U.S. imperialists have many military bases in Taiwan, South Korea, Japan, and in the Philippines, which are all directed against China. China's main attention and policy of struggle are directed to the east, to the west Pacific region, to the vicious and aggressive U.S. imperialism and not to India.... India is not an opponent but a friend of our country. China will not be so foolish to antagonize the U.S. in the east and again to antagonize India in the west... Friends! It seems to us that you too cannot have two fronts.... Is it not so? If it is, here lies the meeting point of our two sides. Will you please think it over?

Nehru personally drafted the response to the Chinese ambassador's démarche, and assessed it as "discourteous." The tragedy lies in the fact that this démarche and its contents were taken by Nehru as a personal affront. The hapless foreign secretary was directed to respond within a week, on May 23, 1959, to say that the statement was "wholly out of keeping with diplomatic usage and courtesies due to friendly countries." Moreover, the astonishing remark was made that "the government of India does not consider or treat any country as an enemy country, howsoever much it may differ from it." (Was Pakistan then a "friendly" country?) Mao would have been deeply offended at Nehru's response.

## Three Current Issues

Let us fast forward to current times. Keeping in mind the historical context and considering China's deep anxiety at present on developments near its eastern seaboard, what then should India make of the latest Chinese offer of a Treaty of Friendship and Cooperation? The first point to underscore is that there exists in the Chinese mind the belief that Indians are by nature rather fond of "vision statements," "joint declarations," "guiding principles," "Five Principles of Peaceful Coexistence," etc. Therefore, offering a Treaty of Friendship and Cooperation to India, at present, would be in line with Chinese thinking about the nature of the

Indian mind and the belief that it can be easily satisfied by initiating, yet again, such high-sounding joint statements.

**The Boundary Dispute**

Second, in the Chinese mind such lofty statements/declarations matter little when placed in the context of real politics practiced by its leadership, as they can be easily ignored or subverted should the need arise. For example, take the Sino-Indian Agreement of April 11, 2005 that set out the "Political Parameters and Guiding Principles" for the settlement of boundary issues. In Paragraph VII it was agreed that, "In reaching a border settlement the two sides shall safeguard the due interests of their settled populations in border areas" [emphasis added]. Any unbiased observer would read this to mean that in the eastern sector of the Sino-Indian Boundary, the two sides had agreed to settle the border on the existing status quo since settled populations exist right up to the boundary. And yet when the political situation turned, the Chinese referred to Paragraph V and said that they could not ignore "national sentiment" and concede so much territory. Further in May 2007, the Chinese Foreign Minister told the Indian External Affairs Minister that "the mere presence of populated areas would not affect Chinese claims on the boundary." In other words, the Chinese were reneging on Paragraph VII.

Therefore the question that arises is how can India pin down the Chinese in concrete terms, so that they cannot escape so easily from commitments they might make in the proposed Treaty of Friendship and Cooperation? And what is the proof of Chinese sincerity?

To begin with, India must not reject the Chinese initiative, as Nehru had so impetuously done in 1959, but play along, for it gives India enough room for diplomatic manoeuver not only with the U.S. but also with states in the South Asian neighborhood. And yet the Chinese must be pinned down in concrete terms. On November 4, 1962, Prime Minister Zhou clarified to Nehru in an official note that in the eastern sector of the Sino-Indian Boundary, the Line of Actual Control "coincides with the McMahon Line." Zhou further said that the Indian government must have a copy of the original McMahon map, negotiated at Simla in 1914 (the Tripartite Conference between British India, China, and Tibet), and therefore it should be easy to read the coordinates line from that copy. That being the case, India should insist that the Chinese live up to Zhou's initiative and not only reaffirm that the Line of Actual Control in the eastern sector conformed to the McMahon Line, but insist that it be demarcated on the ground to avoid any misunderstandings.

If the Chinese government were to agree with its own stipulation, as made by Prime Minister Zhou in November 1962, this indeed would be a concrete proof of Chinese sincerity and a solid basis for negotiating a meaningful Treaty of Friendship. It would also indicate a serious intent on the part of the present Chinese government. Otherwise, the Chinese ambassador's proposal is basically a nonstarter. The boundary question, therefore, is likely to linger.

## The Balance of Trade

Both India, and to some extent the Chinese, recogniz that the huge trade deficit that exists and currently favors China is untenable. Something must be done to ameliorate the situation. It is in this context that the Chinese ambassador offered a Free Trade Agreement between the two countries. It is not in the public domain whether the Chinese authorities have officially proposed the same to India, but nevertheless it is an important development. Before an assessment can be made of India's response, it is imperative to first evaluate the current state of the trade relationship between the two countries.

India's trade relations with China have had a checkered history, and unfortunately continue to remain hostage to political developments between the two countries, albeit considerably less now than earlier. It is to the enormous credit of Prime Minister Rajiv Gandhi that he was the first Indian leader to realize that a solution to the vexed issue of the boundary dispute was not imminent, and therefore to delay normalization of trade and economic relations with China would only be counterproductive. He made the decision to delink the two issues. It was also during his visit to China in December 1988, that for the first time a Joint Economic Group was established. However, it must be pointed out that no one in the Indian leadership at that time paid much attention to this aspect of the relationship, for no one ever anticipated that bilateral trade volumes would develop so fast.

But develop they did. Sino-Indian bilateral trade in 1991 was a paltry US$265 million. It mushroomed exponentially to US$70.7 billion by 2015-16. Interestingly, India's current bilateral trade with China is larger than India's combined bilateral trade with Britain, Germany, and Japan. But the main problem is that India's trade deficit with China is unusually high: in 2015-16 standing at a staggering US$52.7 billion. And it is expected to rise even further this year. This by itself should not be a cause for worry, as India runs deficits with 16 of its top 25 trade partners. The inescapable fact is that India buys more than it sells worldwide.

Almost everyone recognizes the real problem behind this massive trade deficit. India's trade basket consists of cotton, gems and precious metals, copper, and iron ore. All are commodities. China, on the other hand, exports manufactured capital goods, mainly for the power and telecom sectors. India just does not produce enough high-quality manufactured goods even for its own billion-plus consumers, let alone for exports. Therefore it has to rely on quality imports from abroad. Many experts feel that the inordinately high trade deficit between India and China of US$52.7 billion is not a very serious issue for a country such as India that is on its way to establishing an industrial base and seeks high growth rates. Under such circumstances a larger import profile is unavoidable. Since China is the major source of technology-intensive products that are cost-effective, running a high deficit with China appears inevitable.

However, running trade deficits with China may not be necessarily inevitable. According to the Chinese, the problems faced by India are elsewhere, and essentially relate to restrictive labor practices, land and tax laws, rickety infrastructure, and inadequate power supply. In addition, while China is a part of the global supply chain, being the last stop of the manufacturing chain in East Asia, India is nowhere near being a part of this global chain.

Therefore, what would a Free Trade Agreement with China entail, and what would be its implications? Empirical studies show that for India, any such agreement would be a nonstarter, for India is not competitive at all. Such an agreement would not have any major impact on increasing Indian exports to China, for the tariffs that China levies on most items in the Indian export basket already are near zero. Furthermore, the manufacturing skills and abilities currently available in India compared with China are rather low. India's manufacturing industry would be badly hit. Although overall trade between the two countries might grow at a healthy pace, it would be mostly to the advantage of the Chinese. For example, if tariffs levied were to be reduced by five percent across the board, the increase in India's exports would be negligible, whereas those of China would increase by an estimated 18 percent.[1] From the Indian point of view therefore, this proposal is a nonstarter. A selected sector-wise free trade agreement, rather than one across the board, could be one way forward. However, because both India and China find it hard to reconcile their respective positions, progress in negotiations is slow and tedious.

India needs to press the Chinese on opening more facilities and increasing border trade. Right now, trade between India and Tibet across the land borders is very modest in contrast to Sino-Nepal border trade, which stands at US$542 million. There are several reasons. Firstly, the lists of items that can be traded are outmoded and not commensurate with modern requirements. Secondly, the time allotted for trading is very unsuitable, particularly since traders cannot stay overnight in either country. Most border trade points are open only four days a week. The time taken to reach border points is also a factor, since the infrastructure – particularly on the Indian side – is rudimentary at best. For example, the road connecting Siliguri the last railhead to Sikkim and on to Nathu La on the border is about 143 kilometers long, but is a single lane and often subject to landslides. Sikkim has no airport, nor any railhead.

The importance of border trade should be recognized, as it is an important catalyst for poverty reduction in border areas. Border villages are becoming de-populated, because of the lack of jobs, thus posing security concerns for India. In the past, border trade with Tibet helped towns such as Kalimpong, Darjeeling, and even Tawang thrive. If border trade is revived, it can again be a significant dynamic in economic development.

In 1988 when a significant shift happened in Indian policy toward China, it was the fervent hope that goodwill thus generated with normalization in all other sectors would facilitate the settlement of the boundary question. Those hopes have to some extent been belied, but what has also emerged is that the massive trade deficit generated has added an altogether new issue between the two countries. By 2030 the economies of both China and India are expected to be among the top four economies of the world. Unfortunately India still does not have a full-time independent trade negotiator on lines of USTR, and negotiates on an episodic basis.

## One Belt, One Road

The third proposal on the table was the Chinese ambassador's idea of merging China's "One Belt, One Road" concept with India's "Act East Policy" that envisages that only India pays more attention to states east of India, but that special relations with them should be developed.

When the Chinese ambassador spoke of the "One Belt, One Road" connectivity, what exactly did he have in mind? Does it mean that the initiative also includes the US$46 billion Chinese funded China-Pakistan Economic Corridor as an inseparable component? A clear understanding of what is offered is necessary for the study of the proposal's implications. In turn this would facilitate a response from India.

On September 7, 2013, President Xi Jinping made the proposal for a new Silk Road Economic Belt in an address at Nazarbayev University. While addressing the Indonesian Parliament on October 3, 2013, he proposed the new 21st Century Maritime Silk Road. These initiatives were amalgamated and became known as the "One Belt, One Road" concept. The current Chinese leadership has done well to choose this particular name, the Silk Road, for no matter where a person is located in the vast Euro-Asian heartland, the name would always resonate. The Chinese believe that "One Belt, One Road" provides a fresh way of thinking about regional and global cooperation, and that by including both bilateral and multilateral cooperation in political, economic, cultural, and other fields, a new paradigm would be created. The Chinese benefit immensely for the Belt and Road concept takes care of Chinese overcapacity in the steel and cement industries, as well as the desire for utilizing accumulated capital resources to further Chinese ambitions. Its scope would not be limited to Asia, but certainly its success does, to some extent, depend on cooperation that the Chinese receive from important countries such as India. If this initiative comes to fruition, it would link 65 countries and 4.4 billion people.

The Indian position has been that it has never been officially consulted on "One Belt, One Road." The assumption in India is that the China-Pakistan Economic Corridor, in which the Chinese have invested US$46 billion, is an important component of the initiative. In December 2014, the Indian External Affairs Minister stated in Parliament that, "Government has seen reports with regard to China and Pakistan being involved in infrastructure-building activities in Pakistan-occupied Kashmir, including construction of the China-Pakistan Economic Corridor. Government has conveyed its concern to China about their activities and asked them to cease such activities." While the minister was expressing her concern, a Press Trust of India report quoted the Indian High Commissioner to Pakistan as saying that, "India has no worry over construction of the China-Pakistan Economic Corridor, as an economically strong Pakistan would bring stability to the region."

This dichotomy of approach remains to be reconciled, for it seems that it stems from strategic ambiguity. If the past is any guide then in 1965 at Tashkent, India agreed to restore the 1949 ceasefire line and withdrew from areas it occupied across the ceasefire line in the 1965 conflict. Similarly, the whole ethos of the Simla Agreement in 1972 was that Pakistan would accept and at an appropriate time convert the ceasefire line (now called the Line of Control) into an international border. In 1999 as well, India maintained the sanctity of the Line of Control, never crossed the line militarily and used force to oust Pakistani troops and pushed them back and beyond the Line of Control. Thus, it seems India was quite prepared to give up its claims to Pakistan-occupied Kashmir, if Pakistan accepted the Line of Control as an international border. It is not in the public domain if any such concrete offer was ever made in writing to Pakistan [emphasis added]. On the other hand, Prime Minister Modi recently reiterated in his August 15th independence message that Pakistan-occupied Kashmir was indeed sovereign Indian Territory. The question is which of the two strategic modules would India prefer to pursue on a long-term basis?

Thus, if the China-Pakistan Economic Corridor is indeed a vital component of "One Belt, One Road," then it violates Indian Territory, and for India to accept the initiative is a matter of national territorial integrity. On the question of the China-Pakistan Economic Corridor traversing Pakistan-occupied Kashmir, Chinese Foreign Ministry spokesperson Hua Chunying prevaricated on the issue: "With regard to whether the economic corridor passes through [Pak] Kashmir, as far as I have learned, a joint committee for the construction of China-Pakistan Economic Corridor has been established and a second meeting has been held coinciding with the visit of the Pakistani President. I do not know if they have talked about whether the corridor will pass through this region [Pak-Kashmir], but I can tell you that we hope the Kashmir issue can be resolved through consultations and negotiations between India and Pakistan." Clearly the Chinese were hoping to obfuscate the issue and the fact that the China-Pakistan Economic Corridor passed through Pakistan-occupied Kashmir. Recent Chinese press reports have also taken the same view, calling upon India and Pakistan to settle the matter among themselves.

Therefore, if India cannot join "One Belt, One Road" then the Chinese's proposal of joining the "One Belt, One Road" with India's "Act East Policy" clearly becomes a nonstarter. Alternatively, at present India does not have sufficient economic resources or the political heft to put in place either a competitive or an alternative connectivity network on a scale that can offer an alternative option to the Belt and Road initiative. In such circumstances would it be plausible to prudently study those components of the initiative that may improve India's own connectivity to major Central Asian markets, just as India has chosen to join the Chinese-sponsored Asian Infrastructure and Investment Bank and the National Development Bank? For example, India's proposal to build a road cum rail link to Central Asia through the Iranian port of Chahbahar could ostensibly be linked to the Chinese-built routes in the Central Asian region to obtain access to both Central Asian as well as Russian destinations. Would the Chinese be prepared to allow limited participation by India, as opposed to full participation?

If India's resources are indeed limited, then it automatically follows that strategically these must not be spread too thinly as a part of its Act East Policy. As the Indian Ocean area is strategically extremely important for India, it may be more imperative to deploy resources to build an Indian Ocean network of ports, with connecting highways and rail routes, such as the planned Mekong-Ganga corridor and the Sittwe-Mizoram multimodal transport corridor. Plans to develop the deep water port at Trincomalee on Sri Lanka's eastern coast, as a major energy and transport hub, are still in limbo, despite the fact that the Chinese have gone ahead and built the Hambantota port in Sri Lanka and have expanded Colombo port. The Andaman and Nicobar Islands are strategically located in the Bay of Bengal and opposite the Malacca Straits, and yet India continues to treat these islands as distant outposts rather than developing them as important commercial and transportation hubs. The idea of launching a Spice Route, Cotton Route, and even a Mausam project are currently mostly rhetorical ripostes to China's "One Belt, One Road" and to the China-Pakistan Economic Corridor. Much more therefore needs to be done, and clearly some hard thinking needs to be initiated soon.

Notes

1    Chandra Rupa. *"India-China Free Trade Agreement (FTA): Viability, Prospects and Challenges. "IIMB Management Review.*

---

*Ambassador R.S. Kalha is a former Permanent Secretary, Ministry of External Affairs, India. He was also a Member of India's National Human Rights Commission, 2003-08.*

# India and the Emerging Sino-Iranian Partnership

*John W. Garver*
*Vol. 16, No.1*
*2017*

Iran is emerging as an arena of rivalry between China and India. Beijing is using its substantial leverage with Tehran to persuade Iran to expand cooperation in economic, connectivity, political, and security areas. New Delhi fears that elements of expanded Sino-Iranian cooperation may compromise India's national security and add another potentially potent element to the growth of Chinese power in the Indian Ocean region. Analysts have long been attuned to Chinese-Indian rivalry in places like Nepal, Myanmar, Sri Lanka, or the small island states of the Indian Ocean. Now Iran is emerging as a focus. Given Iran's power potential, the outcome of this Sino-Indian contest may be a significant determinant of China's emerging role in the Indian Ocean region.

Dimensions of China's recent courtship of Iran include: war and peace, international connectivity, and enhanced security cooperation. Regarding the issue of war and peace, in 2013-2015 China undertook a high-profile and ultimately successful mediation effort in the Seven Party negotiations over Iran's nuclear program. (The "P5 + 1" + Iran = 7; the "P5" includes the five permanent members of the United Nations Security Council: the United States, UK, France, China, and Russia, plus one, Germany.) Those negotiations led to the Joint Comprehensive Plan of Action (JCPOA) agreement in July 2015 that was successfully implemented by January 2016. In exchange for Iran's scaling back of its nuclear program, many international sanctions against it were lifted. China's mediatory effort represented a bold initiative (for China) that was one manifestation less risk-adverse "pro-active diplomacy" mandated by Xi Jinping after he took power late in 2012. China's mediation effort was also a significant investment of political capital in

Iran's long-term emergence as a major regional power. China's mediation effort in the Seven Party talks stands with China's 1987-1988 role in assisting Tehran escape from war (in that case with Iraq) via a Security Council ceasefire agreement acceptable to Tehran. During the Seven Party talks, China played an important role in convincing Iran to come to terms with international concerns about its nuclear program. Beijing also helped persuade Washington to reach a compromise with Tehran at that juncture. Wikileaks documents show that even prior to the start of the Seven Party talks, China was passing messages between Washington and Tehran, and giving both sides advice about how to move forward in their quest for better ties. China's efforts thus helped Iran avoid a potentially devastating war with Israel and the United States, a war that might have eviscerated Iran's comprehensive national power. The China-mediated nuclear deal secured for Iran the lifting of sanctions, while safe guarding Iran's "right" to non-military use of nuclear energy under the Non-Proliferation Treaty. Comments by Iranian leaders indicate gratitude to China for its "positive and constructive" role. During the Seven Party talks Beijing demonstrated, as it did in 1987-88, that China is Iran's sincere and capable friend on issues of war and peace. Beijing is now using that capital to entice Iran into expanded cooperation.

India sought and secured a degree of detachment from the United States during the debate over Iran's nuclear programs, but undertook nothing comparable to China's high-profile and vigorous mediation effort. Nor did India have the substantial economic leverage with both the United States and Iran that China possessed while advising Washington and Tehran about the nuclear issue. India was also handicapped by its non-inclusion in the United Nations inner circle on the nuclear talks. In contrast to India, China demonstrated to Iran via its JCPOA mediation effort that it could get things done on matters of war and peace.

Regarding international connectivity, with the lifting of international sanctions in January 2016, China is offering Iran very large Chinese investments in Iranian industrialization, especially in the area of infrastructure: railways, highways, telecommunications, energy, harbors, and ports. These proposals were laid out by China's ambassador to Iran shortly before the nuclear deal was completed, and represented, in effect, a Chinese inducement to come to terms over its nuclear program. Once that deal was implemented in January 2016, President Jiang Zemin carried more specific offers to Tehran, promising major Chinese financing and investment if Iran engages with China's One Belt, One Road programs. Xi's visit was the first by a foreign leader to Iran after the successful implementation of the JCPOA. It was also the first visit by China's top leader to Iran since 2002 — 14 years before.

China's vision is of dedicated trains and (perhaps) dedicated rails carrying containers of Chinese goods to Iranian ports for further shipment to the Middle East and western Indian Ocean region. If and when Iranian ports join Kyaukpyu in Myanmar and Gwadar in Pakistan as littoral gateways for Chinese commerce entering the Indian Ocean, China will have gone a good distance toward mitigating its Malacca dilemma. Chinese goods will also have better access to large markets around the Indian Ocean region.

There is apparently a debate underway in Iran over deeper Iranian dependence on China, as opposed to intensified efforts to secure greater European re-engagement with Iran's economy. India has made an effort to limit or counter deeper Iranian economic integration with China. Four months after Xi's visit to Tehran, Indian Prime Minister Narendra Modi conveyed to Tehran India's proposals for expanded cooperation, proposing revival of a harbor, rail, and road project linking Chabahar in Iranian Baluchistan with Delaram in west central Afghanistan and thence with Central Asia. The Chabahar project was paralleled by a tripartite Iran-Afghan-Indian transportation agreement designed to boost trade between India, Russia, and Central Asia via Iran. A third component of Modi's effort was revival of the idea of a north-south corridor involving Russia, Iran, and India, and carrying Caspian Sea region oil and gas to Iranian ports for forward shipment to India and the world, while Indian goods would flow north to Central Asia. In effect, Modi's plan is an effort to moderate Iran's economic dependence on China.

In the area of security, during Xi Jinping's January 2016 visit, Iran and China signed a 25- year Comprehensive Strategic Partnership. The political framework of the agreement included mutual support on "issues pertaining to their core interests," including China's One China policy and Iran's "increasing role in regional and international affairs." In the "regional domain," the two countries supported "multi-polarization of the international system," non-interference in the internal affairs of other countries, and jointly opposed "imposition of unjust sanctions against other countries." All of these provisions were implicitly directed against the U.S. China also undertook to support Iran in the areas of "space" and "peaceful use of nuclear energy." In terms of relations between Chinese and Iranian militaries, there was to be enhanced training, exchange of information, and "equipment and technology." The degree of Chinese alignment with Iran against the United States implicit in the terms of the Comprehensive Strategic Partnership marked a sharp departure from Beijing's earlier careful reluctance to align with Iran against the United States. This too seems to be a manifestation of Xi Jinping's less risk-adverse diplomacy.

Visits to Iranian ports by PLA Navy (PLAN) warships is one concrete manifestation of the expanded Iran-China military partnership. While small PLAN squadrons began calling at Indian Ocean ports in 1985 and greatly increased such activity after Beijing's December 2008 decision to join international anti-piracy operations in the Gulf of Aden, Chinese warships conspicuously avoided Iranian ports. Then in September 2014, two PLAN destroyers made the first-ever visit by PRC warships to Iranian ports. That was two years into Xi Jinping's leadership, at the same time movement toward what became the July 2015 agreement was accelerating. Taken together, the September 2014 PLAN port calls and the Comprehensive Strategic Partnership bode a significantly expanded PRC-IR military partnership.

Nothing in the January 2016 Sino-Iranian joint declaration even insinuates opposition to India. Indeed, Beijing's bid to India is that it should partner with China and other like-minded countries such as Iran, to deal with common concerns with the security of their sea lines of communications in the Indian Ocean. India should, in Beijing's view, take China rather than the United States as its partner in dealing with security matters in the Indian Ocean. That has not thus far been an attractive choice from India's perspective because it would open wider the door to growth of PLAN presence in the Indian Ocean region, ultimately posing the possibility of China becoming a resident power in the South Asia-Indian Ocean Region and the United States could be persuaded to "go home" and leave Asian matters for Asians to deal with. India might then find itself living in a China-dominated SA-IOR.

Commentators in the Indian media have been critical of New Delhi's slow response to China's push for expanded partnership with Iran. Modi's May 2016 visit to Tehran seems to have been recognition of a more vigorous Indian counter to Beijing's efforts. The agreements struck during Modi's visit demonstrate Iranian gains to be had through cooperation with India. In private talks with Iranian leaders, Modi certainly would make clear India's hopes that the evolution of Iran-China ties would not injure India's national security. The Iran card is in play. New Delhi is calling Beijing's bid.

Several macro-structural changes underlie the new Chinese-Indian rivalry. The PLAN's 2009 entry into the Indian Ocean on a permanent and expanding basis has raised the stakes for both China and India. Iran's growing regional influence — in Lebanon, Syria, Iraq, and Yemen — incline Tehran to look for a great power supporter such as its known and trusted friend China. The intensification of India's security partnership with the United States raises the danger for New Delhi that Tehran will drift into opposition to India's alignment with the U.S. Beijing will certainly play up this theme, intensifying the need for India to counter Beijing and demonstrate India's friendship toward Iran. But perhaps the most important influence has been the recession of U.S. power as a regulator of both Chinese and Indian ties with Iran. During the 1990s through the 2000s, Washington used its great influence to dissuade both Beijing and New Delhi from moving too close to Tehran. The volte-face in U.S. policy embodied in the July 2015 agreement made it possible for both Beijing and New Delhi to undertake initiatives toward Tehran based on their own interests, rather than on U.S. policy interests. Simply stated, the withdrawal of U.S. power has led to intensification of Sino-Indian rivalry toward Iran.

*John Garver is Professor Emeritus in the Sam Nunn School of International Affairs at Georgia Institute of Technology, Atlanta, Georgia, and an associate of the China Research Center.*

# China and the Iran Model

*John W. Garver*
*Vol. 14, No.1*
*2015*

A 2011 biography of Mohammad Reza Pahlavi, the shah or king of Iran from 1941 to 1979, lays out a number of haunting similarities between Iran's experience under the shah and the Chinese Communist Party's rule of China today. Authored by Abbas Milani, the director of the Iranian Studies Program at Stanford University and co-director of the Iran Democracy Project at the Hoover Institution, the 488-page book lays bare the processes leading to the popular uprising that toppled the shah's regime in 1979.[1] The parallels between many of those processes and China's experience today are multiple and strong, and not necessarily comforting.

The shah ruled as an authoritarian modernizer in the mold of Mustafa Kemal Attaturk or Japan's Meiji emperor, who used autocratic power to rip a traditional society away from old moorings and hurl it down the path of rapid industrialization, urbanization, secularization, and social mobility. Milani writes:

[In] the last fifteen years of [the shah's] rule, there had been not only unprecedented economic growth, but unparalleled cultural and religious freedom in Iran. Double-digit growth of the GNP was not the exception but the rule. Iran ranked with Turkey, South Korea and Taiwan as the countries that were industrializing most rapidly and were most likely to join the ranks of developed countries.

The shah's authoritarian rule fostered substantial and rapid development. The shah was a leader of the effort by oil producing countries to force consuming nations to pay higher prices. He funneled vast revenues from those oil sales into the rapid development of Iran. Between 1962 and 1974 the percent of GDP represented by the industrial sector grew from 11.7 percent to 17 percent. The number of large-scale industrial enterprises grew from 482 in 1941 to 5,651 in 1974. Land reform freed many farmers from heavy traditional burdens, causing many to move into cities. Education expanded greatly. The number of high schools increased from 351 in 1941 to 2,314 in 1974. The number of universities increased from eight in 1941 to 148 by 1974. The process of educational reform stripped the Islamic clergy of their long-traditional control over education. Tens of thousands of young Iranians went to Europe or the United States for advanced study. Women were major beneficiaries of expanded education. By 1972, 65 percent of students enrolled in tertiary education were female. Women were granted legal equality and emancipated in a number of ways. The middle classes and technocratic classes grew rapidly in size as a result of this swift economic development.

The shah saw himself as the sagacious benefactor of his people. These great advances just outlined were demonstrations of that benevolence, in the shah's view. He expected "his people" to be grateful for the progress and benefits he had conferred on them. The shah, Milani suggests, was "like a traditional Oriental potentate" who believed "society owed him a debt of gratitude for the progress and freedom he had given them." When the people failed to show gratitude, the shah projected responsibility outward onto insidious foreign hidden hands. What the shah didn't comprehend is that the Iranian people did not view these gains as gifts of the shah, but as their natural rights, as Milani points out:

What the shah failed to understand was that it was, in fact, the democratic aspirations of the Iranian people that begat the [opposition] movement against him and that, ironically, his own social and economic policies of the 1960s and 1970s helped created the very social forces — particularly the middle class and the new technocratic class — that united to overthrow him.

The advances and benefits delivered under the shah's rule did not fundamentally legitimize his authoritarian rule.

The CCP today, like the shah in his era, legitimizes its authoritarian rule by appealing to the economic and social benefits its rule has wrought: high rates of economic growth, economic opportunity, increases in standards of living, expanded educational opportunities. That approach did not work for the shah. Will it work for the CCP in the long run? The Iranian people wanted not only higher living standards, though, of course, they wanted those. They also wanted political freedom and democracy. The shah's ambitious and largely successful development efforts greatly strengthened two key groups that turned critically against him: a large urban middle class and a new technocratic elite essential to large-scale industry. There were other important elements of what eventually became the revolutionary coalition in Iran: bazaar merchants, the urban poor, radical clerics, Marxist groups, and some nomadic tribes. But according to Milani, it was the middle class and technocratic elite that the Shah could and should have won to support his rule if he had only undertaken transition to constitutional monarchy.

Liberalization in many areas of culture and religion — but not in politics — is another similarity between the shah's Iran and China today. During the 1960s and 1970s Iranian arts of all sorts — literature, cinema, dance, architecture, and sculpture — enjoyed unprecedented freedoms. There was a virtual effusion of cultural creativity. Old taboos on social relations were eased greatly. Religious freedom waxed. Baha'i were freed from previous persecution and Iranian Jews enjoyed "a golden age." Only in the area of politics was there greater repression. There was freedom for everyone but the political opposition. They were repressed with vigor. In China today the cultural creativity is striking to anyone who travels the land: in painting, sculpture, literature, cinema, dance, music, architecture. Yet in China as in Iran under the shah, artists, authors, or lawyers who sign open letters, manifestos, or petitions to the government are likely to find themselves hounded and imprisoned. Can human freedom really be compartmentalized? In Iran cultural freedom fed expectations of political freedom.

Milani outlines another aspect of the shah's Iran and China today: dual and conflicting identities between, on the one hand, a desire to integrate into the "global march of modernity" and, on the other hand, an "authentic self" rooted in non-globalist traditions (in Iran's case Islam and imperial tradition). "Modernity" includes, for Milani, a political system based on the consent of the people governed and protection of the natural rights of citizens to participate in politics, the collective self-government of citizens. Since a constitutionalist revolution of 1905 the Iranian people have sought to secure the blessings of modern political liberty for themselves and their posterity. That struggle continued into the 1970s and culminated in the ouster of the shah in 1979. Had the shah been willing to transform his monarchy during the 1970s into a constitutional one, allowing politicians selected by democratic elections to run the government — if the shah had been willing to reign but not rule as the 1906 constitution envisioned — the Pahlavi monarchy might have survived, or so Milani suggests. Instead, the shah increased repression of the opposition and strengthened his own personal control over government. The middle class and the new technocratic classes wanted the political freedoms they knew were common elsewhere around the world. As it became apparent the shah would not accept modern political freedoms, these urban classes gravitated increasingly to radical Islamic clergy, who offered a seemingly modernized version of Shiite Islam accommodating modern political freedom.

Again the similarities with China are many and marked. China, like Iran, is torn between embrace of global modern political norms (the self-defensively CCP dubs those norms "Western") and more authentic, non-globalist political forms rooted in China's distinctive tradition — Confucianism, the Imperial era, Marxism-Leninism-Mao Zedong Thought. China's 1911 revolution, like Iran's 1905 revolution, sought to establish modern political institutions. Though both efforts failed in large part, popular movements for that same objective have punctuated China's modern history, as they have Iran's. It can even be argued that anti-democratic minorities hijacked attempted democratic revolutions of both countries. In the several years after 1945, the popular uprising that toppled Chiang Kai-shek and brought the CCP to power rallied behind a banner of "new democracy" that called for free elections and an end to "one-party dictatorship," censorship and political imprisonment. Once in power, however, that democratic camouflage was discarded and Stalinism imposed. In Iran, Islamic clerics paved the way to embrace of Ruhollah Khomeini as leader of the revolution by popularizing what seemed to be a modernized version of Shiite Islam. Khomeini in the critical months of 1978 masqueraded adroitly as a democrat, a believer in women's rights and secular government, who had no desire himself to rule. He made no mention of his doctrine of Islamic theocracy. His publications containing his advocacy of that doctrine were unavailable because the shah had long suppressed them. Khomeini passed for a modern man — until power was in his hands. Might Chinese groups seeking a Fifth (political) Modernization someday in the future be once again tricked by extremist groups masquerading as democrats? Where might that take China?

Another similarity between the shah's Iran and today's China is the interweaving of a strong sense of national humiliation and belief in a vast international conspiracy as the cause of that humiliation. By the 20th century the once powerful Persian empire had come under the domination of Russia or Britain. This produced Iranian "souls humiliated by a sense of historic defeat — at the hands of the Russians, the West, Fate…." The shah claimed that his reforms, combined with the vast military power he acquired for Iran, was wiping out Iran's humiliation and establishing Iran as a world power. This view of historic loss combined with a sense of individual powerlessness to produce widespread belief in conspiracy explanations of Iran's woes. Iranians widely believed that the United States, Britain, or the Soviet Union were the real masters of events in Iran. Milani puts it this way:

A people who have lost faith in their messiah but have yet to reach social mastery of their own fate need conspiracy theories to assuage their anxieties and satisfy their existential human urge to have a narrative explanation — a history of their lives and what has befallen them.

Thus when the Carter Administration began stressing the human rights shortcomings of the shah's regime in 1977-78, the conspiracy mentality of many Iranians led them to conclude that the American masters of Iran had decided to get rid of the shah, and this sense of his new vulnerability gave a fillip to Iranian opposition to the shah's regime.

In China, of course, the claim to ending and wiping out the stain of the century of national humiliation is at the core of the CCP's claim to legitimacy. Embrace of this ideational complex is widespread in China, as is the notion that the Americans or some other malevolent power is working to encircle, contain or split China, deny it its rightful position of respect and eminence, working to overthrow China's government casting it into anarchy and civil war, and so on. In Iran this sense of humiliation of conspiracy combined to help lead the Iranian people away from the political liberty many of them sought.

The most striking difference between Iran under the shah and China today involves, of course, Islam. The shah viewed middle class nationalists and Marxists as his most dangerous opposition, and regarded the Islamic clergy as a bulwark against Marxism and the Soviet Union. The moderate clergy was left free to propound its views and organize a network based on mosques. There seems to be nothing comparable in China. But China today possesses one artifact absent in the shah's Iran: autonomous nationalist movements which on the one hand pressure the government on foreign affairs, but on the other hand are controlled by the state and serve to vent opposition anger and legitimize the regime.

*Notes*
1   Abbas Milani, *The Shah*, London: Palgrave Macmillan, 2011.

---

*John Garver is Professor Emeritus in the Sam Nunn School of International Affairs at Georgia Institute of Technology, Atlanta, Georgia, and an associate of the China Research Center.*

*Politics and International Relations*

## China Rules the World?

*John W. Garver*
*Vol. 15, No.2*
*2016*

A panel on the traditional East Asian tributary system at the annual convention of the Association of Asian Studies in Seattle in early April produced a fascinating discussion on the subject of whether China really ever ruled the world, or at least the East Asian portion of the world that China's pre-modern emperors understood to be the world. This arcane debate touches on the self-identity of rising China. Many of China's "citizen intellectuals" who now opine in print and online about China's mission in the emerging world order argue that China must once again become the dominant power in the world, replacing the United States in that role and dispensing a morality superior to the conflict-prone individualistic materialism peddled by the United States. Since the notion that China in fact "ruled the world" for several millennia constitutes a key premise of this new Chinese nationalist hubris, it is important to ask: Did China ever really once dominate East Asia as the idea of the traditional pre-modern tributary system maintains? Close examination of that proposition suggests that the answer is "no," it did not.

The idea of a "tributary system" ordering relations for two millennia between China's successive imperial dynastic states (Han, Tang, Song, Ming, Qing, etc.) and other states in East Asian, Central Asian and Southeast Asian was developed by Western scholars after World War II. Harvard Professor John King Fairbank was a pioneer in formulating the tributary system model. The "East Asian tributary system" became the standard model of Western sinology, and several generations of scholars delved into aspects of this system. Papers presented at the Seattle conference continued this effort by investigating the operation of the tributary system during the Qing-French confrontation over Vietnam in 1884 and during the Qing-Meiji confrontation over Chosen (Korea) in 1894.

The tributary system supposedly worked like this: China's emperor, the Son of Heaven, claimed – and to a significant degree exercised universal authority over (similar to the Pope in Medieval Europe) – all kings and potentates ruling civilized lands and lands aspiring to become civilized. Rulers of other lands recognized China's superior ways and voluntarily entered into subordinate relations with China's Son of Heaven in order to gain his sage advice and practical help. China's imperial states typically had superior economic wealth and military power, but it was superior virtue – reflected in China's prosperous and orderly society – that really distinguished China's Son of Heaven from other powerful rulers. The ideal relation between China's emperor and foreign rulers was analogous to the relation between a wise and benevolent father and a dutiful son: obedient submission in exchange for benevolent treatment.

The standard model laid out several key modalities of the tributary relation. China's Son of Heaven invested foreign kings, conferring symbols of celestial authority that were handy in guarding against coups, usurpations, and rebellions. The Son of Heaven also supplied a calendar that accurately reflected the agricultural cycle and predicted celestial events (eclipses, comets, and such), powerfully demonstrating the Son of Heaven's close relation with the cosmos. "Gifts" were also exchanged between the Son of Heaven and the foreign ruler. In theory the foreign ruler's gifts were tribute to the Son of Heaven in recognition of the latter's august supremacy. But since benevolence toward "obedient" subordinates was required of the Son of Heaven, Chinese gifts to the foreign ruler typically far outweighed in value the foreign gifts to China. This can be seen as a way of buying the foreign ruler's "obedience," but was, in any case, often less expensive than war and more effective than building great walls. In exchange for "obedience" to imperial Chinese "instructions," the foreign potentate ruled their lands with little Chinese interference and with broad Chinese support. Given China's wealth and power, foreign rulers often found these handy things to have, in dealing with rebellions or foreign invasion, for example.

Many of China's contemporary "citizen intellectuals" commenting in the space for discourse created by the government's declaration of China's "peaceful rise" and "dream" of "great rejuvenation of the Chinese nation" assert that China must work to establish a modern variant of the traditional tributary system, perhaps in Asia and perhaps over the whole world, replacing the United States as global hegemon.[1] China's rapidly growing power and influence suggest, to these citizen intellectuals, that the time has come for China to restore its historically normal place – per the tributary system – as leading global power.

A number of considerations indicate that the notion of many centuries of Chinese domination of its known world via the tributary system is, in fact, a scholarly simplification that became a myth.

First of all, "barbarian" states were often more powerful that China's imperial states. This was especially the case with the horse-riding states that emerged to China's north and whose highly mobile armies of mounted archers were often able to ride circles, quite literally, around Chinese armies. In dealing with these militarily potent "barbarian" states, China's imperial rulers often resorted to extremely generous "gifts" to stave off worse fates. China would try to frame this payoff of blackmail within the framework of the tribute system. But if that failed, China would pay up while still writing the records dutifully reporting that the foreign potentate obediently kowtowed before China's Son of Heaven. The tributary system in these cases became a framework not for China's hegemony, but its weakness.

Major East Asian states refused to accept ritual subordination to China. Japan and Russia were the most important of these. Except for a brief period in the early 15thcentury, Japan's imperial court adamantly refused to agree that China's ruler was superior to Japan's.[2] Japan's ruler, like China's, was a "celestial emperor" not a mere "king," Japan's royal court insisted. Japan's lese majeste made direct communication between China and Japan's rulers virtually impossible. Relevant here, however, is the reality that Japan did not live under Chinese hegemony via the tributary system. It refused.

Regarding Russia, arrival of Russian adventurers in the 17th century to lands north of what is today China's northeast led to decades of low-grade conflict between Qing China and Romanov Russian forces. That conflict ended in1659 when the two states concluded a treaty delineating their mutual boundary. Drafted by Jesuit priests in service to the Qing court and written in Latin, the Treaty of Nerchensk embodied European notions of equality of sovereign states – both of which are ideas antithetical to the tributary system's hierarchy and universal rule. Most important, the treaty led to a de facto military alliance against the Mongol states still dominating much of Central Asia lying between the Qing and Romanov realms. While Chinese scribes and historians certainly did their best to fit Qing ties with Romanov Russia into the tributary mold, the reality was that an aggressive and powerful Russian state was China's equal, and did not pay tribute to or kowtow before the Son of Heaven.

During the Yuan (Mongol) dynasty (1279-1368 CE) the modalities of the tribute system were adapted to aggressive imperialism. The great Mongol khans ruling – also, as the Sons of Heaven – typically began new conquests with demands for ritual subordination via the tributary system. If and when those solicitations were rejected, powerful Yuan armies and fleets followed. This was certainly hegemony, although the additional descriptor "Chinese" may not apply. More to our point, the tributary system of the Yuan dynasty did not involve voluntary submission out of recognition of superior civilization. Nor did it involve loose and indirect Chinese rule; Mongol rule was heavy and harsh.

The notion of voluntary subordination to China's Son of Heaven out of recognition of China's superior civilization – a notion popular with many contemporary Chinese nationalists – does not comport well with the more messy realities of Asia's history. Even countries like Korea and Vietnam that drew deeply on China's civilization had complex feelings about their tributary relation with China. The relationship had many advantages, including avoidance of wars with China for "disobedience" to its wishes. But a close relation with China also required periodic defense against bouts of Chinese aggressiveness. Vietnam, especially, survived as an independent state in China's civilizational orbit by developing a political culture centered on the idea that they were NOT Chinese and would resist Chinese attempts to make them so.

Then there were the seaborne European maritime powers. The arrival of Portuguese, Spanish, Dutch, and English merchant ships in the western Pacific in the 16th and 17thcenturies plugged East Asia into an emerging global economy. With new designs, European ships could sail the wild Atlantic and Pacific Oceans, delivering much sought-after East Asian goods to European markets. These merchant powers chaffed at the restrictions of the tributary system which Ming and Qing governments imposed on this trade. Ultimately, in the 19th century, those Western grievances would lead to wars toppling the tribute system in favor of free trade. But even while the Ming and Qing states were healthy, Chinese control over this dynamic East Asian maritime trade began and ended at water's edge. China's imperial states were, with a very few exceptions, continental land powers.[3] Chinese naval fleets generally operated in coastal waters. Ming and Qing China simply did not exercise hegemony over the seas of the Western Pacific, let alone the Oceanic highways beyond. Rather, those maritime lines of communication were dominated by powers other than China.

On close examination the standard model of the East Asian tributary system depicting long centuries of Chinese dominance is a crude simplification of a far more complex reality. It may work fairly well in understanding China's ties with a small set of countries (Korea, Vietnam, and Siam), but set in a larger, fuller context must be seen as one piece of a more diverse, Rube Goldberg-like "system."

It may well be that all academic theories are simplifications of sorts. But when some Chinese nationalists today envision China restoring the long-lost golden age of a China-centric hierarchical state order in Asia or the world, with China delivering greater security, prosperity, and order than the United States, they are turning an academic simplification into a myth. It would be unfortunate if China's rise in the 21stcentury were guided by a myth about its pre-20th century role in

East Asia.

## Notes

1   *Official sources carefully eschew such bold ideas. The idea that ordinary Chinese citizens seize upon policies laid out by the Party center to comment in print and in cyberspace and within a fairly wide range on centrally approved policies is one of the key ideas scholars of contemporary China use to understand political discourse in contemporary China.*

2   *The early 15th century exception came during a period of Chinese navalism, exemplified by Admiral Cheng He's bold expeditions into the Indian Ocean. Cheng He's naval expeditions came only about 125 years after the nearly successful Mongol invasion of Japan defeated only by the "divine wind" that shattered the Mongol invasion fleet.*

3   *The notable exceptions were the Yuan and the early Ming periods.*

*John Garver is Professor Emeritus in the Sam Nunn School of International Affairs at Georgia Institute of Technology, Atlanta, Georgia, and an associate of the China Research Center.*

# Manifesto of China's Reformers: David Shambaugh's China's Future?

*John W. Garver*
*Vol. 15, No.2*
*2016*

A leading U.S. authority on China's politics, David Shambaugh of George Washington University, has authored what amounts to a manifesto of China's reformers who are dismayed by the recent return to hard authoritarianism under President Xi Jinping. These moderates believe that the current retreat from both deeper marketization of the economy and gradual political liberalization and return to hard-line repression not seen since the immediate aftermath of the Beijing massacre of June 4, 1989, will ultimately undermine rather than strengthen Communist Party rule over China. China's reformers cannot themselves write an open and direct critique of China's current direction under Xi, so Dr. Shambaugh has given them voice. In effect, China's reformers have aired their views through a well-connected American Sinologist. Anyone desiring to understand the debate over China's future underway among China's top leadership can do no better than Shambaugh's concise book. (172 pages exclusive of notes).

The upheaval that began with the autonomous student movement in Beijing in April 1989 continued through the collapse, one-after-the-other, of the East European Communist states and culminated in the disintegration of the USSR at the end of 1991. It was a profound shock for China's rulers, a near-death experience. A consensus quickly emerged within the CCP top leadership. The decision to impose the Party's will in June 1989 had been "correct." Political liberalization allows opposition to emerge and leads to mounting challenges to Party leadership that may require highly risky confrontation with large and mobilized sections of the population. This was the fundamental "lesson" of the 1989-1991 upheavals.

Don't relax or lose control. Don't allow opposition to emerge and coalesce. Insist on upholding Party leadership. Don't share power. This is the perspective that inspires the current return to hard-line authoritarianism under Xi Jinping.

By the mid-1990s, however, and according to Shambaugh, a different interpretation of the "lesson" of the Soviet collapse emerged among CCP leaders. From this perspective, the fundamental cause of the Soviet collapse was not Gorbachev's much-belated efforts at reform starting in the mid-1980s, but the increasing bureaucratization and rigidity of Communist rule, plus a disregard for the desires of the people of the Soviet Union going back to the 1920s and 1930s. These things, this ossification of Communist rule, had made Gorbachev's desperate efforts necessary. The overthrow of Soviet Communist rule in 1991 was the result of six decades of repression and stagnation. This was the great danger the CCP needed to avoid. The Party needed to forge a more "consultative" type of rule with a more independent media, legislature, judiciary, economic activity, and civil society. The Party needed to pay greater heed to the desires of the people, and less attention to imposing its will. The Party needed to give up a degree of control – to the judiciary, to legislative bodies, the media, the intelligentsia, to enterprises. Changes along these lines, the reformers argued, ultimately would strengthen CCP rule. Refusal to become more inclusive was the path to ultimate regime demise.

From 1998 to 2008 the moderate reformers' views prevailed, and under the tutelage of Jiang Zemin and Hu Jintao, China followed a "soft authoritarianism" course. Autonomous civil society organizations were tolerated. The media were given freer rein. People's Congresses and the "democratic parties" were given a broader role in "consultation." Private entrepreneurs were subsumed within the realm of "socialism" and given political voice. Foreign entities operating in China were given loose rein. Late in 2008, however, a conservative coalition coalesced around deep suspicious about the previous decade of soft authoritarianism and progressive weakening of Party control. This coalition included the Party propaganda apparatus, ministries of state and public security, the People's Liberation Army and the People's Armed Police, and inefficient state-owned enterprises. Party control was reinstituted across a range of policies, turning China away from soft to hard authoritarianism under Xi Jinping.

The crux of Shambaugh's argument – and, I believe, that of the CCP moderates he is speaking for – is that China now faces a series of very serious problems which cannot be adequately addressed under hard-line authoritarian policies inspired by fear of CCP loss of control. Rather, genuine solutions of these problems will require loosening of Party control over the allocation of capital and labor, higher education and intellectual inquiry generally, civil society, and even institutions of state and the political process to a significant degree. CCP moderates do not envision liberal democracy for China. Their inspiration is Singapore, where a single party perpetuates its rule but with autonomous technocratic organs of government (including legal and judicial organs), and wide if still limited scope for free debate and discussion.

Shambaugh piles up a long list of pressing problems: An aging population and exhaustion of low-cost labor supply. Future costs of caring for the elderly. Property and stock market bubbles. Huge levels of debt carried by local governments and state-owned enterprises. A heavy burden of non-performing loans carried by banks. Massive over-building of industrial plants. Sub-optimal allocation of capital via state fiat to state-owned banks. Informal loans provided by non-official lenders that are largely unregulated, very important for the private sector and, thus highly risky. Degradation of arable land and usable water. Air pollution. Normalizing the status of China's vast population of migrants illegally inhabiting its cities. Meeting the rising expectations of an ever-larger middle class deeply plugged into global events (including uprisings against autocratic regimes around the world) via the internet. Maintaining positive relations with the United States and with China's neighbors. Adequate solutions to these problems will require a greater openness and a greater role for markets – with a corresponding rollback of state control. China's leaders generally understand this, Shambaugh argues, and have laid out policies to address these problems in authoritative statements of previous Central Committee Plenums. Yet those earlier policy prescriptions have been ignored. Fearing loss of control and dominated by the conservative coalition, CCP leaders have drawn back from real reform, relying instead on administrative control and repression. This, Shambaugh maintains, is the CCP path to Soviet-style stagnation, bureaucratic ossification, and popular alienation.

Two key and interrelated threads of Shambaugh's argument have to do with: 1) escaping the middle-income trap by shifting to high value-added production, and 2) the role of free intellectual inquiry in fostering scientific and technological innovation.

A middle-income trap occurs when a newly industrializing country succeeds in becoming a producer of low-cost, labor-intensive export goods utilizing brands, product designs and production technology supplied by richer, more technologically advanced countries. On this basis, the country accomplishes a comfortable mid-range of income and development. It fails, however, to move past this stage of development and become a rich country or leading global economy. China's leaders recognize this danger. A State Council investigation found that only 13 of 101 industrializing economies had succeeded in escaping this "trap" and becoming rich economies. "Successes" included Japan, South Korea, Taiwan, Hong Kong, Singapore, Israel, Puerto Rico, and Mauritius. Economies that remained "trapped" included Russia and other post-Soviet states. To escape the mid-level income trap, China needs to shift from massive investment in fixed assets (transportation infrastructure, housing, and expansion of heavy industrial facilities) and production of goods for export to production of goods and services for Chinese consumers. Massive state spending and easy bank loans under state guidance drives China's current "middle income" production structure. China's most efficient, dynamic, and innovative firms tend to be private companies outside the state sector and disesteemed by China's formal financial system. China's leaders understand, Shambaugh says, that deep market reforms are necessary if China is to escape the "middle-income trap" and become a rich and leading economy. But confronted by a slowdown in China's economic growth rate combined with sluggish foreign demand for China's exports, China's conservative control-minded leaders, fearing loss of control, have fallen back on an old tried and proven method of state fiat and administrative direction.

In terms of free intellectual inquiry, Shambaugh's argument is that such freedom is required for path-breaking scientific and technological innovation that leads to new products and processes that become embedded in high value-added goods and services. Indigenous innovation is thus a key driver of escape from the middle-income trap. China's leaders clearly recognize this problem and have spent significant money on research and development and on elite universities. China now produces an abundance of journal articles and files a large number of patents. It woos accomplished ethnic Chinese engineers and scientists to "return" from Europe and the U.S. to China to continue their investigations. Yet the payoff of these efforts in terms of basic innovation has been paltry. Shambaugh attributes this to a Confucian emphasis on rote memorization and a preference (once again) for state direction and control. Major breakthroughs in understanding – new ways of looking at things – are difficult to accomplish in an atmosphere of insistence on ideological correctness and orthodoxy. Creating a genuine innovation economy and thus escaping the middle-income trap will require that China embrace a culture of free intellectual inquiry and debate, Shambaugh argues.

Shambaugh outlines several possible trajectories for the CCP. The good outcome, he suggests, would be a return to power of a reform coalition at the next Party Congress in 2017. China's post-Mao politics has been characterized, Shambaugh notes, by a shift every several years between a period of *"fang"* or relaxation, followed by several years of *"shou"* or tightening. The current post-2008 tightening may be merely the most recent iteration of this *fang-shou* cycle, to be followed by renewed efforts at reform – perhaps after the global economy has escaped its current doldrums. Shambaugh also raises the possibility that strongman Xi Jinping might be pushed aside at the 2017 Party Congress, or perhaps even before that, in some sort of intra-Party coup.

On the other hand, if the current conservative hard authoritarianism continues, the CCP state might be sliding into its "Brezhnev period" of several decades of bureaucratic ossification and alienation from those it rules. In such a situation, Shambaugh suggests, CCP leaders might attempt to re-legitimize their rule by giving the Chinese people what they crave: demonstrable establishment of China as a leading – perhaps "the" leading – global power. Hard authoritarianism internally combined with aggrieved nationalism externally would be a gloomy development.

---

*John Garver is Professor Emeritus in the Sam Nunn School of International Affairs at Georgia Institute of Technology, Atlanta, Georgia, and an associate of the China Research Center.*

# About the Editors

**James R. Schiffman**: Dr. Schiffman is an Assistant Professor in the Mass Communication Department at Georgia College & State University in Milledgeville, Georgia. Previously, he served as Chief Copy Editor at CNN International, where he was involved in editorial decision making, network style, hiring, and training. Prior to joining CNN, Dr. Schiffman was a staff correspondent for The Wall Street Journal in Atlanta and The Asian Wall Street Journal in Hong Kong, Seoul, and Beijing. As a correspondent in Beijing between 1986 and 1988, Dr. Schiffman reported extensively on Chinese economic reforms, the role of foreign investment, and Chinese politics and culture at a time of rapid change and turmoil. Dr. Schiffman speaks Mandarin Chinese, and lectures occasionally to academic and community groups. He earned a Ph.D. in Communication at Georgia State University in May 2012 and is the editor of China Currents.

**Penelope B. Prime**: Beginning with her first visit to China in 1976, Dr. Prime has more than 40 years of experience studying the dynamic Chinese economy. After majoring in Chinese studies and studying Mandarin as an undergraduate, she earned a Ph.D. in economics at the University of Michigan. Dr. Prime is currently Clinical Professor in the Institute of International Business, J. Mack Robinson College of Business, Georgia State University. She is also Founding Director of the China Research Center and Managing Editor of China Currents. Dr. Prime's research focuses on China's economy and business environment, including topics such as China's foreign trade and investment, domestic market reforms, and provincial and local-level development, as well as applied business and economics cases on China and Asia.

CPSIA information can be obtained
at www.ICGtesting.com
Printed in the USA
FFOW01n2109151017
41138FF